A HANDS-ON
APPROACH TO
TEACHING
ABOUT AGING

Hallie E. Baker, PhD, is Associate Professor, Psychology Department, Muskingum University. Dr. Baker supports traditional and nontraditional students through both face-to-face and online pedagogy as she teaches courses in psychology and the health sciences. Currently she teaches Adulthood and Aging, Adolescence and Young Adulthood, Lifespan Development, Introduction to Psychology, Social Gerontology, and Health Policy. She has taught Behavioral Statistics, Research Methods, and Sociology of the Family in recent years. Her research interests include online pedagogy, disability and aging, long-term care, research ethics, and the pedagogy of gerontology. Currently, Dr. Baker works to train her peers in the best practices in online teaching and works to improve the resources available for online students at Muskingum University. She is also a Licensed Social Worker in Ohio with past experience in geriatric social work.

Tina M. Kruger, PhD, is Associate Professor and Chair, Department of Multidisciplinary Studies, Indiana State University (ISU). Dr. Kruger developed an undergraduate Gerontology certificate program at ISU. She has taught Society and Aging, Health Promotion and Aging, Family Relationships, Health Biostatistics, and Research Methods and is active in several research projects. Dr. Kruger has been recognized for her teaching efforts through the Rising Star Junior Faculty Honor from the Association for Gerontology in Higher Education (AGHE) and the Faculty Outstanding Community Engagement Award from the College of Nursing, Health, and Human Services at ISU. Her research interests include health behaviors and aging, sustainability and aging, art and aging, and the pedagogy of gerontology. Her work includes several community-based participatory research studies related to physical and mental health, primarily conducted with residents of low resource areas.

Rona J. Karasik, PhD, is Professor and Director, Gerontology Program, St. Cloud State University, where she has taught since 1993. She is a Fellow of both AGHE and the Gerontological Society of America and received the AGHE Distinguished Teacher Award in 2010. Dr. Karasik is the author of several articles on intergenerational service-learning, internships, and gerontological education. Currently she teaches a wide range of courses, including Introduction to Gerontology, Health and Aging, Dementia, Aging and Community, and Housing and Transportation Options for Older Adults. Her research interests include gerontological pedagogy, experiential learning and community engagement, and specialized housing for older adults.

A HANDS-ON APPROACH TO TEACHING ABOUT AGING

32 Activities for the Classroom and Beyond

Hallie E. Baker, PhD

Tina M. Kruger, PhD

Rona J. Karasik, PhD

Editors

SPRINGER PUBLISHING COMPANY

Springer Publishing Company, LLC
11 West 42nd Street
New York, NY 10036
www.springerpub.com

Acquisitions Editor: Sheri W. Sussman
Compositor: diacriTech

ISBN: 978-0-8261-4916-9
ebook ISBN: 978-0-8261-4917-6

Downloadable Worksheets are available to all readers at springerpub.com/baker
Worksheets ISBN: 978-0-8261-4921-3:

17 18 19 20 21 / 5 4 3 2 1

The author and the publisher of this Work have made every effort to use sources believed to be reliable to provide information that is accurate and compatible with the standards generally accepted at the time of publication. The author and publisher shall not be liable for any special, consequential, or exemplary damages resulting, in whole or in part, from the readers' use of, or reliance on, the information contained in this book. The publisher has no responsibility for the persistence or accuracy of URLs for external or third-party Internet websites referred to in this publication and does not guarantee that any content on such websites is, or will remain, accurate or appropriate.

Library of Congress Cataloging-in-Publication Data
Names: Baker, Hallie E., editor.
Title: A hands-on approach to teaching about aging : 32 activities for the classroom and
    beyond/Hallie E. Baker, PhD, Tina M. Kruger, PhD, Rona J. Karasik, PhD, editors.
Description: New York, NY : Springer Publishing Company, LLC, [2018] |
    Includes bibliographical references and index.
Identifiers: LCCN 2017036060| ISBN 9780826149169 | ISBN 9780826149176 (ebook)
    | ISBN 9780826149213 (worksheets)
Subjects: LCSH: Gerontology—Study and teaching (Higher)—Activity programs.
    | Aging—Study and teaching (Higher)—Activity programs.
Classification: LCC HQ1061 .H3367 2018 | DDC 305.26071/1—dc23 LC record available at
    https://lccn.loc.gov/2017036060

Printed in the United States of America.

CONTENTS

CONTRIBUTORS

Carrie Andreoletti, PhD   Professor of Psychological Science and Coordinator of Gerontology, Central Connecticut State University, New Britain, Connecticut

Monika Ardelt, PhD   Associate Professor of Sociology, University of Florida, Gainesville, Florida

Hallie E. Baker, PhD, LSW   Associate Professor, Muskingum University, New Concord, Ohio

Connie Beran, MSG   Registrar/Faculty, Concordia University, Texas; Concordia University Nebraska (Adjunct); University of Indianapolis Center for Aging and Community (Adjunct), Austin, Texas.

Cheryl Bouckaert, MSN, RN   Assistant Professor of Nursing, Nebraska Methodist College, Omaha, Nebraska

Pamela Pitman Brown, PhD, CPG   Assistant Professor of Sociology, Albany State University, Albany, Georgia

Jacquelyn Browne, PhD, LCSW   Director, Master of Arts in Gerontology, Nova Southeastern University, Fort Lauderdale, Florida

Maria Claver, PhD, MSW   Associate Professor, California State University, Long Beach, California

Eleanor Krassen Covan, PhD   Professor Emerita, University of North Carolina Wilmington, North Carolina

K. Jason Crandall, PhD, ACSM-CEP   Associate Professor, School of Kinesiology, Recreation, and Sport, Western Kentucky University, Bowling Green, Kentucky

Filipa Cunha, MS   Psychologist, Inspiring Future Association, Lisbon, Portugal

Sharon A. DeVaney, PhD   Professor Emeritus, Purdue University, and Editor, *Family & Consumer Sciences Research Journal*

Susan Dillmuth-Miller, AuD, CCC-A   Assistant Professor, East Stroudsburg University, East Stroudsburg, Pennsylvania

Mary C. Ehlman, PhD, CHES, HFA   Associate Professor of Gerontology—College of Nursing and Health Professions, Director, Center for Healthy Aging and Wellness, University of Southern Indiana, Evansville, Indiana

Kimberly S. Farah, PhD   Professor, Lasell College, Newton, Massachusetts

Rachel Filinson, PhD   Professor of Sociology and Gerontology Coordinator, Rhode Island College (Gerontology Center at RIC), Providence, Rhode Island

Elizabeth Fugate-Whitlock, PhD   Lecturer, University of North Carolina Wilmington, North Carolina

Filomena Gerardo, PhD   Researcher, Instituto Universitário de Lisboa (ISCTE-IUL) and University of Paris, Lisbon, Portugal

Casey Goeller, MS, MA   Lecturer, California State University, Long Beach, California

Phyllis A. Greenberg, PhD, MPA   Associate Professor, St. Cloud State University, St. Cloud, Minnesota

Elena Ionescu, MS   Lecturer, California State University, Long Beach, California

Rona J. Karasik, PhD   Professor and Director, Gerontology, St. Cloud State University, St. Cloud, Minnesota

Kyoko Kishimoto, PhD   Professor, Ethnic and Women's Studies, St. Cloud State University, St. Cloud, Minnesota

Lisa Knecht-Sabres, DHS, OTR/L   Associate Professor, Midwestern University, Downers Grove, Illinois

Tina M. Kruger, PhD   Associate Professor, and Chair, Department of Multidisciplinary Studies, Indiana State University, Terre Haute, Indiana

Sibila Marques, PhD   Assistant Professor, Instituto Universitário de Lisboa (ISCTE-IUL), CIS-IUL, Lisbon, Portugal

Jennifer Mendez, PhD   Director Co-Curricular Programs & Assistant Professor, Wayne State University School of Medicine, Detroit, Michigan

Joana Mendonça, MS   PhD Candidate, Instituto Universitário de Lisboa (ISCTE-IUL), CIS-IUL, Lisbon, Portugal

Joann M. Montepare, PhD Director, Center for Research on Aging and Intergenerational Studies Professor of Psychology, Auburndale, Massachusetts

Kelly Niles-Yokum, PhD, MPA Associate Professor, Director, Gerontology Program, University of La Verne, La Verne, Georgia

Preeya Prakash, BA Year 3 Medical Student, Wayne State University School of Medicine, Detroit, Michigan

Ricardo Borges Rodrigues, PhD Researcher and Invited Assistant Professor, Instituto Universitário de Lisboa (ISCTE-IUL), CIS-IUL, Lisbon, Portugal

Heather R. Rodriguez, PhD Assistant Professor of Sociology, Central Connecticut State University, New Britain, Connecticut

Elaine M. Shuey, PhD, CCC-SL Professor, Department of Communication Sciences & Disorders, East Stroudsburg University, East Stroudsburg, Pennsylvania

Nina M. Silverstein, PhD Professor of Gerontology, University of Massachusetts Boston

Colleen Steinhauser, MSN, RN-BC, FNGNA Assistant Professor of Nursing, Nebraska Methodist College, Omaha, Nebraska

Sasha Stine, MS Year 3 Medical Student, Clinical Volunteer Opportunities Coordinator, Wayne State University School of Medicine, Detroit, Michigan

April Temple, PhD, NHA Associate Professor, James Madison University, Harrisonburg, Virginia

Christin-Melanie Vauclair, PhD Researcher, Instituto Universitário de Lisboa (ISCTE-IUL), CIS-IUL, Lisbon, Portugal

Minetta Wallingford, DrOT, OTR/L Associate Professor, Midwestern University, Downers Grove, Illinois

Russell J. Woodruff, PhD Associate Professor of Philosophy, St. Bonaventure University, St. Bonaventure, New York

PREFACE

Welcome! If you are looking for innovative ways to incorporate aging content into your courses, trainings, and workshops for students or professionals, you have come to the right place. The activities found within offer hands-on approaches to engage students of all backgrounds—from social workers to family caregivers, medical students to demographers, nurses to community planners, personal care attendants to students in introduction to gerontology courses. These faculty-tested, peer-reviewed educational activities cover topics ranging from physical aging, media, and demographic portrayals of older adults to disaster planning, public policy, and diversity among older adults.

This collection started as a conversation at the 41st Annual Meeting and Educational Leadership Conference of the Association for Gerontology in Higher Education (AGHE), held in Nashville, Tennessee, in 2015. As we reflected on some of the challenges inherent in teaching about aging and older adults, each of us recalled strategies we used and wanted to share or activities that our peers used with their students or professionals. We agreed it was time to organize a collection of activities spanning multiple topics within the field of aging from a variety of disciplines.

During the fall of 2015, a call for activities went out through AGHE and other sources. The result was astounding. Thanks to 12 wonderful peer reviewers, we were able to review, revise, and finally accept 32 unique and interesting activities for inclusion in the book. The end result is the educational resource book before you now.

Each activity in this collection comes with detailed instructions, basic background information, a materials list, and an explanation of how the specific content aligns with one or more of the AGHE competencies for undergraduate and graduate education in gerontology (www.aghe.org/images/aghe/competencies/gerontology_competencies.pdf). Additionally, all royalties from this book benefit the AGHE and its mission to "foster the commitment of higher education to the field of aging through education, research, and public service" (AGHE, retrieved 2016 from www.aghe.org). We are proud to support this wonderful organization. If you are unfamiliar with AGHE, we encourage you to find out more about it.

Hallie E. Baker
Tina M. Kruger
Rona J. Karasik

As an aid to using the activities included in this book, all forms and worksheets have been made available as PDFs that can be completed digitally or printed for distribution. To download this supplemental material, go to www.springerpub.com/baker.

ACKNOWLEDGMENTS

The editors would like to thank the following reviewers for contributing to the development of this book:

- **Carrie Andreoletti, PhD** Professor of Psychological Science and Coordinator of Gerontology, Central Connecticut State University, New Britain, Connecticut
- **Pamela Pitman Brown, PhD, CPG, FAGHE** Assistant Professor of Sociology, Albany State University, Albany, Georgia
- **Elisabeth O. Burgess, PhD** Director, Gerontology Institute, Associate Professor of Gerontology and Sociology, Georgia State University, Atlanta, Georgia
- **Christine Ferri, PhD** Associate Professor of Psychology, Stockton University, Galloway, New Jersey
- **Janet C. Frank, MSG, DrPH** Adjunct Associate Professor, Faculty Associate, UCLA Center for Health Policy Research, UCLA Fielding School of Public Health, Los Angeles, California
- **Kristina Hash, LICSW, PhD** Professor and Director, Gerontology Certificate Program, School of Social Work, West Virginia University, Morgantown, West Virginia
- **Joann M. Montepare, PhD** Professor of Psychology, Lasell College, Newton, Massachusetts
- **Anabel Pelham, PhD** Professor Emerita, Gerontology, San Francisco State University President, National Association for Professional Gerontologists, Founding Director, CAFÉ Center for Age-Friendly Excellence, Los Altos Community Foundation, Los Altos, California
- **Amy J. Plant, MA, CDP, CPG** Adjunct Faculty Instructor, Research and Consulting Associate, Youngstown State University, Youngstown, Ohio
- **Nina M. Silverstein, PhD** Professor, University of Massachusetts Boston

- **Jim Tift, MA** Assistant Professor, Interprofessional Education, St. Catherine University, St. Paul, Minnesota
- **Andrea Gossett Zakrajsek, OTD, OTRL** Associate Professor & Aging Studies Program Director, Eastern Michigan University, Ypsilanti, Michigan

The editors would also like to thank the following individuals for their contributions in editing and supporting the development of this book: **Troy Gray, Elena Hafner,** and **Jennifer Kruger.**

CHAPTER

TEACHING COURSES ON AGING: EXPERIENTIAL LEARNING ACTIVITIES TO ENGAGE STUDENTS*

Rona J. Karasik, Tina M. Kruger, and Hallie E. Baker

Amid the backdrop of "instant information" and staccato sound bites, how do we move students beyond the belief that all one really needs to know is how to "ask Siri" or enter a few key words into a search engine? How do we make learning "real" for them? Experiential education is an answer that ironically dates back long before the Internet. From the traditional apprenticeship model and John Dewey's classic revelation that "all genuine education comes through experience" (Dewey, 1938, p. 25) to Kolb's experiential learning theory (Kolb, 1984, 2014), "hands-on" learning is a tried, true, and oft reinvented complement to more didactic models of education. Done well, contemporary active learning strategies have been shown to positively impact student learning, interest, and empathy (Altpeter & Marshall, 2003; Eymard, Crawford, & Keller, 2010; Henry, Ozier, & Johnson, 2011).

*Authors' Note: Use of "they" and "their" as singular pronouns herein reflects modern, accepted practice that acknowledges both the non-binary nature of gender and the importance of using inclusive, anti-oppressive language whenever possible (LaScotte, 2016).

As a strategy for teaching about aging and older adults, experiential learning activities also have the potential to engage students in a field that might not seem "sexy" or appealing in our youth-oriented society (Karasik, 2012). Indeed, despite current demographic trends and career-rich predictions, the number of students initially interested in studying aging falls remarkably short of what is needed (Harahan, 2010; Lee & Sumaya, 2013; Warshaw & Bragg, 2016). Bergman, Erickson, and Simons (2014), on the other hand, found that experiential learning was related to higher interest in aging-related careers. Similar findings have been shown with regard to students' interest in elder care work (Augustin & Freshman, 2015), physicians selecting a geriatric specialization (Flacker, 2015), and nurses' desire to work with older adults (Parsons, MacDonald, Hajek, & Moody, 2016).

GETTING THE MOST OUT OF EXPERIENTIAL LEARNING ACTIVITIES

Experiential learning activities ranging from intergenerational service-learning to age-simulations and role-playing have also been shown to reduce ageist attitudes and increase empathy for the experiences of older adults (e.g., Dauenhauer, Steitz, Aponte, & Fromm Faria, 2010; Henry et al., 2011; Koren et al., 2008; Schuldberg, 2005). Not all experiential activities, however, will have positive or lasting outcomes. Diachun, Dumbrell, Byrne, and Esbaugh (2006), for example, found that initial gains from experiential learning in geriatric medical students do not appear to last, although they speculate that the one time experience may not have been long enough for a long-term impact. Conversely, Gugliucci and Weiner (2013) describe having medical students and health professionals live in nursing homes (24/7) for 2 weeks as being a "life altering" activity.

To make the most of experiential learning activities, educators must consider a number of factors. Content, not surprisingly, is a core component for which activities need to be thoughtfully selected and matched to specific intended learning outcomes (Majeski & Stover, 2007; Schmall, Grabinski, & Bowman, 2008). As part of making the connections and applicability of a particular activity clear to the participants, Schmall et al. (2008) advocate post-activity "debriefing," which is also essential to measuring what has been learned (intentionally or otherwise). Care must be taken to minimize or redress negative outcomes (e.g., reinforcing ageist stereotypes). Without follow-up assessment, it is impossible to know what information has been transmitted and how it has been interpreted.

Similarly, instructor preparation is another key consideration for activity success. In addition to avoiding potentially negative learning outcomes, activity facilitators are responsible for creating and maintaining an appropriate learning atmosphere throughout the activity (Schmall et al., 2008). Like any other educational format, this includes having a basic understanding of the content presented as well as being aware of one's own biases related to the subject matter. Ageism, for example, is prevalent throughout society, including among students, educators, practitioners, and elders themselves (Chonody & Wang, 2014; Eymard & Douglas, 2012; Palmore, 2015).

On a more practical level, preparation includes having all the necessary materials ready to use in advance of implementation. Taking the activity for a "test drive" (think focus group testing) might be a way to work out any unforeseen glitches. It will come as no surprise to seasoned facilitators that not everyone will be comfortable with role-playing, nor will every student or topic be a good match for intergenerational service-learning (Goldenberg, Andrusyszyn, & Iwasiw, 2005;

Karasik, Maddox, & Wallingford, 2004). While it is not possible or practical to plan for every eventuality, having a contingency plan (or two) never hurts when trying out a new activity (or even one that is tried and true) on a new group of participants.

WHY A COLLECTION OF AGING ACTIVITIES?

Devising or locating activities that are relevant, appealing, and appropriate can be a challenge for new faculty and veteran educators alike. Moreover, the inherently interdisciplinary nature of aging studies requires instructors to access expertise in a broad range of disciplines and content areas. For some, gerontology and geriatrics may be their main content area. For others, the extent of their aging content knowledge may be more limited. This book should prove useful for anyone incorporating aging content into their courses, regardless of experience teaching aging-related material. The peer-reviewed activities in this book provide instructors from disciplines including but not limited to counseling, family studies, gerontology, geriatrics, medicine, psychology, public administration, public health, nursing, social work, sociology, and speech pathology with teaching strategies to readily engage students in the exploration of aging and older adults.

The effort to create this volume was inspired by faculty at three member institutions of the Association for Gerontology in Higher Education (AGHE). Recognizing the challenges of creating new, exciting, and engaging activities to capture student interest and facilitate learning of aging-related material, we also recognized the wide array of activities instructors had already created or found, and sought to bring them together in one place. The ultimate purpose of the 32 activities contained in this volume is to facilitate student learning of age-related course content through application of "high-impact" practices (Kuh, 2008), which have the potential to "enhance student engagement and increase student success" (p. 21). Furthermore, by engaging in meaningful and fun ways with aging content, students are more likely to remain both in college and in gerontology programs.

Another motivation for creating this book was to facilitate instructors addressing the AGHE *Gerontology Competencies for Undergraduate and Graduate Education*. As the field of gerontology moves toward competency-based education, it is vital that educators have clear strategies for meeting core and optional competencies. Each activity included in this book identifies the AGHE competencies addressed by that activity. This book will serve as a useful tool for helping programs ensure that their course offerings address required competencies and provide a structure for planning to assess the extent to which the competencies are being met.

GETTING THE MOST OUT OF THIS COLLECTION

The activities in this book are organized into 10 broad topical areas. Each chapter provides a brief introduction to the topic's key components, as well as a description of how the specific activities in the chapter relate to the overall topic area. Each activity within the chapter includes information on the activity type, level of difficulty, activity introduction, key terms, learning goals, AGHE competencies addressed, recommended number of activity participants, an estimate of the time and setting needed to implement the activity, and any materials that are required or optional for the activity. Activity procedures include information on preparation, introduction, implementation, discussion/reflection, wrap-up or follow-up if recommended, and assessment materials. Each activity also features additional information and implementation tips from the authors.

Each chapter and each activity is self-contained, so feel free to browse through the book in any order that suits you. Some activities will take some time to prepare before implementing (e.g., making arrangements with sites to visit, seeking institutional review board [IRB] approval), so it is recommended that you review topics of interest while you are preparing your courses and syllabi. Other activities require very little prep time, on the other hand, so if you ever need a last-minute activity for class, don't hesitate to search through the options in this book. We hope that there is something here for everyone and that implementing activities contained in this book will help to ensure that the learning experience in any class (be it online or face-to-face) is fun, exciting, and helpful for increasing students' awareness of the challenges and opportunities presented by the aging of the world's population.

REFERENCES

Altpeter, M., & Marshall, B. (2003). Making aging "real" for undergraduates. *Educational Gerontology, 29*(9), 739–756.

Augustin, F., & Freshman, B. (2015). The effects of service-learning on college students' attitudes toward older adults. *Gerontology & Geriatrics Education, 37*(2), 123–144. doi:10.1080/02701960.2015.1079705

Bergman, E. J., Erickson, M. A., & Simons, J. N. (2014). Attracting and training tomorrow's gerontologists: What drives student interest in aging? *Educational Gerontology, 40*(3), 172–185.

Chonody, J. M., & Wang, D. (2014). Ageism among social work faculty: Impact of personal factors and other "isms." *Gerontology & Geriatrics Education, 35*(3), 248–263.

Dauenhauer, J. A., Steitz, D. W., Aponte, C. I., & Fromm Faria, D. (2010). Enhancing student gerocompetencies: Evaluation of an intergenerational service learning course. *Journal of Gerontological Social Work, 53*(4), 319–335.

Dewey, J. (1938). *Experience and education.* New York, NY: Macmillan.

Diachun, L. L., Dumbrell, A. C., Byrne, K., & Esbaugh, J. (2006). . . . But does it stick? Evaluating the durability of improved knowledge following an undergraduate experiential geriatrics learning session. *Journal of the American Geriatrics Society, 54*(4), 696–701.

Eymard, A. S., Crawford, B. D., & Keller, T. M. (2010). "Take a Walk in My Shoes": Nursing students take a walk in older adults' shoes to increase knowledge and empathy. *Geriatric Nursing, 31*(2), 137–141.

Eymard, A. S., & Douglas, D. H. (2012). Ageism among health care providers and interventions to improve their attitudes toward older adults: An integrative review. *Journal of Gerontological Nursing, 38*(5), 26–35.

Flacker, J. M. (2015). Experiential learning and "selling" geriatrics. In B. A. Bensandon (Ed.), *Psychology and geriatrics: Integrated care for an aging population* (pp. 207–221). San Diego, CA: Academic Press.

Goldenberg, D., Andrusyszyn, M.-A., & Iwasiw, C. (2005). The effect of classroom simulation on nursing students' self-efficacy related to health teaching. *Journal of Nursing Education, 44*(7), 310–314.

Gugliucci, M. R., & Weiner, A. (2013). Learning by living: Life-altering medical education through nursing home-based experiential learning. *Gerontology & Geriatrics Education, 34*(1), 60–77.

Harahan, M. (2010). A critical look at the looming long-term-care workforce crisis. *Generations, 34*(4), 20–26.

Henry, B., Ozier, A., & Johnson, A. (2011). Empathetic responses and attitudes about older adults: How experience with the aging game measures up. *Educational Gerontology, 37*(10), 924–941.

Karasik, R. J. (2012). Engaged teaching for engaged learning: Sharing your passion for gerontology and geriatrics. *Gerontology & Geriatrics Education, 33*(2), 119–132.

Karasik, R. J., Maddox, M., & Wallingford, M. (2004). Intergenerational service-learning across levels and disciplines: "One size (does not) fit all." *Gerontology & Geriatrics Education, 25*(1), 1–17.

Kolb, D. A. (1984). *Experiential learning: Experience as the source of learning and development.* Englewood Cliffs, NJ: Prentice-Hall.

Kolb, D. A. (2014). *Experiential learning: Experience as the source of learning and development* (2nd ed.). Upper Saddle River, NJ: Pearson.

Koren, M. E., Hertz, J., Munroe, D., Rossetti, J., Robertson, J., Plonczynski, D., . . . Ehrlich-Jones, L. (2008). Assessing students' learning needs and attitudes: Considerations for gerontology curriculum planning. *Gerontology & Geriatrics Education, 28*(4), 39–56.

Kuh, G. D. (2008). *High-impact educational practices: What they are, who has access to them, and why they matter.* Washington, DC: Association of American Colleges and Universities.

LaScotte, D. K. (2016). Singular they: An empirical study of generic pronoun use. *American Speech, 91*(1), 62–80.

Lee, W. C., & Sumaya, C. V. (2013). Geriatric workforce capacity: A pending crisis for nursing home residents. *Frontiers in Public Health, 1.* doi:10.3389/fpubh.2013.00024

Majeski, R., & Stover, M. (2007). Theoretically based pedagogical strategies leading to deep learning in asynchronous online gerontology courses. *Educational Gerontology, 33*(3), 171–185.

Palmore, E. (2015). Ageism comes of age. *Journals of Gerontology Series B: Psychological Sciences and Social Sciences, 70*(6), 873–875.

Parsons, K., MacDonald, S., Hajek, A., & Moody, J. (2016). Increasing attitudes and interest in caring for older adults in first year nursing students using innovative teaching and learning strategies. *Journal of Nursing Education and Practice, 5*(9), 63–71.

Schmall, V., Grabinski, C. J., & Bowman, S. (2008). Use of games as a learner-centered strategy in gerontology, geriatrics, and aging-related courses. *Gerontology & Geriatrics Education, 29*(3), 225–233.

Schuldberg, J. (2005). It is easy to make judgments if it's not familiar: The use of simulation kits to develop self-awareness and reduce ageism. *Journal of Social Work Education, 41*(3), 441–455.

Warshaw, G. A., & Bragg, E. J. (2016). The essential components of quality geriatric care. *Generations, 40*(1), 28–37.

CHAPTER 2

AGEISM AND AGING IN THE MEDIA

Tina M. Kruger

If media (TV, commercials, magazines, advertisements, etc.) portrayed an accurate picture of society, we would expect to see relatively few people of color, working class or lower class individuals and families, and certainly few older adults (particularly any with disabilities) in the real world. Media portrayals of aging are far from accurate though, with older adults being vastly underrepresented and the diversity of the aging experience being virtually nonexistent (Vickers, 2007).

Typical students in college classes (those age 18–24) are exposed to an average of 58.78 hours of media (TV, radio, TV-connected devices like console games or DVDs, personal computers, smartphones, or tablets) per week, according to the fourth quarter Nielsen Company (2015) Comparable Metrics Report (and the numbers are even higher in older age groups). Cultivation theory (Gerbner & Gross, 1976) posits that the more TV people watch, the more they come to believe that TV's portrayal of society is realistic and accurate. Thus, many students in college classrooms are likely to believe the misrepresentation (and underrepresentation) of older adults conveyed through various media sources.

Milner, Van Norman, and Milner (2012) describe four types of ageism (personal, institutional, intentional, and unintentional), explaining how media perpetuates ageism in a variety of ways. They go on to describe various negative outcomes for older adults who are exposed to such negative portrayals of aging, including decreases in physical and cognitive performance, heightened stress responses, lower likelihood of engaging in health promoting behaviors, and reduction in life expectancy (among other outcomes). Younger people exposed to such messages are more likely to fear aging and older adults, treat older people with contempt, and perpetuate microaggressions against older adults. A recent article on the *Huffington Post* (Brenoff, 2015) highlights various ways people (both young and old) undermine the value of aging in our society and propagate ageism.

AGEISM AND AGING EDUCATION EXERCISES

To facilitate learning about aging, we as teachers must first tear down these beliefs students (and ourselves) have internalized through years of exposure to inaccurate media representations of aging. The activities presented in this chapter help to do just that.

Activity 2.1, Aging as Portrayed in Children's Picture Books, challenges students to think critically about the earliest messages people receive about aging. By examining representations of aging in picture books, students begin to see how early negative or inaccurate messages about aging are conveyed to children.

Similarly, through Activity 2.2, Aging in the Movies, students examine the ways in which aging is portrayed in various popular films, again critically reviewing the accuracy of those portrayals and the impact movies have on viewers' beliefs. In Activity 2.3, imAGES: Intervention Program to Prevent Ageism in Children and Adolescents, students work in multigenerational groups to examine sources and contents of their beliefs about aging and work together to generate an awareness campaign about aging to disseminate locally. This activity promotes efforts to confront inaccurate beliefs held by people of multiple generations and develop messages to counter ageism.

Activity 2.4, Examining the Social Clock Through YouTube, facilitates challenges to the idea that there is a "typical" path people follow through life, highlighting the facts that people over 60 maintain active and satisfying sex lives and that childbirth is not the sole province of 20-, 30-, or even 40-, or 50-somethings. Together or individually, these activities should foster critical self-reflection, intense discussion, and, ideally, reduction of ageist beliefs among participants.

REFERENCES

Brenoff, A. (2015). 10 microaggressions older people will recognize immediately. *The Huffington Post*. Retrieved from http://www.huffingtonpost.com/entry/10-microaggressions-of-ageism-that-are-not-ok-to-ignore_us_564f7155e4b0d4093a57ab9d

Gerbner, G., & Gross, L. (1976). Living with television: The violence profile. *Journal of Communication, 26*(2), 172–199.

Milner, C., Van Norman, K., & Milner, J. (2012). The media's portrayal of aging. In J. R. Beard, S. Biggs, D. E. Bloom, L. P. Fried, P. Hogan, A. Kalache, & S. J. Olshansky (Eds.), *Global population ageing: Peril or promise* (pp. 25–28). Geneva, Switzerland: World Economic Forum.

Nielsen Company. (2015). The comparable metrics report: Q4 3015. Retrieved from http://www.nielsen.com/us/en/insights/reports/2016/the-comparable-metrics-report-q4-2015.html

Vickers, K. (2007). Aging and the media: Yesterday, today, and tomorrow. *Californian Journal of Health Promotion, 5*(3), 100–105.

ACTIVITY 2.1 AGING AS PORTRAYED IN CHILDREN'S PICTURE BOOKS

Pamela Pitman Brown

ACTIVITY INFORMATION

Type

__X__ In class

_____ Online

__X__ Take home

__X__ In community

Difficulty

__X__ Introductory

__X__ Intermediate

_____ Advanced

OVERVIEW

Images and suggestions, whether through art, literature, or other media, push stereotyping/ageism into the forefront of our accumulated knowledge base of older adults. Children's books play a critical role within socialization of children toward cultural norms and expectations. Picture books are often the first books children see and have read to them. Research has previously indicated that picture books provide gendered stereotyping, and age stereotyping/ageist attitudes, as well as biases toward older adults. Stereotypes are "learned, widely shared, socially validated general beliefs about categories of individuals. While usually inaccurate, they are widely shared as truth and are very powerful" (Turner-Bowker, 1996, p. 461). Stereotyping of older adults is often in relation to older adults' memory, their physical abilities/appearance, their taste in clothing, their skill sets, and what grandmothers/grandfathers do with their "free" time.

KEY TERMS

Ageism
Stereotyping

ACTIVITY LEARNING GOALS

Following this activity, students should be able to . . .

- Critique and analyze a children's picture book based upon ageist stereotypes of older adults.

- Relate the author's words and the artist's drawings to common stereotyping of older adults.
- Synthesize suggestions to the author/artist to combat the ageism or stereotypes of the older adults portrayed within the story.

ASSOCIATION FOR GERONTOLOGY IN HIGHER EDUCATION COMPETENCIES

- Develop comprehensive and meaningful concepts, definitions, and measures for well-being of older adults and their families, grounded in humanities and arts.
- Develop a gerontological perspective through knowledge and self-reflection.
- Critique and analyze assumptions, stereotyping, prejudice, and discrimination related to age (ageism) at both personal and public levels.
- Analyze how older individuals are portrayed in public media and advocate for more accurate depictions of the diverse older population using research-based publications and multi-media dissemination methods.

MINIMUM/MAXIMUM NUMBER OF PARTICIPANTS

- 5 to 50

TIME NEEDED TO IMPLEMENT ACTIVITY

- 1 week

SETTING(S)

- Library
- Classroom

MATERIALS

Required

- Children's picture books from library

Optional

- Bring children's picture books that you have previously selected to use during class.
- Examples of excellent age-friendly books can be found at the following links:
  - http://library.lmunet.edu/booklist
  - www.aghe.org/publications/books-for-k-primary-students

PROCEDURES

Preparation

Students should have covered ageism and stereotyping of older adults prior to the activity. If students are to select the books, prepare them for the visit to the library by discussing what they will need to search for in the children's book section (see the introduction script). It is usually a good idea to call ahead, notifying the librarian that the class will be searching for picture books, and ask that a librarian be available for assistance. Do not tell the students exactly what the activity will consist of as prior activities have shown that students will find books that include almost no older adults, or they will find one that they do not find offensive (or go with their old standby favorite).

Introduction

(SCRIPT): Today we will be searching for a children's picture book that has older adults featured in the text and in the pictures. I would like for you to search for a book that you think will interest you. Do not read the book ahead of time, but you may glance at the pictures to give you an idea of whether you would like the story or not. When you have completed your search, you should immediately check the book out, complete your book information slip, and turn it in to me (see Appendix 2.1A for Book Information Slips).

After the student hands in the Book Information Slip, hand the student the Activity Sheet to complete for homework (see Appendix 2.1B for Activity Sheet).

Activity

Students will complete the Activity Sheet at home as homework and then will return to class during the next class period to share their book and findings either with the class as a whole (if the class is small) or with a small group if the class is larger.

Discussion/Reflection

Students are allowed to make changes to their Activity Sheets if they choose after having discussed the book/findings with their peers.

Wrap-Up

Go around the room and have each student tell one thing learned from this activity or one thing that was similar among the books of their group. Also ask the students whether they enjoyed the activity and why, as well as what they liked/disliked about the activity.

Assessment

Students will turn in their Activity Sheet for a grade. I use this as a critical thinking piece, and offer between 25 and 50 points for the activity (see Appendix 2.1C for Rubric).

REFERENCE

Turner-Bowker, D. M. (1996). Gender stereotyped descriptors in children's picture books: Does "curious Jane" exist in the literature? *Sex Roles, 35*(7/8), 461–488. doi: 10.1007/BF01544132

APPENDIX 2.1A: BOOK INFORMATION SLIPS

BOOK INFORMATION SLIP:

Name: _____

Name of Book: _____

Author(s): _____

Artist(s): _____

BOOK INFORMATION SLIP:

Name: _____

Name of Book: _____

Author(s): _____

Artist(s): _____

BOOK INFORMATION SLIP:

Name: _____

Name of Book: _____

Author(s): _____

Artist(s): _____

BOOK INFORMATION SLIP:

Name: _____

Name of Book: _____

Author(s): _____

Artist(s): _____

BOOK INFORMATION SLIP:

Name: _____

Name of Book: _____

Author(s): _____

Artist(s): _____

BOOK INFORMATION SLIP:

Name: _____

Name of Book: _____

Author(s): _____

Artist(s): _____

APPENDIX 2.1B: ACTIVITY SHEET: CHILDREN'S PICTURE BOOK

Name: _____

Activity Sheet: Children's Picture Book

Name of Book: _____

Author(s): _____

Artist(s): _____

Characters in the book (include relationships/approximate ages).
Write a synopsis of the plot/storyline of the book (one to two paragraphs).
Write about the roles of the older adults.

Author:
What stereotyping/ageism do you see within the text of the book?
Relate the author's words to common stereotyping of older adults.
From your list of stereotypes from the previous question, synthesize suggestions to the author to combat the ageism or stereotypes of the older adults portrayed within the story.
Integrate what we discussed in our textbook/class on ageism and stereotyping.

Artist:
What stereotyping/ageism do you see within the pictures of the book?
Relate the artist's drawings to common stereotyping of older adults.
From your list of stereotypes from the previous question, synthesize suggestions to the artist to combat the ageism or stereotypes of the older adults portrayed within the story.
Integrate what we discussed in our textbook/class on ageism and stereotyping.

APPENDIX 2.1C: RUBRIC

Name: _____

Name of Book: _____

Author(s): _____

Artist(s): _____

	4	3	2	1	0
Book Choice	Book meets/exceeds criteria, including older adults featured prominently in the text/pictures.	Book meets criteria, including older adults in the text/pictures.	Book somewhat meets criteria, with at least one older adult in the text/pictures.	Book has an older adult in either the text or the picture.	Book has no older adults in text or pictures.
Characters in the Book	Student meets/ exceeds criteria and lists all characters in the book, as well as includes relationships/ approximate ages.	Student meets criteria and lists all characters in the book, as well as includes most of the information of relationships/ approximate ages.	Student somewhat meets criteria and lists most of the characters in the book, but has little information on relationships/ages.	Student lists some characters but no information on relationships/ ages.	Student fails to list characters and provides no information on relationships/ ages.
Synopsis (one to two paragraphs)	Student writes one to two paragraphs, with full controlled explanation of plot/ storyline. Includes specific details.	Student writes one to two paragraphs, but does not capture plot or storyline sufficiently.	Student writes one paragraph synopsis (five sentences/ more). Incomplete work.	Student writes less than one paragraph synopsis (fewer than four sentences).	Student fails to write synopsis of plot/storyline.

(continued)

	4	3	2	1	0
Roles of the Older Adult	Student discusses adult(s) character(s) role (e.g., grandmother/grandfather, teacher), and interaction within story line. Clarity of meaning.	Student discusses adult(s) character(s) role (e.g., grandmother/grandfather, teacher), and interaction within story line. Lacks clarity of meaning.	Student discusses adult(s) character(s) role (e.g., grandmother/grandfather, teacher), but fails to integrate fully with storyline.	Student discusses adult(s) character(s) role (e.g., grandmother/grandfather, teacher) only.	Student fails to discuss adult character's(') role(s).
Author	Student clearly states stereotyping/ageism within the text of the book, relays author's words to describe stereotyping/ageism, and synthesizes to text using specific examples/details to fully address question. Uses page numbers of book/text.	Student states stereotyping/ageism within the text of the book, relays author's words to describe stereotyping/ageism, and relates to text using limited examples/details to answer question.	Student states a few examples of stereotyping/ageism within the text of the book, relays author's words to describe stereotyping/ageism, and relates to text using limited examples/details to answer question.	Student states an example of stereotyping/ageism within the text of the book, relays author's words to describe stereotyping/ageism, and fails to relate to text.	Student lists author's words to describe stereotyping/ageism.

Artist	Student clearly states visualized stereotyping/ageism within artist's drawings, relates artist's drawings to common visual stereotyping/ageism, and synthesizes suggestions to artist for overcoming visual stereotyping/ageism. Uses page numbers of book/text.	Student states visualized stereotyping/ageism within artist's drawings, relates artist's drawings to common visual stereotyping/ageism, and offers limited suggestions to artist for overcoming visual stereotyping/ageism.	Student states one to two examples of stereotyping/ageism within artist's drawings, limited information given to relate artist's drawings to common visual stereotyping/ageism, and offers limited suggestions to artist for overcoming visual stereotyping/ageism.	Student states one to two examples of stereotyping/ageism within artist's drawings, limited information given to relate artist's drawings to common visual stereotyping/ageism, and offers no suggestions to artist for overcoming visual stereotyping/ageism.	Student states one to two examples of stereotyping/ageism within artist's drawings, gives no information to relate artist's drawings to common visual stereotyping/ageism, and offers no suggestions to artist for overcoming visual stereotyping/ageism.
Mechanics/ Conventions	Student's writing has clear, correct simple/complex/compound sentences with correct punctuation. No errors.	Student's writing has clear, correct simple/complex/compound sentences with correct punctuation. One to three errors.	Student's writing has limited, correct simple sentences with correct punctuation. One to three errors.	Student's writing has limited, correct simple sentences with correct punctuation. Four or more errors.	Student's writing has numerous errors in both usage and mechanics, with sentence fragments. Errors interfere with meaning.

ACTIVITY 2.2 AGING IN THE MOVIES

April Temple

ACTIVITY INFORMATION

Type

_____	In class
_____	Online
__X__	Take home
_____	In community

Difficulty

__X__	Introductory
_____	Intermediate
_____	Advanced

OVERVIEW

Despite an aging demographic, older adults are consistently underrepresented in popular media, including television and movies. For example, although people age 65 and above represent about 13% of the population, this group accounts for fewer than 2% of prime-time television characters (Dahmen & Cozma, 2009). Furthermore, the media often portrays older adults in a negative light, reinforcing age-based stereotypes of dependence, decline, incompetence, and worthlessness, with women being particularly vulnerable to ageism and ageist roles (Dahmen & Cozma, 2009). Even when aging is portrayed in a seemingly positive manner, the media often depicts an unrealistic image of older adults who have defied the aging process (Milner, Van Norman, & Milner, 2012). Given the portrayal of older people in the mass media is predominately negative, this exposure perpetuates ageist attitudes and stereotypes within society and impacts the views older people have of themselves, even contributing to worsening health and functional decline (Dahmen & Cozma, 2009; Milner et al., 2012). Although realistic images of aging in the media are beginning to emerge, a more balanced approach toward the portrayal of the challenges and successes of aging is needed.

The purpose of this activity is for students to identify and evaluate the depiction of older adults and/or the aging process as presented in popular movies. Students use critical thinking skills to recognize relevant gerontological concepts as well as analyze whether the content was accurately portrayed based on content knowledge. This activity also contributes to an overall understanding of ageism and stereotypes in the mass media. It is a well-received activity particularly in undergraduate, introductory gerontology courses.

KEY TERM

Ageism

ACTIVITY LEARNING GOALS

Following this activity, students should be able to . . .

- Identify relevant gerontology concepts from a selected movie.
- Substantially relate the concepts presented in the movie to course content (e.g., in lectures, textbook readings, and/or outside research).
- Evaluate whether concepts were accurately portrayed in the movie based on learned information.

ASSOCIATION FOR GERONTOLOGY IN HIGHER EDUCATION COMPETENCIES

- Utilize gerontological frameworks to examine human development and aging.
- Relate biological theory and science to understanding senescence, longevity, and variation in aging.
- Relate psychological theories and science to understanding adaptation, stability, and changes in aging.
- Relate social theories and science of aging to understanding heterogeneity, inequality, and context of aging.
- Develop comprehensive and meaningful concepts, definitions, and measures for well-being of older adults and their families, grounded in humanities and arts.
- Distinguish factors related to aging outcomes, both intrinsic and contextual, through critical thinking and empirical research.
- Develop a gerontological perspective through knowledge and self-reflection.

MINIMUM/MAXIMUM NUMBER OF PARTICIPANTS

This activity works best in small to moderate class sizes up to approximately 60 students.

TIME NEEDED TO IMPLEMENT ACTIVITY

As a take home activity, students view the movie and complete the writing assignment outside of class time. It may take approximately 1 hour of class time to provide a contextual background of aging in the media and to explain the guidelines for the activity (see Appendix 2.2). Upon completion of the activity, the instructor may also wish to use a class meeting to facilitate a discussion of the gerontology concepts identified in the movies and the portrayal of older adults and/or the aging process in television/film.

SETTING(S)

Students complete the assignment on their own time outside of class. The initial introduction of the activity and final reflection occur within class meeting(s).

MATERIALS

Required

Students are responsible for viewing the movie selected for the assignment. Suggested movies to include on an approved list are *Driving Miss Daisy* (1989), *About Schmidt* (2002), *Away From Her* (2006), *The Notebook* (2004), *Fried Green Tomatoes* (1991), *The Bucket List* (2008), *Calendar Girls* (2003), *The Curious Case of Benjamin Button* (2008), *UP* (2009), *Hope Springs* (2012), *R.E.D.* (2010), *The Best Exotic Marigold Hotel* (2012), *In Her Shoes* (2005), *Still Alice* (2015), and *The Intern* (2015). Students may be given the option to select other movies as approved by the instructor.

PROCEDURES

Preparation

To prepare for this activity, instructors will need to become familiar with the movies included on the approved list. Instructors may also wish to adapt the list of movies according to certain themes or topics that are particular to a specific gerontology course (such as only movies that pertain to a Psychology of Aging course). The instructor should review the relevant content sources listed at the end of this activity to gain a general overview of ageism and the portrayal of older adults in the media. Last, the instructor will need to review and potentially adapt the assignment guidelines included in Appendix 2.2.

Introduction

It should take approximately 30 minutes to 1 hour to introduce the activity. The introduction should include a brief contextual background of ageism and aging in the media (see content sources listed at the end of this activity). The instructor should also discuss and review the objectives of the activity and the guidelines and evaluation criteria of the written assignment (see Appendix 2.2).

Activity

For this activity, students are first instructed to view a movie from the approved list (or others as approved in advance by the instructor) outside of class time. Most movies are available to borrow through the university or local library or as an inexpensive rental through services such as Amazon Instant Video or Netflix.

While viewing the movie, students need to identify the two to three most salient gerontology concepts presented in the movie (e.g., physical changes in aging, death and dying, caregiving, long-term care, dementia, retirement, sexuality).

After viewing the movie, each student will write a short, four- to five-page paper that relates two to three gerontology concepts presented in the movie to what the student has learned about those topics from class lectures, readings from the textbook, and/or outside research. The paper should also include a discussion of whether these concepts were accurately portrayed in the movie based on learned material.

Sample instructions for students are included in Appendix 2.2.

Discussion/Reflection

Upon submission of the activity, the instructor may wish to use a class meeting to facilitate a discussion and evaluation of the gerontology concepts identified in select movies. This discussion could take the form of a larger class discussion or students could be put into smaller groups based on shared movies. Discussion questions could include,

- What were the salient course topics identified in each movie?
- For each concept, was it accurately portrayed in the movie? If not, what content was lacking or misrepresented?
- How could the movie have captured a more realistic view of the topic(s)?
- Did the movie depict age-based stereotypes and/or ageism?
- What influence may this movie have on the audience's perspective of aging/ older adults?

Wrap-Up

In addition to the discussion/reflection described earlier, the instructor can wrap-up the activity by relating the assignment more broadly to the portrayal of older adults and/or aging in the media as well the implications of age-based stereotypes. See Appendix 2.2 for suggested content sources.

Follow-Up

By reading individual student papers, the instructor will be able to grasp whether students have a solid understanding of various gerontology concepts. Individual follow-up with students can be conducted by providing feedback on their papers. If there are common misconceptions or misinformation across several papers, the instructor has the opportunity to provide clarification to the whole class.

Assessment

The topics of individual papers will vary depending upon the movie selected and the gerontology concepts identified within each movie. A sample grading rubric based on the Association of American Colleges and Universities (2009) *Critical Thinking VALUE Rubric* can be used.

REFERENCES

Association of American Colleges and Universities. (2009). Critical thinking VALUE rubric. Retrieved from https://www.aacu.org/value/rubrics

Dahmen, N. S., & Cozma, R. (2009). Media takes: On aging. Retrieved from http://www.ilc-alliance.org/images/uploads/publication-pdfs/Media_Takes_On_Aging.pdf

Milner, C., Van Norman, K., & Milner, J. (2012). The media's portrayal of ageing. In J. R. Beard, S. Biggs, D. E. Bloom, L. P. Fried, P. Hogan, A. Kalache, & S. J. Olshansky (Eds.), *Global population aging: Peril or promise?* (Chap. 4, pp. 25–28). Retrieved from http://www3.weforum.org/docs/WEF_GAC_GlobalPopulationAgeing_Report_2012.pdf

APPENDIX 2.2: AGING IN THE MOVIES—ASSIGNMENT SHEET

AGING IN THE MOVIES: SAMPLE GUIDELINES FOR STUDENTS

The objectives of this assignment are to: (a) identify relevant gerontology concepts from a selected movie; (b) substantially relate the concepts presented in the movie to course content (in lectures, textbook readings, and/or outside research); and (c) evaluate whether concepts were accurately portrayed in the movie based on information learned in the course.

The following popular movies illustrate real life issues faced by older adults that are covered in this gerontology course, including physical changes in aging, death and dying, utilization of long-term care, caregiving, dementia, retirement, and sexuality. Select *one* of the following approved movies to view on your own time outside of class: *Driving Miss Daisy* (1989), *About Schmidt* (2002), *Away From Her* (2006), *The Notebook* (2004), *Fried Green Tomatoes* (1991), *The Bucket List* (2008), *Calendar Girls* (2003), *The Curious Case of Benjamin Button* (2008), *UP* (2009), *Hope Springs* (2012), *R.E.D.* (2010), *The Best Exotic Marigold Hotel* (2012), *In Her Shoes* (2005), *Still Alice* (2015), and *The Intern* (2015). Other movies may be *selected if approved by the instructor in advance.*

The final outcome of this assignment is a four- to five-page paper that identifies, relates, and discusses gerontology concepts within the selected movie to material learned in the course. The paper must include the following:

- Identify two to three of the most salient gerontology concepts in the selected movie.

- For each concept or topic identified, provide a contextual background that describes how it was depicted in the movie.

- Substantially relate each concept or topic to course content using evidence from lectures, textbook readings, and/or outside research. Do not simply summarize the movie but rather integrate specific learned material to demonstrate a sophisticated understanding of each concept. Be sure to include appropriate in-text citations and a full reference page.

- Evaluate whether or not each concept was accurately portrayed in the movie based on content knowledge.

ACTIVITY 2.3 IMAGES: INTERVENTION PROGRAM TO PREVENT AGEISM IN CHILDREN AND ADOLESCENTS

Sibila Marques, Christin-Melanie Vauclair, Ricardo Borges Rodrigues, Joana Mendonça, Filomena Gerardo, and Filipa Cunha

ACTIVITY INFORMATION

Type

  __X__   In class

  _____   Online

  __X__   Take home

  _____   In community

Difficulty

  _____   Introductory

  __X__   Intermediate

  _____   Advanced

OVERVIEW

The imAGES intervention program was originally developed for children and adolescents in the K-12 group. Nevertheless, it may also be extended to undergraduate students, with some adaptations to make the activities more interesting for this age group. Additionally, the intergenerational activities foreseen in this intervention program rely on the voluntary collaboration of active adults over 60 years old.

The term *ageism* refers to generalized negative opinions, attitudes, and practices toward individuals based solely on their age (Nelson, 2002). Evidence shows that older people are special targets of this type of negative evaluation (Marques, 2011; Marques, Lima, Abrams, & Swift, 2014; Marques et al., 2015). Ageism has negative consequences for older people, affecting their mental and physical capabilities (Levy, 1996; Whitbourne & Sneed, 2002).

Age is a fundamental dimension along which children organize their perceptions of people in their social world (Lewis & Brooks-Gunn, 1979). Children's perceptions of older adults tend to be negative: children as young as 3 years old have been found to have negative ideas about older people (e.g., Middlecamp & Gross, 2002). When comparing older to younger adults, children report preferring to spend time with younger people (Seefeldt, 1987) and present negative views of aging, classifying older people as helpless, stubborn, and senile (Pinquart, Wenzel, & Sörensen, 2000). There is also evidence showing that this preference prevails throughout adolescence and adulthood (e.g., Falchikov, 1990; Levy, 2003; Marques et al., 2014). Emphasizing the great diversity that exists within the older population, for example, by presenting information that contradicts what is usually expected from this group, can be an effective way to change such stereotypical perceptions (Garcia-Marques & Mackie, 1999). Similarly, intervention programs aiming to promote intergenerational contact between younger and older individuals are promising strategies to counter ageist beliefs and behaviors (Pettigrew & Tropp, 2006).

ACTIVITY LEARNING GOALS

Following this activity, students should be able to . . .

- Understand the interindividual diversity within the group of older people.
- Apply positive behavioral intentions when interacting with older people.

ASSOCIATION FOR GERONTOLOGY IN HIGHER EDUCATION COMPETENCIES

- Promote quality of life and positive social environment for older persons.
- Employ and design programmatic and community development with and on behalf of the aging population.
- Engage in research to advance knowledge and improve interventions for older persons.
- Develop a gerontological perspective through knowledge and self-reflection.

MINIMUM/MAXIMUM NUMBER OF PARTICIPANTS

- Learning sessions: one class of 20 to 30 students.
- Contact session: one class of 20 to 30 students and the same number of older adults.

TIME NEEDED TO IMPLEMENT ACTIVITY

- First learning session: 1 hour and 15 minutes
- Second learning session: 45 minutes
- Contact session: 1 hour and 15 minutes

SETTING(S)

- Learning sessions: classroom with chairs.
- Contact session: classroom with several tables with chairs around them, where younger and older participants should be seated by teams, alternating by age: younger, older, younger, older, and so on.

MATERIALS

Required

- For the two learning sessions: computer, slideshow, whiteboard, markers, work-sheet, identification cards, characters' masks, homework sheet, pretest question-naire, posttest questionnaire.
- For the contact session: computer, slideshow, whiteboard, markers, worksheet, blank posters, handwork materials (such as color pencils, markers, scissors, glue, and cardboards), posttest questionnaire, a light snack.

PROCEDURES

Introduction

The imAGES intervention program to prevent ageism in children and adolescents is based on a theoretical model comprising the main factors referred to in the litera-ture as having influence in changing negative stereotypes (Figure 2.1).

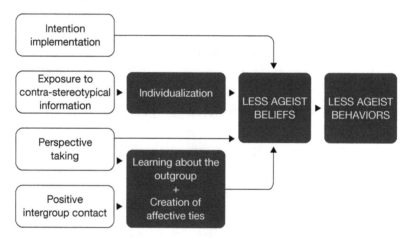

Figure 2.1 Theoretical Model of the imAGES Intervention Program.

Studies suggest that learning about the out-group, that is, acquiring new and pos-itive information about its members and creating affective ties, for example, when engaging in conversations and activities that foster emotional closeness, results in less negative perceptions about discriminated groups (Pettigrew & Tropp, 2006).

Perspective taking, that is, assuming the perspective and role of other people, counters stereotypical perceptions by allowing one to realize what it is like to be the object of discrimination, as well as the positive characteristics and experiences of others (Galinsky & Moskowitz, 2000).

Positive intergroup contact has been shown to be effective in decreasing preju-dice, as it has the potential to increase perspective taking and affective ties between groups, leading to more positive views regarding the other group (Kenworthy, Turner, & Hewstone, 2005).

Exposure to counter-stereotypical information is another effective method to challenge stereotypes. For example, presenting examples that contradict what is usually expected in a group has been shown to result in a more individualized view of its members, by giving the idea that not everyone is alike (Garcia-Marques & Mackie, 1999).

Implementation intention strategies that encourage individuals to think of behavioral alternatives when interacting with members of the discriminated group also promote positive and nondiscriminatory modes of interaction (Mendoza, Gollwitzer, & Amodio, 2010).

Based on this theoretical model, the imAGES intervention program targets these multiple factors with the goal of reducing ageism. To accomplish this, the intervention comprises a set of activities based on sociocognitive training along with direct contact experiences. More specifically, two learning sessions are held to promote the discussion of real examples of older people and, consequently, to raise awareness on the part of younger participants to the heterogeneity of this age group. A contact session involving intergenerational activities is also carried out, allowing younger participants to create affective ties with older individuals and learn more about their age group.

Activity

First learning session

The trainer begins the first learning session by welcoming the participants and explaining the goal of the session: to learn more about age. This is followed by an "icebreaker" in which all participants are asked to say their name and mention one characteristic that society commonly attributes to older people. The trainer writes all these characteristics on the board.

Participants then form small groups, and each group is given an identification card that describes a positive and active example of a real older person for all members to analyze together. After that, each group selects a spokesperson to impersonate this real example and introduce oneself to the class, while wearing a mask with the face of the older person. Before starting, the trainer demonstrates how to perform the presentation. The trainer also writes the main characteristics mentioned for each older person on the board during the presentations.

Afterwards, the trainer compares the two groups of characteristics written on the board: those of real older people and those attributed to them by society. While promoting this discussion, the trainer deconstructs the stereotypes about older people and highlights the diversity that exists within this age group.

Before ending the session, the trainer gives two homework assignments for the following session. In the first assignment, participants are asked to choose, among the real examples of older people, both whom they liked the most and whom they would like to be in the future. In the second assignment, participants are asked to imagine how they would interact with an older person they know. The trainer makes sure they understand the assignments and gives some examples. Finally, the trainer ends the session by thanking everyone for their participation and reminding the date of the next session.

Second learning session

At the start of the second learning session, the trainer asks participants whether they did their homework and whether they had any doubts. To analyze the homework, the trainer asks for their answers to the first assignment, emphasizing that ageing involves different outcomes for each person. Similarly, the trainer asks for their answers to the second assignment, allowing them to discuss the many behaviors possible when interacting with older people.

Following the homework analysis, the trainer presents several stereotypical sentences about older people, while also deconstructing them and showing why they are false. The trainer also compares these sentences with the real examples of older people discussed in the previous session. The trainer then ends the session by highlighting once again the great diversity that exists regarding older people.

Contact session

In the contact session, the trainer welcomes the participants and explains the goal of the session: to create an awareness campaign to improve their city. This is followed by the creation of small groups containing the same number of older and younger participants.

After sitting in chairs around tables, they form intergenerational pairs within each group for an icebreaker. This activity involves getting to know their partner by asking several questions given by the trainer, including their name; whether they live in the city; if so, for how long; and what they enjoy doing there. In the last question, both partners jointly answer which place in the city they would like to go together. Afterwards, the trainer asks each pair to share their response to the final question and writes their answers on the board.

Before starting the main intergenerational activity, the trainer presents the theme of the campaign and highlights its importance, mentioning that there are many different people living in the city and that everyone should feel included in its community. The trainer asks each group to create a poster with appealing messages to motivate others to make their city a better place to live.

After distributing one poster per group and other necessary materials, the trainer gives an initial orientation, suggesting that the title should be written before creating the rest of the poster and encouraging participants to think together about what should be changed in the city to make it better and more inclusive for everyone. During the poster development, the trainer makes sure that all members of each group are participating, preventing their exclusion or isolation, and ensures that the activity is completed within the available time.

After the groups finish their posters, the trainer congratulates all the groups for their excellent work and points out that their suggestions on how to improve the city were very important and should be shared with others. For that reason, the trainer informs that the posters will be displayed in the classroom to be seen by all. Finally, the trainer thanks everyone for their participation and invites them for a light snack.

Discussion/Reflection

In the first learning session, the discussion of real examples of positive and active ageing, including the comparison with negative societal perceptions toward older people, aims to expose younger participants to counter-stereotypical information about this age group, thus promoting a more balanced and diversified idea of older people and making the younger participants realize that the consequences of ageing are different for each person. Additionally, the impersonation of these real examples has the goal of stimulating perspective taking and making younger participants learn more about older people.

Besides reinforcing what participants had learned during the first session, the homework assignments for the second learning session also aim to promote perspective taking, by asking them to think about their own ageing, as well as positive behavior intentions, by asking them to think about future interactions with older people.

The goal of the contact session is to promote a situation of positive intergroup contact between younger and older people, allowing them to learn about the other group while facilitating the development of affective ties. In this intergenerational activity, younger and older people are invited to work in teams toward a common goal. The choice of a theme unrelated to ageing, yet relevant and known to both age groups, is instrumental to establish a relationship of equality between them. Last, the light snack provided to all participants at the end of the session also intends to promote further interaction between the two age groups.

Assessment

Assessing the impact of the imAGES program requires the administration of self-report questionnaires in three different stages: a pretest questionnaire applied 1 week before the intervention, and a posttest questionnaire applied two times: after the second learning session and after the contact session. This questionnaire is available in Marques et al. (2015) listed in the Content Sources at the end of this activity. This book is available as open-access and is an important guide to this activity.

To measure stereotypical perceptions about older and younger people, both questionnaires include an age stereotyping scale for each group ("Thinking about older/younger people, in what degree do you think they are . . ."), based on the Stereotype Content Model (Fiske, Cuddy, Glick, & Xu, 2002). The scale is composed of six items divided into two subscales: competence (three items: capable, confident, and skilled) and warmth (three items: friendly, sincere, and trustworthy). All items are rated on Likert-like scales ranging from 1 ("They are nothing like that") to 7 ("They are a lot like that"). Since older people tend to be rated high on warmth but low on competence (Fiske et al., 2002), a successful intervention should lead participants to perceive older individuals as both warm and competent. Thus, the imAGES intervention should result in significant increases in competence ratings as after the second learning session and especially after the contact session.

Other optional questions may also be included to collect control and supplementary data, such as frequency and quality of contact with older people and their grandparents, open questions about participants' perceptions regarding older people and the contact session, as well as demographic questions. Ideally, the intervention group should be compared with a control group, to make sure that the differences between the different stages in the intervention are due to the impact of the learning and/or contact sessions rather than to other uncontrolled/external factors that may co-occur between the sessions.

ADDITIONAL CONSIDERATIONS

imAGES is a promising intervention program to reduce ageism in younger generations, with positive results in three different European cultural backgrounds: Portugal, Austria, and Lithuania. Testing and disseminating this program in other countries would be of great importance to evaluate its impact across different cultures. It is preferable to apply the entire intervention, including both learning sessions and the contact session, as this is the modality that yielded more significant changes in participants' perceptions of older people. The degree of previous contact with older people should also be an important point to consider in the application of the imAGES intervention program.

REFERENCES

Falchikov, N. (1990). Youthful ideas about old age: An analysis of children's drawings. *International Journal of Aging and Human Development, 31*(2), 79–99.

Fiske, S. T., Cuddy, A. C., Glick, P., & Xu, J. (2002). A model of (often mixed) stereotype content: Competence and warmth respectively follow from perceived status and competition. *Journal of Personality & Social Psychology, 82*(6), 878–902.

Galinsky, A. D., & Moskowitz, G. B. (2000). Perspective-taking: Decreasing stereotype expression, stereotype 64 accessibility, and in-group favoritism. *Journal of Personality and Social Psychology, 78*, 708–724.

Garcia-Marques, L., & Mackie, D. M. (1999). The impact of stereotype-incongruent information on perceived group variability and stereotype change. *Journal of Personality and Social Psychology, 77*(5), 979.

Kenworthy, J. B., Turner, R. N., & Hewstone, M. (2005). Intergroup contact: When does it work, and why? In J. F. Dovidio, P. Glick, & L. A. Rudman (Eds.), *On the nature of prejudice: Fifty years after Allport* (pp. 278–292). Malden, MA: Blackwell.

Levy, B. (1996). Improving memory in old age through implicit self-stereotyping. *Journal of Personality and Social Psychology, 71*(6), 1092–1107.

Levy, B. R. (2003). Mind matters: Cognitive and physical effects of aging self-stereotypes. *The Journals of Gerontology: Series B: Psychological Sciences and Social Sciences, 58B*(4), P203–P211. doi:10.1093/geronb/58.4.P203

Lewis, M., & Brooks Gunn, J. (1979). Toward a theory of social cognition: The development of self. *New Directions for Child and Adolescent Development, 1979*(4), 1–20.

Marques, S. (2011). *A discriminação social das pessoas idosas* [Social discrimination of older people]. Colecção de Ensaios da Fundação Francisco Manuel dos Santos. Lisbon, Portugal: Relógio D´Água Editores.

Marques, S., Lima, M. L., Abrams, D., & Swift, H. (2014). Will to live in older people's medical decisions: Immediate and delayed effects of aging stereotypes. *Journal of Applied Social Psychology, 44*(6), 399–408. doi:10.1111/jasp.12231

Marques, S., Swift, H. J., Vauclair, C. M., Lima, M. L., Bratt, C., & Abrams, D. (2015). 'Being old and ill'across different countries: Social status, age identification and older people's subjective health. *Psychology & Health, 30*(6), 699–714. doi:10.1080/08870446.2014.938742

Mendoza, S. A., Gollwitzer, P. M., & Amodio, D. M. (2010). Reducing the expression of implicit stereotypes: Reflexive control through implementation intentions. *Personality and Social Psychology Bulletin, 36*, 512–523.

Middlecamp, M., & Gross, D. (2002). Intergenerational daycare and preschooler´s Attitudes about aging. *Educational Gerontology, 28*, 271–288. doi:10.1080/036012702753590398

Nelson, T. D. (2002). *Ageism: Stereotyping and prejudice against older persons.* Cambridge, MA: MIT Press.

Pettigrew, T. F., & Tropp, L. R. (2006). A meta-analytic test of intergroup contact theory. *Journal of Personality and Social Psychology, 90*(5), 751–783.

Pinquart, M., Wenzel, S., & Sörensen, S. (2000). Changes in attitudes among children and elderly adults in intergenerational group work. *Educational Gerontology, 26*(6), 523–540. doi:10.1080/03601270050133883

Seefeldt, C. (1987). The effects of preschoolers' visits to a nursing home. *The Gerontologist, 27*(2), 228–232.

Whitbourne, S. K., & Sneed, J. R. (2002). The paradox of well-being, identity processes, and stereotype threat: Ageism and its potential relationships to the self in later life. In T. D. Nelson (Ed.), *Ageism: Stereotyping and prejudice against older persons* (pp. 247–273). Cambridge, MA: MIT

CONTENT SOURCE

This is the relevant content source that the reader needs to be aware of to be able to try this activity.

Marques, S., Vauclair, C. M., Rodriges, R., Mendonça, J., Gerardo, F., Cunha, F., . . . Leitão, E. (2015). *imAGES: Intervention program to prevent ageism in children.* Lisbon, Portugal: Santa Casa da Misericórdia & Leya.

ACTIVITY 2.4 EXAMINING THE SOCIAL CLOCK THROUGH YOUTUBE

Rachel Filinson

ACTIVITY INFORMATION

Type

__X__	In class
__X__	Online
__X__	Take home
_____	In community

Difficulty

__X__	Introductory
_____	Intermediate
_____	Advanced

OVERVIEW

Social gerontologists study later life through the *life course* framework, investigating how social change in the public sphere can affect entire cohorts of individual biographies in the private sphere. Social stratification based on class, race, or gender as well as the circumstances of early life further influence the trajectory of the life course, the sequence of transitions and turning points that occur throughout it, and their timing. Recognized in this perspective, therefore, are the limits to human agency in shaping one's own life journey. The life course can be disrupted by societal catastrophe and personal misfortune, but even without such disturbance, the life course is constrained by social dictates known as *age norms*. These are the unwritten, informal rules that determine the standard deadlines for entering and exiting significant social roles related to education, work, and family.

We tend to believe that vital life events are governed by biology, but age norms regarding these major decisions are only loosely based on biology. The social nature of norms is evident in their substantial cross-cultural and historical variations that exceed biological differences. The norms with respect to the appropriate age for entering or leaving social roles follow a *social clock*. In U.S. contemporary society, the early hours of our "social clock" are traditionally devoted to completing education, finding a mate, and leaving the parental home. In the later hours, it is customary to raise children and establish a career. At the latest hours of the social clock, withdrawal from work and family responsibilities are anticipated.

Age norms and the social clock serve as a template for a predictable, organized progression of major adulthood landmarks, but historical events, early experiences, and social disadvantages can impede conformity to them, and life satisfaction can be diminished as a consequence, particularly when deviations engender sanctions. At the same time, adherence to age norms and the social clock can have unfavorable outcomes if the norms are so prescriptive that they prohibit or stifle beneficial behavior or encourage unhealthful behavior, such as social disengagement.

KEY TERMS

Life course
Age norms
Social clock

ACTIVITY LEARNING GOALS

Following this activity, students should be able to . . .

- Explain the concepts of life course, age norms, and social clock.
- Apply these concepts to online videos that demonstrate stark departures from the conventional life course.
- Analyze differing reactions to divergent rejections of age norms.

ASSOCIATION FOR GERONTOLOGY IN HIGHER EDUCATION COMPETENCIES

- Utilize gerontological frameworks to examine human development and aging.
- Relate social theories and science of aging to understanding heterogeneity, inequality, and context of aging.
- Develop a gerontological perspective through knowledge and self-reflection.

MINIMUM/MAXIMUM NUMBER OF PARTICIPANTS

- At least 10 individuals to provide multiple viewpoints; 30 is an ideal maximum for active engagement.

TIME NEEDED TO IMPLEMENT ACTIVITY

- Open-ended when done online; a traditional in-person class setting would require 45 minutes for the lecture, 10 minutes to view the videos, and an additional 20 to 30 minutes for recording and circulating reactions to videos if this were done in class.

SETTING(S)

- Could be done in a classroom with equipment for accessing the Internet but lends itself to remote instruction.

MATERIALS

Required

- Computer that will access Internet videos

PROCEDURES

Preparation

The instructor prepares an online lecture about the life course perspective, age norms, and the social clock. Two suitable videos that relate to the defiance of age norms are identified and made accessible to students in the course (see Appendix 2.4).

Introduction

Students review an online lecture about the life course perspective, age norms, and the social clock. In a traditional delivery mode of instruction, the lecture could be presented in the classroom.

An excerpt from the lecture with illustrative references is provided in the text that follows. The lecture should emphasize the social rather than biological determinants of the life course and age norms; the power of age norms over decisions and transitions related to education, family and work; and the heterogeneity of age norms and the corresponding social clocks across cultures and time periods.

Activity

After reviewing the lecture, students download two videos in an online course or alternatively are shown two videos in a conventional classroom setting. The two videos are:

1. "Still Doing It" available at www.youtube.com/watch?v=NVgcdULvtX0
2. "66-Year-Old Woman Gives Birth to Triplets" available at www.youtube.com/watch?v=W5clXPEcKGM

A detailed explanation of the choice of these videos is offered in Appendix 2.4.

Discussion/Reflection

Questions are posed regarding the reaction to the videos. In the online version of the activity, students are asked to post on the discussion board whether they supported the choices of the individuals shown in each video and to explain their positions. They are further asked to review their peers' reactions that were posted on the discussion board and determine whether one of the videos received more support than the other.

If the activity were conducted in a traditional classroom setting, students would be asked to prepare written journal entries of their attitudes toward the videos. The comments of all students would then need to be circulated so that they could be shared for purposes of comparison.

Wrap-Up

Students submit an assignment in which they (a) reiterate their reactions to the videos that were posted on the discussion board; (b) analyze how each video demonstrates the concepts of life course, age norms, and social clock, summarizing each concept; (c) determine whether the class as a whole was more positively oriented toward one video rather than the other; and (d) use critical thinking skills to explain why the differences in evaluation of the videos would occur, again utilizing concepts from the lecture.

Students submit the assignment by uploading it to an online learning management platform in the distance learning course and could submit it in the form of a short written paper in an in-person classroom.

Follow-Up

In the online version of the activity, online grader feedback prods students who have not sufficiently made the links between the key concepts and their video analysis to recognize the connections. In a traditional classroom setting, a classroom discussion that follows assignment submission could be used to summarize and reinforce the application of the concepts and to interpret the differing reactions to the two videos. Typically students admit to discomfort from both videos, acknowledging that ageist, misinformed opinions may account for these feelings in relation to the "Still Doing It" video but not for their visceral objections to the "66-year-old Women Gives Birth to Triplets" video. Students could be asked to reflect on how their responses were affected by the gender and cultural background of the individuals depicted in the videos.

Assessment

A rubric that measures the achievement of the learning goals—derived from an Association of American Colleges & Universities rubric for critical thinking—is used to grade the assignment. The rubric considers four areas:

1. Does the student present a clear summary of the key concepts (social clock; age norms; life course) that are expected to be utilized in this activity?
2. Is the student able to analyze the selected videos by applying the key concepts and, through differentiating their application to the two videos, demonstrate an understanding of them?
3. Does the student offer a logical explanation of their (typically) varied reactions to the videos, integrating the key concepts within the explanation?
4. Is the student able to synthesize peers' responses to the videos and critically compare them to their own?

ADDITIONAL CONSIDERATIONS

While the two videos selected for this activity are excellent for prompting discussion of the life course, others that depict irregularities in the traditional life course could be substituted. For example, a video depicting an adult moving back to the parental home after a divorce or unemployment or an older adult embarking on the pursuit of higher education or a new career could be used.

Social gerontologists study later life through the *life course* framework, examining the "interplay between human lives and changing social structures" (American Sociological Association, n.d.) Historical events and social change playing out in the public sphere are seen to affect entire cohorts of individual biographies in the private sphere. For example, wars or economic downswings can result in delayed or foregone marriage, childbearing, and career building for the generation coming of age during this time period (cf. Elder, 1999), the impacts of which extend into old age. Social stratification, based on class, race, or gender (cf. Institute for Social Research, n.d.) and the circumstances of early life (cf. Kamiya, Doyle, Henretta, & Timonen, 2014) further influence the trajectory of the life course, the sequence of transitions and turning points that occur throughout it, and their timing (Hutchison, 2007). Recognized in this perspective, therefore, are the limits to human agency in shaping one's own life journey.

The life course can be disrupted by societal catastrophe and personal misfortune, but even without such disturbance, the life course is constrained by social dictates known as *age norms*. These are the unwritten, informal rules that determine the standard deadlines for entering and exiting significant social roles related to education, work, and family (cf. Settersten & Hagestad, 1996a, 1996b). Such rules also exist for more minor decisions, such as whether it's deemed appropriate for an older person to dress "young" or learn weight lifting. We tend to believe that vital life events like marriage or childbearing (or starting or finishing education) are governed by biology, but age norms regarding these major decisions are only loosely based on biology. The social nature of norms is evident in their substantial cross-cultural and historical variations that exceed biological differences (cf. Matthews & Hamilton, 2009). The temporal fluctuations in age norms are illustrated by recent increases in the United States in the age at which men and women marry for the first time, have their first child, complete education, and enter retirement (cf. Associated Press/NORC Center for Public Affairs Research, 2013).

The norms with respect to the appropriate age for entering or leaving social roles are primarily socially constructed ideas and follow a *social clock*. In U.S. contemporary society, the early hours of our "social clock" are traditionally devoted to completing education, finding a mate, and leaving the parental home. In the later hours, it is customary for children to be raised and a career established. At the latest hours of the social clock, withdrawal from work and family responsibilities are anticipated. Age norms and the social clock serve as a template for a predictable, organized progression of major adulthood landmarks but historical events, early experiences, and social disadvantages can impede conformity to them and life satisfaction can be diminished as a consequence (Ferraro, 2013), particularly when deviations engender sanctions. At the same time, adhering to age norms and the social clock can have unfavorable outcomes if the norms are so prescriptive that they prohibit or stifle beneficial behavior or encourage unhealthful behavior, such as social disengagement. Levin (2013) details the loosening age norms for education, work, and family transitions, and the breakdown of the life course. With increasing flexibility, the life course becomes increasingly liberated from strict timetables and age-based roles.

REFERENCES

American Sociological Association. (n.d.). Section on aging and the life course. Retrieved from http://www.asanet.org/sections/aging-and-life-course

Associated Press/NORC Center for Public Affairs Research. (2013). National survey: Working longer—Older Americans' attitudes on work and retirement. Retrieved from http://www.apnorc.org/PDFs/Working%20Longer/NORC-AP-NORC-Working-longer.pdf

Elder, G. H. (1999). *Children of the Great Depression: Social change in life experience*. Boulder, CO: Westview Press.

Ferraro, K. F. (2013). The time of our lives: Recognizing the contributions of Mannheim, Neugarten, and Riley to the study of aging. *The Gerontologist, 54*(1), 127–133. doi:10.1093/geront/gnt048

Hutchison, E. D. (2007). A life course perspective. Retrieved from http://www.cor-win .com/upm-data/16295_Chapter_1.pdf

Institute for Social Research. (n.d.). Growing older in America: The health and retirement study. Retrieved from http://hrsonline.isr.umich.edu/index.php?p= dbook

Kamiya, Y., Doyle, M., Henretta, J. C., & Timonen, V. (2014). Early-life circumstances and later-life loneliness in Ireland. *Gerontologist, 54*(5), 773–783. doi:10.1093/ geront/gnt097

Levin, J. (2013). *Blurring the boundaries: The declining significance of age.* London, UK:\ Routledge.

Matthews, T. J., & Hamilton, B. E. (2009, August). Delayed childbearing: More women are having their first child later in life. *NCHS Data Brief, 21,* 1–8. Retrieved from http://www.cdc.gov/nchs/data/databriefs/db21.pdf

Settersten, R. A., & Hagestad, G. O. (1996a). What's the latest? Cultural age deadlines for family transitions. *The Gerontologist, 36*(2), 178–188. doi:10.1093/geront/36.2.178

Settersten, R. A., & Hagestad, G. O. (1996b). What's the latest? II. Cultural age deadlines for educational and work transitions. *The Gerontologist, 36*(5), 602–613. doi:10.1093/geront/36.5.602

APPENDIX 2.4: INSTRUCTIONS FOR ACTIVITY

The activity follows a lecture centered on the life course perspective, age norms, and the social clock. At levels above the introductory one, the lecture could additionally highlight how cumulative disadvantage in the early part of life has cascading impacts on the life course and its outcomes.

After reviewing the lecture, students are shown two videos:

1. "Still Doing It," available at www.youtube.com/watch?v=NVgcdULvtX0
2. "66-year-old Woman Gives Birth to Triplets," available at www.youtube.com/watch?v=W5clXPEcKGM

These two videos were selected because of their brevity and provocative content that piques student interest and generates strong reactions. They were also selected because their contrast facilitates an understanding of the key concepts being taught. In both videos, deviation from the typical life course, age norms, and social clock are depicted, but the degree of acceptance of the deviation is likely to significantly differ, a difference that hinges on the social implications of their behavior. In the first video, older women discuss their continued interest and engagement in sexual relations. This is a behavior that would normally not be observable by others; its private nature distinguishes it from the visible social actions—recognized milestones—associated with the major educational, familial, and work transitions comprising the life course. These would include, for instance, graduating from college, getting married, becoming widowed, or starting or ending a career. As a primarily concealed behavior that concerns mainly the participating partners, sexual activity may be less subject to societal guidance and reaction than behaviors that occur in the open. It can be contained in the micro world rather than crossing the boundaries to the macro world. Moreover, by defying the norm of the asexual older female, the women in the video appeared to gain in life satisfaction.

In comparison, the second video describes the situation of a 66-year-old woman in India who has given birth to triplets after fertility treatments. In this situation, the aberrant timing of a major life event—childbirth—is not just the culmination of a series of personal choices. It has been made possible by available technology that overrides natural limitations of childbearing, policy permitting physicians to provide fertility treatment to women of advanced age, the cultural demands for genetic intergenerational bonds to premise inheritance, and other social factors. This event of the woman's life course garners the public gaze to the degree that media attention is extensive. The video emphasizes the aggravated health risks that arise from circumvention of the natural age restrictions to childbearing. Furthermore, the elderly mother's choice to not abide by the rules of the accepted social clock has effects not only for her but also for the children she has produced, even the larger society, should she not be able to care for her children.

Following the viewing of the brief videos, students are asked to write brief entries (in an online discussion board or in "free-write" journals) that indicate whether or not they supported the choices of the individuals shown in each video and to explain their positions. They are further asked to review their peers' reactions, which are made available to them.

The final, written assignment consists of students (a) reiterating their reactions to the videos; (b) analyzing how each video demonstrates the concepts of life course, age norms, and social clock and summarizing each concept; (c) determining whether the class as a whole was more positively oriented toward one video rather than the other; and (d) using critical thinking skills to explain why the differences in evaluation of the videos would occur, again utilizing concepts from the lecture.

CHAPTER 3

DEMENTIA
Rona J. Karasik

While old age and dementia are often seen as intertwined, the reality is that most older people *do not* have dementia, nor is every person with dementia "old." For example, according to the Alzheimer's Association (2015), in the United States:

- Less than 11% of those aged 65 years and older have dementia.
- Risk of developing dementia increases with age.
- Approximately 32% of those older than age 85 have some form of dementia.
- Approximately 200,000 persons younger than age 65 are thought to have early-onset Alzheimer's (one form of dementia).

While these percentages remain relatively low, the overall number of cases of dementia is increasing (due in part to increases in the overall population size, increasing life expectancies, and earlier diagnosis). Moreover, the challenges of having dementia are considerable and reach far beyond those with the diagnosis and their immediate caregivers.

WHAT IS DEMENTIA?

In earlier versions of the *Diagnostic and Statistical Manual*, "dementia" was a broad *diagnostic category* representing the development of some or all of the following symptoms at a level severe enough to interfere with daily functioning. These symptoms include impairments of:

- Memory
- Judgment
- Abstract reasoning
- Speech/communication
- Sense of time
- Emotional responses
- Coordination

It is important to recognize that these symptoms may also be caused by a wide range of other, *non-dementia*-related factors, including:

- Visual or hearing impairments
- Medications
- Nutritional issues
- Emotional factors (e.g., grief, stress)
- Fatigue
- Overload
- Other illnesses

In other words, many people demonstrating symptoms associated with dementia do not have dementia at all. It is essential, therefore, to look further as to the cause of the symptoms. While some forgetfulness and cognitive misfiring is normal for everyone, symptoms that interfere with a person's daily functioning and/or become progressively worse should be evaluated further (Agronin, 2014; Mace & Rabins, 2011).

In 2013, the *Diagnostic and Statistical Manual of Mental Disorders* (5th ed.; *DSM-5*) replaced the diagnostic category of "dementia" with a similar diagnostic category, "Neurocognitive Disorders (Major and Minor)" (American Psychiatric Association, 2013; Regier, Kuhl, & Kupfer, 2013). The term *dementia*, however, is still commonly used.

WHAT IS THE DIFFERENCE BETWEEN ALZHEIMER'S DISEASE AND DEMENTIA?

Alzheimer's disease (AD) is one of roughly 70 different disorders that produce the symptoms associated with the diagnostic category of dementia. Alzheimer's is the most common dementia-producing disease. In other words, AD is one form of dementia.

Other dementia-producing disorders include vascular dementia, Lewy-body dementia (LBD), frontotemporal degeneration (FTD), and Huntington's disease. The National Institute of Neurological Disorders and Stroke (NINDS) is a good source for up-to-date information on specific dementia-producing disorders (www.ninds.nih.gov). While, by definition, dementia-producing disorders share many similar symptoms, each disorder is unique in cause, manifestation, and progression.

Alzheimer's Disease

Characterized by neurofibrillary tangles and beta amyloid plaques, Alzheimer's is a nonreversible neurodegenerative disorder that has at least two forms: the relatively rare early onset (before age 65) and the more common later onset. The disease tends to progress gradually over a number of years and stages, with increasing confusion and severity of cognitive impairment.

Lewy-Body Dementia

A common cause of dementia, LBD is a neurodegenerative disorder that, in addition to dementia-like progressive cognitive decline, also features Parkinson-like symptoms (e.g., resting tremors, bradykinesia) and fluctuations in cognitive function. Visual hallucinations and depression are also possible.

Vascular Dementia

Vascular dementia is a subcategory of dementias (e.g., multi-infarct dementia, subcortical vascular dementia) resulting from damage caused by cardiovascular problems impairing blood supply to the brain. Symptoms may appear to progress in a step-wise fashion and/or as more localized rather than global cognitive deficits, depending on the specific areas of the brain that are affected (such as speech, memory, or mobility).

Frontotemporal Degeneration

A subcategory of dementias is associated with impairment to the frontal and temporal lobes of the brain. Associated symptoms include changes in behavior (e.g., reduced social screens, lack of empathy, disinhibition) and/or difficulties with speech and language. Memory and spatial skills may appear less affected early on than in other dementias.

WORKING WITH PERSONS WITH DEMENTIA

Interacting with persons with progressive declines in cognitive function poses a wide range of challenges, not only for families and care providers, but for the person with dementia as well. It is essential to keep the following in mind:

- Caring for a person with dementia can be an exhausting, frustrating, and frightening experience. It can be a rewarding and positive experience as well.

- People with dementia have feelings and value. A person with dementia is a person first—there's more to a person than their dementia.

- Every person with dementia is an individual and has unique experiences.

- While most dementia is progressive, one's abilities do not diminish all at once. Focus on a person's remaining abilities.

- Having dementia can be an exhausting, frustrating, and frightening experience.

- Behavior is in the eye of the beholder. Actions that may appear disruptive or inappropriate are likely the result of a person trying to communicate their needs as best as possible, given the cognitive challenges.

DEMENTIA EDUCATION ACTIVITIES

The following two activities offer participants opportunities to develop and apply positive approaches to interacting with persons with dementia.

In Activity 3.1, Dementia Communication and Empathy, participants are asked to role-play scenarios where persons with dementia endeavor to communicate with their caregiver. Insight and increased empathy are promoted through the challenges participants experience, not only in understanding the message being communicated, but also the challenges of conveying even a simple message while impaired by physical and/or cognitive limitations.

Activity 3.2, Enhancing Students' Therapeutic Interaction Skills With Older Adults With Dementia, brings participants into the community to interact directly with persons with dementia. By working one on one with persons with dementia in an adult day center or similar situation, participants are afforded the opportunity to apply their content knowledge and hone their interpersonal skills. Persons with dementia, and the agencies that serve them, also stand to benefit from the added individualized attention and assistance with programming.

REFERENCES

Agronin, M. (2014). *Alzheimer's disease and other dementias: A practical guide* (3rd ed.). New York, NY: Routledge.

Alzheimer's Association. (2015). 2015 Alzheimer's disease facts and figures. *Alzheimer's & Dementia, 11*(3), 332. Retrieved from https://www.alz.org/facts/downloads/facts_figures_2015.pdf

American Psychiatric Association. (2013). *Diagnostic and statistical manual of mental disorders* (5th ed.). Arlington, VA: American Pyschiatric Publishing.

Mace, N., & Rabins, P. (2011). *The 36-hour day: A family guide to caring for persons with Alzheimer's disease, related dementing illness and memory loss in later life* (5th ed.). Baltimore, MD: Johns Hopkins University Press.

National Institute of Neurological Disorders and Stroke. (2016). Retrieved from http://www.ninds.nih.gov

Regier, D. A., Kuhl, E. A., & Kupfer, D. J. (2013). The *DSM-5:* Classification and criteria changes. *World Psychiatry, 12*(2), 92–98.

ACTIVITY 3.1 DEMENTIA COMMUNICATION AND EMPATHY

Rona J. Karasik

ACTIVITY INFORMATION

Type

__X__	In class
_____	Online
_____	Take home
__X__	In community

Difficulty

_____	Introductory
__X__	Intermediate
_____	Advanced

OVERVIEW

Communication is complex, involving multiple modes (verbal, nonverbal), goals (such as understanding someone and making oneself understood), and contexts (such as environments, roles, emotions, and expectations). Everyday challenges of communication may be amplified when one or more of the persons trying to communicate is experiencing cognitive and/or physical impairments (e.g., dementia, stroke, aphasia, traumatic brain injury).

The progressive nature of dementia makes communication even more complicated as new declines and challenges are likely to emerge. Not very long ago, persons with moderate to severe dementia were thought to be incapable of meaningful communication. Now it is understood that even though a person with dementia may struggle with more traditional forms of communication, that person can and does communicate. Moreover, actions that were once regarded as undesirable "dementia-related behaviors" may now be viewed as important, albeit potentially difficult to interpret, forms of communication (Power, 2010).

Research suggests that communication skills training for professionals and families can be beneficial and effective in improving comprehension and facilitating positive interactions with persons experiencing symptoms of dementia (Eggenberger, Heimerl, & Bennett, 2013). Trying on the role, even briefly, of a person attempting to communicate while impaired by cognitive and/or physical limitations has the potential to increase one's empathy and understanding for those who face these challenges on a daily basis. This role-playing activity was created to simulate the obstacles persons with and without dementia (or other impairment) may experience when attempting to communicate with each other in order to (a) develop the understanding that communicative limitations are not the same as having nothing to communicate; (b) provide insight into some of the difficulties and frustration that can be associated with not understanding or being able to make oneself understood; (c) foster empathy both for persons with cognitive and/or physical impairments and the persons they interact with (such as caregivers); and (d) enhance students' and practitioners' skills for communicating with persons with dementia and/or other impairments.

ACTIVITY LEARNING GOALS

Following this activity, students should be able to . . .

- Recognize that the behavior of a person with a cognitive and/or physical impairment is a form of communication.
- Empathize with communication challenges persons with cognitive and/or physical impairments may face.
- Communicate more effectively with persons with cognitive and/or physical impairments.

ASSOCIATION FOR GERONTOLOGY IN HIGHER EDUCATION COMPETENCIES

- Develop a gerontological perspective through knowledge and self-reflection.
- Engage, through effective communication, older persons, their families, and the community in personal and public issues in aging.
- Promote older persons' strengths and adaptations to maximize well-being, health, and mental health.
- Promote quality of life and positive social environment for older persons.

MINIMUM/MAXIMUM NUMBER OF PARTICIPANTS

- 10 to 30

TIME NEEDED TO IMPLEMENT ACTIVITY

- 45 to 75 minutes

SETTING(S)

- Classroom or other room with sufficient space and furniture to allow for pairs to work together face to face. *Note*: Activity can get noisy so adequate space for pairs is recommended.

MATERIALS

Required

- Dementia and Communication: A Brief Overview (Appendix 3.1A)
- Dementia Communication Challenge Cards (Appendix 3.1B)
- Improving Our Communication Strategies (Appendix 3.1C)

Optional

- Pre/post assessments (Appendix 3.1D)
- Physical and/or sensory impairment simulators (e.g., vision impairment simulation goggles, earplugs); assistive mobility devices (such as walkers, wheelchairs)

PROCEDURE

Preparation

- Review content materials provided.
- Create Dementia Communication Challenge Cards (Appendix 3.1B) by copying the challenge cards included onto card stock and cutting them into individual vignettes and/or creating your own cards which identify (a) tentative diagnosis, (b) the communication challenge(s) the person with dementia/care recipient is experiencing, and (c) the message the person with dementia/care recipient wishes to communicate.
- Print optional pre/post assessments (if using; Appendix 3.1D).

Introduction

- Administer optional pretest assessment (if using).
- Introduce participants to the topic with the Dementia and Communication: A Brief Overview mini-lecture (Appendix 3.1A).
- Information may be delivered via lecture, discussion, and/or handout format.

Activity

- Divide participants into pairs and have them spread out as far as the room allows so that they are less likely to be distracted by the work of other pairs.
- Have each pair identify who will take on the role of "care recipient" and who will take on the role of "caregiver."
- Distribute a Dementia Communication Challenge Card to each "care recipient," with instructions *not* to show the card to the "caregiver" partner. (*Note*: It is recommended that each pair be given a different card so that pairs are not all trying to communicate the same message at the same time.)
- Ask the "care recipients" to review the information on their card and attempt to communicate their "message" as best they can to their "caregiver" within the constraints of assigned communication challenges.

- Monitor pairs' progress—they will not all "reach an understanding" of the message at the same rate.

- When a pair completes a communication (e.g., the "caregiver" has successfully identified the message the "care recipient" is trying to convey), have the partners switch roles and repeat the process using a different communication card.

- Repeat by rotating challenge cards and alternating roles as time allows and switching pair groupings if desired. (*Note*: Some pairs work more efficiently together than others. For pairs that are struggling or complete the task too easily, it can be beneficial to regroup participants into different pairs.)

Discussion/Reflection

- After each member of the pair has had the chance to experience each role at least once (but preferably multiple times—particularly for pairs that seem to finish their challenges early), conduct a group discussion to reflect on their experiences.

Reflection questions might include the following:

- Which message did you find the most difficult to communicate?
- Which message did you find the easiest to communicate?
- Which challenge(s) did you find the most limiting?
- Which challenge(s) did you find the least limiting?
- What frustrated you as you were trying to communicate?
- How clearly were you able to communicate/understand the message? Why?
- What did you learn from this experience? How/why?
- How might you improve your communication strategies in the future?
- How might this experience translate into your interactions with persons with dementia and/or who have communication challenges?

Wrap-Up

Following the group discussion, provide participants with the information in Improving Our Communication Strategies (Appendix 3.1C).

- Information may be delivered via lecture, discussion, and/or handout format.
- Demonstration and practice of successful communication strategies (optional).
- If time and interest allow, have participants role-play applying some of the strategies to situations on the communication cards (or other communication scenarios).

Assessment

At the conclusion of the wrap-up, administer the postsurvey assessment (Appendix 3.1D) if using.

ADDITIONAL CONSIDERATIONS

- This activity can produce a fair amount of noise, so try to find a venue where others will not be disturbed.

- Some participant pairs will take the activity more seriously than others, and some individuals may find role-playing to be uncomfortable or embarrassing at first.

- It may be necessary to provide additional challenge cards to pairs that finish early so that the other pairs have time to finish at least one set experiencing each role.

- It can also be beneficial to change pairings to create different communication dynamics.

REFERENCES

Eggenberger, E., Heimerl, K., & Bennett, M. I. (2013). Communication skills training in dementia care: A systematic review of effectiveness, training content, and didactic methods in different care settings. *International Psychogeriatrics, 25*(3), 345–358.

Power, G. A. (2010). *Dementia beyond drugs. Changing the culture of care.* Baltimore, MD: Health Professions Press.

RECOMMENDED RESOURCES

There are many good sources regarding the basics of dementia, benefits of communication skills training, and person-centered nonpharmaceutical approaches to dementia care based on the premise that dementia "behaviors" represent communication. Popular dementia educator Teepa Snow offers a number of informative training videos at her website: teepasnow.com. Additional resources include the following:

Alzheimer's Association. (2016). *Communication: Tips for successful communication at all stages of Alzheimer's disease* (Publication No. 770-10-0018). Chicago, IL: Author.

National Institute of Neurological Disorders and Stroke. (2017). Website. Retrieved from http://www.ninds.nih.gov

Regier, D. A., Kuhl, E. A., & Kupfer, D. J. (2013). The *DSM-5:* Classification and criteria changes. *World Psychiatry, 12*(2), 92–98.

APPENDIX 3.1A: DEMENTIA AND COMMUNICATION: A BRIEF OVERVIEW

While many people tend to focus on memory concerns, persons with dementia may experience a range of communication challenges that can (a) interfere with a person's remaining cognitive abilities; (b) vary with the stage or degree of the dementia-producing disorder; and (c) be caused by factors other than and/or unrelated to dementia. Some communication challenges identified by the Alzheimer's Association (2016) include the following:

- Difficulty finding desired word (word finding, word substitution)
- Describing rather than naming objects
- Difficulty organizing thoughts/words (e.g., word hash)
- Repeating familiar words (perseveration)
- Difficulty maintaining train of thought
- Speaking less/gesturing more
- If applicable, reverting to a native language

  Additional challenges include the following:
- Understanding what words mean
- Paying attention during long conversations
- Frustration if communication isn't working
- Being very sensitive to touch and to the tone and loudness of voices (ADEAR, 2012, p. 1)

In the past, persons with moderate to severe dementia often were thought to be incapable of meaningful interaction. Now we have come to understand that even though persons with dementia may struggle with more traditional forms of communication, they can and do communicate and actions that were once viewed as undesirable "dementia-related behaviors" are now being seen instead as attempts at communication (Power, 2010).

COMMUNICATION TRAINING

Communication is an interactive experience consisting of verbal (words), nonverbal (e.g., emotional cues, body language), and context elements (e.g., environment, time of day, surrounding events, and interpersonal relationships). With dementia, verbal abilities tend to decline, increasing the importance of nonverbal cues (Williams & Herman, 2011).

Everyone involved contributes to the ease or difficulty of communication (Jones, 2015). Therefore, as the communication abilities of a person with dementia decline, it is important for those without cognitive impairment to "step up their game" and find ways to compensate for dementia-associated changes. In other words, when a person with dementia is struggling, it is up to everyone else to improve their communicative efforts.

While changing one's communication approach can be difficult, research shows that communication training for family members and professional caregivers can be effective both in increasing positive interactions with persons with dementia, as well as improving their overall quality of life (Eggenberger, Heimerl, & Bennett, 2013; Haberstroh, Neumeyer, Krause, Franzmann, & Pantel, 2011).

The following role-playing activity is designed to simulate some of the challenges persons with cognitive impairment may experience when attempting to communicate, as well as to provide participants with the opportunity to find ways to improve their end of the communication partnership.

REFERENCES

Alzheimer's Association. (2016). *Communication: Tips for successful communication at all stages of Alzheimer's disease* (Publication No. 770-10-0018). Chicago, IL: Author.

Alzheimer's Disease Education and Referral Center. (2012). *Alzheimer's caregiving tips: Changes in communication skills.* Silver Spring, MD: National Institute on Aging.

Eggenberger, E., Heimerl, K., & Bennett, M. I. (2013). Communication skills training in dementia care: A systematic review of effectiveness, training content, and didactic methods in different care settings. *International Psychogeriatrics, 25*(3), 345–358.

Haberstroh, J., Neumeyer, K., Krause, K., Franzmann, J., & Pantel, J. (2011). TANDEM: Communication training for informal caregivers of people with dementia. *Aging & Mental Health, 15*(3), 405–413.

Jones, D. (2015). A family living with Alzheimer's disease: The communicative challenges. *Dementia, 14*(5), 555–573.

Power, G. A. (2010). *Dementia beyond drugs. Changing the culture of care.* Baltimore, MD: Health Professions Press.

Williams, K. N., & Herman, R. E. (2011). Linking resident behavior to dementia care communication: Effects of emotional tone. *Behavior Therapy, 42*(1), 42–46.

APPENDIX 3.1B: DEMENTIA COMMUNICATION CHALLENGE CARDS

Use these prompts or create your own.

Tentative Diagnosis: • Mid- to late-stage dementia (possibly Lewy body) **Communication Challenge(s):** • Vocalization but no intelligible speech • Resting tremors **Message to Be Communicated:** • "I am hungry."	**Tentative Diagnosis:** • Mid-stage dementia (unknown type) **Communication Challenge(s):** • Limited speech • Hearing impairment **Message to Be Communicated:** • "When am I going home?"
Tentative Diagnosis: • Stroke, possible dementia **Communication Challenge(s):** • Limited speech • Right side paralysis **Message to Be Communicated:** • "I need to go to the bathroom."	**Tentative Diagnosis:** • Mid-stage dementia (unknown type) **Communication Challenge(s):** • Limited speech • Difficulty finding specific words **Message to Be Communicated:** • "I don't feel well."
Tentative Diagnosis: • Mid- to late-stage dementia **Communication Challenge(s):** • Vocalization but no intelligible speech • Vision impaired from cataracts • Confusion as to time and location (used to live on a farm) **Message to Be Communicated:** • "It's time to milk the cows."	**Tentative Diagnosis:** • Mid stages of dementia (possibly Alzheimer's) **Communication Challenge(s):** • Confusion as to time and location • Difficulty finding specific words **Message to Be Communicated:** • "I feel like dancing. Will you dance with me?"

(continued)

(*continued*)

Tentative Diagnosis: • Mid stages of dementia (possibly Alzheimer's) **Communication Challenge(s):** • Difficulty finding specific words • Confusion as to time and location **Message to Be Communicated:** • "I can't find my purse. I think someone stole it. It had all my money. My mother will be very angry."	**Tentative Diagnosis:** • Mid stages of dementia (unknown type) **Communication Challenge(s):** • Confusion as to time and location • Difficulty finding specific words • Agitation **Message to Be Communicated:** • "I don't know where my husband is. Have you seen him? He is supposed to be here to pick me up."
Tentative Diagnosis: • Mid- to late-stage dementia, cause of mobility issues unknown **Communication Challenge(s):** • Vocalization but no intelligible speech • Extremely limited mobility **Message to Be Communicated:** • "I have an itch on the middle of my back and I cannot reach it."	**Tentative Diagnosis:** • Mid stages of dementia (possibly Alzheimer's) **Communication Challenge(s):** • Garbled speech • Overly vocal **Message to Be Communicated:** • "These cookies remind me of my mother's. May I have another?"
Tentative Diagnosis: • Stroke, possible dementia **Communication Challenge(s):** • Limited speech • Right side paralysis • Requires wheelchair **Message to Be Communicated:** • "What is your name?"	**Tentative Diagnosis:** • Mid-stage dementia (unknown type) **Communication Challenge(s):** • No short-term memory • Keeps trying to walk out the door **Message to Be Communicated:** • "Let's go for a walk outside and pick flowers."
Tentative Diagnosis: • Mid-stage dementia **Communication Challenge(s):** • Limited speech • High level of agitation/urgency **Message to Be Communicated:** • "All this noise is bothering me. I want to leave."	**Tentative Diagnosis:** • Mid-stage dementia (unknown type) **Communication Challenge(s):** • Limited speech • Difficulty finding specific words **Message to Be Communicated:** • "I don't know where I am or who you are, and I am scared."

(*continued*)

(*continued*)

Tentative Diagnosis: • Mid-stage dementia **Communication Challenge(s):** • Repetitive speech • Crying/agitation **Message to Be Communicated:** • "Have you seen my dog Millie? I can't find her, and she is not coming when I call her. Do you think she is lost? Will you help me find her?"	**Tentative Diagnosis:** • Mid stages of dementia (possibly Alzheimer's) **Communication Challenge(s):** • Confusion as to time and location • Difficulty finding specific words **Message to Be Communicated:** • "I haven't seen you in a long time; where have you been?"
Tentative Diagnosis: • Mid stages of dementia (possibly Alzheimer's) **Communication Challenge(s):** • No short-term memory • Confusion as to time and location (thinks still a grade school teacher) **Message to Be Communicated:** • "Why haven't you turned in your homework yet? You need to go to the principal's office."	**Tentative Diagnosis:** • Mid stages of dementia, arthritis **Communication Challenge(s):** • Limited speech • Difficulty finding specific words • Arthritic hands with limited mobility **Message to Be Communicated:** • "I like your sweater. I used to knit all the time. Did you knit this yourself? Did you use a pattern to make it?"
Tentative Diagnosis: • Mid-stage frontotemporal degeneration **Communication Challenge(s):** • Limited social screens (appropriateness) • Difficulty finding words • Often uses curse words **Message to Be Communicated:** • "I do not want to go anywhere. Leave me alone!"	**Tentative Diagnosis:** • Mid to later stages of dementia **Communication Challenge(s):** • Profound confusion (thinks you are a relative) • Perseveration **Message to Be Communicated:** • "Is it time to go home yet? I am ready to go home now."

APPENDIX 3.1C: IMPROVING OUR COMMUNICATION STRATEGIES

The following tips are adapted from the Alzheimer's Association and additional sources. (Alzheimer's Association, 2012; 2016; ADEAR, 2012; Coste, 2003; & Hodgeson, 1995).

Communication is interactive, involving both the *sending of messages to others* (production) and the *understanding of messages sent by others* (comprehension). Cognitive impairment associated with dementia can interfere with the communication process, leading to frustration and confusion for everyone involved. Understanding the communication challenges that a person with dementia may be facing and working to improve our own communication may have a positive impact on the interaction. An important first step is recognizing that communication includes not only the **words** we use, but also our **tone, body language**, and **actions**. It is not what we say or do, but how we say or do it that matters most. Additional ways to improve communication include the following:

Practice Listening! Take Time to Receive the Other Person's Communication

- Listen and watch the person's body language.
- Be patient and wait for the person's response (do not interrupt or rush).
- Focus on the emotional (nonverbal) cues.
- Double check that you understand what the individual has communicated.

If a Person Cannot Find the Right Word

- Encourage the person to act out the meaning.
- Encourage the person to "talk around" what they are trying to say.
- Say what you think the person is trying to communicate (persons may be able to recognize words they cannot generate on their own).
- Avoid correcting "wrong" words (this can be frustrating or embarrassing).

If a Person Digresses or Loses the Train of Thought

- Repeat the last words said.
- Summarize what has been discussed so far.
- Ask relevant questions.
- Show respect for the feelings expressed, even if the facts are wrong (avoid arguing).

Improve Your Own Verbal Communication

- Think before you speak.
- Avoid distractions (such as competing noise from TV), and keep your voice calm and friendly.
- Avoid "talking down" to the person or talking as if they are not there.
- Avoid "elder speak" (e.g., overly slow, overly simplified "baby talk").
- Start each time by introducing yourself (e.g., giving your name, role) and saying why you are there.

- Explain what is going to happen.
- Use short, simple sentences (but avoid "elder speak"—mentioned earlier).
- Avoid using conjunctions (such as "and" and "but"), which make sentences longer and more complex.
- Be specific, direct, and explicit about what you mean.
- Use concrete and common words (avoid abstract or fancy words).
- Avoid clichés, idioms, sayings, generalizations, and colloquialisms (is it really "raining cats and dogs"?).
- Use proper names and common nouns (avoid pronouns).
- Give the most important information at the **end** of sentences (e.g., "Do you want coffee or tea?").

If a Person Is Having Trouble Understanding You

- Remember that pain, illness, fatigue, and vision/sight impairments can interfere with communication.
- Repeat, revise, and/or restate what you are saying using different words.
- Avoid logical discussions or debates (instead, respond to feelings the individual is expressing).
- Provide immediate feedback, reassurance, and rewards.
- Assume that the person can understand more than the person can express.
- Remember that people with dementia will probably forget, so you may need to repeat yourself.

When Asking Questions

- Avoid open-ended questions.
- Limit the number of choices possible to two.
- Give lots of time for a response.
- If needed, repeat or reword questions.

When Giving Instructions

- Break instructions into smaller steps.
- Give only one direction at a time.
- Allow the person to finish each instruction **before** giving the next.
- Give directions close to when they must be followed.
- Give positive directions that say what to do (e.g., "Come with me") rather than what not to do (e.g., "Don't go in there").

Improving Your Nonverbal Communication

- Understand that facial expressions, tone, and gestures are more meaningful than words.
- Gently get a person's attention by being sure they can see you before saying anything.
- Approach the person from the front (and in that person's visual field) so they can see you.

- Use more than one of the five senses (e.g., say their name and touch their shoulder).
- Use a calm, pleasant, low-pitched tone of voice.
- Use open, friendly, relaxed body language.
- Move slowly and gently.
- Maintain appropriate eye contact (consider cultural implications here as well).
- Use positive facial gestures (e.g., smile).
- Respect personal space (do not stand too close or too far from the person).
- Try to converse at eye level beside or in front of the person (not from behind the person).
- Use objects and pictures to illustrate your message.
- Use physical actions to illustrate your message.
- When giving instructions, demonstrate the action.
- Be aware of the person's culture.
- Be sure that your verbal and nonverbal communication match.
- Keep trying and be supportive (would you want someone to give up on you?).

REFERENCES

Alzheimer's Association. (2012). *Communication: Best ways to interact with a person with dementia* (Publication No. 770-10-0018). Chicago, IL: Author.

Alzheimer's Association. (2016). *Communication: Tips for successful communication at all stages of Alzheimer's disease* (Publication No. 770-10-0018). Chicago, IL: Author. Retrieved from http://www.alz.org/national/documents/brochure_communication.pdf

Alzheimer's Disease Education and Referral Center. (2012). *Alzheimer's caregiving tips: Changes in communication skills.* Silver Spring, MD: National Institute on Aging. Retrieved from https://www.nia.nih.gov/sites/default/files/alzheimers-caregiving-tips-changes-in-communication-skills.pdf

Coste, J. K. (2003). *Learning to speak Alzheimer's: A groundbreaking approach for everyone dealing with the disease.* New York, NY: Houghton Mifflin Harcourt.

Hodgeson, H. (1995). *Alzheimer's: Finding the words. A communication guide for those who care.* Minneapolis, MN: Chronimed.

APPENDIX 3.1D: SAMPLE PREACTIVITY ASSESSMENT

Please rate the level to which you agree or disagree with the following statements:

	Strongly Disagree	Somewhat Disagree	Neither Agree nor Disagree	Somewhat Agree	Strongly Agree
It is normal for persons with dementia to shout or cry for no reason.					
People with dementia do not really care what you say or do.					
You should never lie to a person with dementia.					
It is important to correct people with dementia if they say something that is not true.					
I am often uncomfortable being around people with dementia.					
If someone with dementia does not respond immediately, you should help the person by carrying on both sides of the conversation.					

(continued)

(continued)

	Strongly Disagree	Somewhat Disagree	Neither Agree nor Disagree	Somewhat Agree	Strongly Agree
It is not what you say but how you say it that is most important.					
I feel frustrated when I do not understand what someone is trying to tell me.					
I feel frustrated when someone does not seem to understand what I am trying to say.					
People with dementia often can understand more than they can say.					
Once a person is unable to speak, the person is no longer able to communicate.					
I have no idea what to say when talking with persons with a physical impairment.					
I have no idea what to say when talking with persons with a cognitive impairment.					

(continued)

(continued)

	Strongly Disagree	Somewhat Disagree	Neither Agree nor Disagree	Somewhat Agree	Strongly Agree
Changing how I communicate can help a person with dementia to better understand me.					
Changing how I communicate can help me to better understand a person with dementia.					
There is not really much you can do to help a person who has dementia.					

SAMPLE POSTACTIVITY ASSESSMENT

Please rate the level to which you agree or disagree with the following statements:

	Strongly Disagree	Somewhat Disagree	Neither Agree nor Disagree	Somewhat Agree	Strongly Agree
It is normal for persons with dementia to shout or cry for no reason.					
I feel more confident about talking with persons with dementia.					

(continued)

(continued)

	Strongly Disagree	Somewhat Disagree	Neither Agree nor Disagree	Somewhat Agree	Strongly Agree
You should never lie to a person with dementia.					
It is important to correct people with dementia if they say something that is not true.					
I am often uncomfortable being around people with dementia.					
If someone with dementia does not respond immediately, you should help that person by carrying on both sides of the conversation.					
It is not what you say but how you say it that is most important.					
I have no idea what to say when talking with persons with a physical impairment.					
I have no idea what to say when talking with persons with a cognitive impairment.					

(continued)

(continued)

	Strongly Disagree	Somewhat Disagree	Neither Agree nor Disagree	Somewhat Agree	Strongly Agree
If a person has dementia, there is not really much you can do to help that person.					
People with dementia often can understand more than they can say.					
People with dementia do not really care what you say or do.					
Once a person is unable to speak, that person is no longer able to communicate.					
Changing how I communicate can help a person with dementia to better understand me.					
Changing how I communicate can help me to better understand a person with dementia.					

ACTIVITY 3.2 ENHANCING STUDENTS' THERAPEUTIC INTERACTION SKILLS WITH OLDER ADULTS WITH DEMENTIA

Minetta Wallingford and Lisa Knecht-Sabres

ACTIVITY INFORMATION

Type

_____ In class

_____ Online

_____ Take home

___X___ In community

Difficulty

_____ Introductory

___X___ Intermediate

_____ Advanced

OVERVIEW

AD and other dementias impact millions of Americans. Since dementia is more prevalent in the senior population, the incidence is expected to rise because of the increase in the aging population (Alzheimer's Association, 2013). Even though students may learn about dementia in their coursework, many students may not have had the opportunity to interact or work directly with a person who has dementia. Students may have preconceptions, misconceptions, or questions about this population. Adult day-care centers that focus on serving older adults with dementia can be excellent community partners for a variety of educational activities and may provide an opportunity for students to interact with this population. Likewise, the adult day-care center may welcome additional assistance and ideas for activities. Therefore, this activity was created to meet the needs of an adult day-care center, while providing an intergenerational educational experience for students to learn about and work with older adults with dementia. This activity is designed to provide clients at an adult day-care facility who may typically receive more "group" programming with the opportunity to participate in an "individualized" activity session designed by a student and based on the client's past or current personal interests. Hence, the activity provides the older adult with some individual attention and augments the center's programming.

Moreover, this activity affords students with the opportunity to interact directly with an older adult and to enhance their comfort and skills in working with older adults with dementia. This learning experience is designed for students to intentionally consider the older adults' interests and abilities as they plan their sessions with the goal of enhancing this person's engagement in meaningful activities. They also apply their knowledge and understanding of dementia while planning and conducting these activities. Thus, the students apply and refine clinical reasoning, interpersonal, communication, and self-assessment skills. Through this experience, students have an opportunity to better understand the older adult as an individual unique person and not just a person with dementia. Therefore, another potential benefit of these intergenerational interactions between students and older adults is that they may lead to enhanced students' attitudes toward working with older adults and older adults with dementia in the future.

ACTIVITY LEARNING GOALS

Following this activity, students should be able to . . .

- Understand key attributes of dementia in order to design and implement an individualized activity with an older adult with dementia.
- Analyze and critique their own comfort and skills and interpersonal interactions in working with older adults with dementia.
- Plan and organize materials to engage an older adult in a meaningful activity session based on their interests and abilities to promote the older adult's strengths and enhance quality of life.
- Plan, implement, and modify an activity to match older adults' interests and abilities to maximize their participation in the activity (given time parameters and the environment).
- Apply clinical reasoning, interpersonal, and communication skills to effectively interact and collaborate with the older adults with dementia to facilitate engagement in a meaningful activity.
- Analyze an older adult's responses throughout the session and respond in the moment to enhance the individual's engagement in the activity.
- Analyze the activity to anticipate and prevent any potential safety concerns.
- Analyze the session relative to the older adult's performance in promoting and facilitating their social participation and engagement in the activity.

ASSOCIATION FOR GERONTOLOGY IN HIGHER EDUCATION COMPETENCIES

- Develop a gerontological perspective through knowledge and self-reflection.
- Engage collaboratively with others to promote integrated approaches to aging.
- Promote older persons' strengths and adaptations to maximize well-being, health, and mental health.
- Promote quality of life and positive social environment for older persons.

MINIMUM/MAXIMUM NUMBER OF PARTICIPANTS

This activity may be structured to accommodate a few (3) or many (50) participants. The number of participants depends on numerous factors (class size, number of clients at the site/sites, clients' abilities, staff and faculty familiarity with clients, facility environment, supervisor/student ratio, number of staff and/or faculty supervisors, student to client ratio, etc.). Ideally, only one or two students are assigned to work directly with one older adult at a time. A low student to supervisor (e.g., 2–1, 4–1, or 6–1) ratio provides opportunities for more individualized supervision. However, these ratios may vary depending on the environment and the activities that are being conducted. Therefore, it is important to consider who will be supervising the students (e.g., faculty, staff, or both faculty and staff) to determine how many students can be supervised at a time.

TIME NEEDED TO IMPLEMENT ACTIVITY

This activity requires upfront planning time as well as time spent with the clients at the adult day-care center. The time required to implement this assignment depends on the number of students, student/supervisor ratio, and student/client ratio.

Planning the experience may take 2 to 8 hours, depending on a number of factors. It may take time to identify and develop a relationship with an appropriate community partner and collaboratively plan this experience to ensure it meets the needs of both partners. Planning is discussed in more detail in the "Procedures" section.

The actual time faculty spends with students at the site depends on whether faculty or staff are directly supervising the students. An individualized session with an older adult may be 40 to 45 minutes with an additional 15 to 20 minutes allowed for setup, cleanup, and processing the session with the students. Therefore, the course director may need to schedule 1 hour for each student or pair/group of students. Sessions may be conducted on one or more days depending on the number of clients at the site and the number of students enrolled in the course.

SETTING(S)

- Adult day-care center that serves older adults with dementia.
- **Note:** This activity is designed for students who will be working with older adults and may encounter older adults with dementia. This activity could be modified for a number of students in different disciplines (e.g., students in therapeutic recreation, gerontology, clinical psychology, social work, nursing, and allied health professions). It could be conducted with similar types of community partners such as senior centers, continuing retirement communities, assistive living facilities, dementia care units, or skilled nursing facilities. This activity and the objectives could be modified to be used with older adults at the previously noted facilities who do not have dementia or a specific impairment.

MATERIALS
Required

Students should plan the activity/activities and prepare a materials list for their sessions based on the older adult's interests, abilities, and other considerations such as the cost of materials. Materials may be available through the educational program, at the site, or from common household items that the student brings from home (e.g., items for making a no-bake snack or crafts or participating in games) or special items that need to be purchased by students or faculty. It will be the students' responsibility to obtain any materials that are not available through their educational program or the adult day-care center to conduct the activity. Therefore, policies related to reimbursement or nonreimbursement for the cost of materials should be addressed by the course director as part of the syllabus or during discussion about the assignment. Regardless of the activities, students need to consider the environment and the older adult's safety in planning the activities and materials.

PROCEDURES

Preparation

The steps for preparing for this experience are the following:

1. Identify a community partner and meet with the site to discuss the activity and identify and address any policies, procedures, or agreements that may be required by both organizations.
2. Ascertain information on the client's past and current interests and abilities from the site (i.e., information obtained from staff, facility records, and/or client's family).
3. Collaborate with the site to set up and schedule the intergenerational experience.
4. Provide students with relevant course content and objectives and details of the assignment (e.g., expectations, evaluation methods, site address and contact information, schedule).
5. Provide students with relevant educational content related to the assignment (e.g., communicating with individuals who have dementia).
6. Assign students to clients and share clients' interests and background information.
7. Review students' planned activities and provide feedback to enhance older adults' active participation and enjoyment in the experience.
8. Orient site staff to the supervision process if they are assisting with supervision.
9. Orient students to the facility and staff prior to the start of the session.

Once a community organization has agreed to partner with your institution on this collaborative experience, it is important to follow any policies and procedures that may be required by either organization. This may involve a verbal agreement or a more formal agreement between the organizations.

The next steps in collaborating with the adult day-care site may entail gathering and organizing information related to each individual client's interests and abilities; creating a schedule to match students with an older adult; and providing each student with a specific date, time, and any pertinent written information that is relevant to their particular experience.

Suggested lecture points

In order to prepare and plan for the experiences, students' coursework should cover content related to understanding the normal aging process as well as the etiology and functional impact of dementia. This knowledge is important in differentiating symptoms and behaviors that are a result of dementia versus normal aging. Therefore, students should have an understanding of some of the behaviors that they may observe in people with dementia and be familiar with strategies for communicating with individuals with dementia (McGhee, 2011, p. 45; Robinson & Cubit, 2007). McGhee (2011) is one resource that provides communication strategies for interacting with older adults with dementia. The Alzheimer's Association is another good resource for content related to understanding dementia and AD.

In addition, it is important to clearly explain the intergenerational assignment, and grading criteria. The course director can discuss some of the individuals' interests and facilitate a discussion with the class on how they may modify the activities. Students will need to consider how to plan, grade, and adapt an activity given their individual older adult's interests, abilities, and the environment of the day-care center. The course director can provide an example of a specific activity or activities and students can discuss what materials are needed, how to set up the environment and activity, how to provide simple instructions, or how to demonstrate the actions. The students can discuss any potential challenges they anticipate they may encounter and the class may come up with some strategies to address those potential challenges. The course director should also answer students' inquiries, and provide feedback regarding their preliminary ideas. Students should be oriented to the facility (e.g., where to park, what to expect) prior to the experience.

An additional consideration in planning is supervision. The experience can be designed so that faculty or staff members may supervise two or more student sessions at a time. This works well if the student/older adult sessions are located within close proximity. Staff who are involved in supervision should be oriented to the assignment and assessment materials. Students are encouraged to plan for at least two or three meaningful activities for each 40-minute session. Therefore, one or more students may be assigned to work with the same older adult in a specific session. When more than one student works with the same person, it is recommended that each student have a clearly defined role and plan for the session (e.g., student A is responsible to conduct the first activity and student B conducts the second activity). This approach allows each student to take ownership in planning and conducting part of the session. Suggestions for modifications to this activity are listed in the "Additional Considerations" section.

Introduction

It is suggested that staff inform the clients and/or clients' families that students will be working with them prior to the experience. This may be done via a weekly or monthly calendar or as a formal or informal announcement in advance of the experience. On the day of the activity, the students or their supervisors should introduce themselves to appropriate staff and their assigned clients prior to the beginning of the session. Students should inquire how the older adult would like to be addressed (e.g., Mrs., Miss, Mr., Dr., or by their first name).

Activity

Background

This assignment provides students with the experience of interacting with older adults and is intended to enhance their comfort and skills in working with older adults with dementia. The faculty member sets up the experiential experience with the facility and collaborates with the staff. The students plan a 40-minute session based on the information provided by the faculty, family, and staff. Students are required to critically think about potential options for meaningful activities that may be feasible for the older adult to complete within this session given personal, financial, and environmental considerations. This involves considering the demands of the activity, the materials required, and the individual's interests, skills, and abilities. Given the nature of this experience, it is designed to increase students' interaction, clinical reasoning, and self-assessment and self-reflection skills through the experience of interacting directly with an older adult with dementia. These skills are described in more detail in the text that follows.

Interaction skills

The students should establish rapport with the older adults; collaborate with them while directing the activity; and modify the activity, their interpersonal approach, and communication style as needed throughout this experience. This requires that students think proactively to anticipate and overcome any challenges that they may encounter during this interaction. Students may need to provide very simple instructions, demonstrate an action, or provide assistance when appropriate. However, it is recognized that many individuals in this population have limited communication skills and may only be able to participate to a limited capacity.

Clinical reasoning

Students apply their clinical reasoning skills in all phases of this experience to maximize the individuals' safe participation in this experience. Students should consider and apply their knowledge of interacting with individuals with dementia as early as the initial planning phase. Preparation involves planning the activity/activities to match the older adults' interest and abilities, obtaining and organizing materials, anticipating safety concerns, and considering ways to modify the activity, the materials, or the environment within the given time parameters. Some activity sessions may involve light cooking, arts, crafts, puzzles, cards, board games, or gross motor activities (e.g., dancing, bags game, bowling, golfing, and table tennis). Therefore, students need to anticipate environmental and time considerations, requiring that the students complete some of the initial preparation ahead of time. Thus, they may select activities such as decorating prebaked cookies and donuts, filling a cannoli, or preparing no-bake snacks and desserts in order to involve the older adult in a cooking activity in the allotted time. In other words, students are challenged to think about and anticipate the demands of the activities, the environment, and the individual's cognitive, communication, and motor abilities when designing and implementing these activities with the older adults with dementia.

When students are implementing the activity with the older adult, they will need to use their clinical reasoning skills in the moment to respond to the individual's verbal and nonverbal communication and performance to facilitate engagement in the activity. This may involve adapting the materials or the setup of the environment, modifying the task, or adapting their interpersonal approach. For example, a student designing a golf "putting" activity may need to change the size and distance of the targeted hole numerous times throughout the session in order to provide the "just right challenge" for this person. Therefore, students may have to apply clinical reasoning to upgrade and downgrade the activity as well as adjust their interaction style throughout the session to maximize the individual's engagement in the experience.

Discussion/Reflection

Reflection and self-assessment
This experience also provides an opportunity for students to reflect on their knowledge and skills and examine their own interactions. This starts with the planning stage, in which students should formulate and present their preliminary questions and ideas to faculty for feedback prior to this intergenerational interaction. This process is the beginning of the opportunity for students to reflect and modify their approach to enhance the potential for a successful outcome. Faculty or knowledgeable staff trained to complete the student evaluation should be present at the facility to support and supervise the students and provide feedback while they are working with the older adult. This real-time feedback allows students to receive guidance and refine their approach and interaction skills in the moment to enhance the experience for the older adult. Students should have the opportunity to discuss and process their encounter with their supervisor once the session has been completed.

Wrap-Up

Students should provide closure with the older adults at the end of the session by thanking them for their time and reviewing the experience. Students may also ask the older adults whether they enjoyed the activity.

Ideally, the faculty member or the staff supervisor will meet with each assigned student(s) immediately following the activity session to reflect on the experience and to provide verbal feedback. Students should reflect on their session by answering some of the following questions: What is your overall impression of this interaction? What went well? What did not go as planned? What would you change or do differently in the future? What did you learn about working with individuals with dementia? Students may benefit from completing a written self-reflection either in addition to, or instead of, the verbal reflection. See the "Self-Reflection: Geriatric Experience" form in Appendix 3.2A.

The faculty member should follow up with the site after the experience to gain an understanding of the staff and older adults' perceptions of the experience. This can be an informal or formal process, such as utilizing a site evaluation tool. This process can provide valuable feedback on the planning, implementation, and the impact of the experience as a whole. This is an extremely important step for evaluating the assignment, as well as making any necessary modifications for future collaborations.

Suggested lecture points
It is also beneficial for the course director and students to discuss and reflect on the experience with the whole class during the next class session. The students and course director can discuss what students observed and learned from working with the older adults with dementia. This provides the opportunity for students to learn from each other as they hear about other students' unique experiences. Some sample discussion questions may include the following: What were some of the behaviors or symptoms associated with dementia that they observed? What strategies did they use in their interactions that worked well? What were some of the challenges?

The overall purpose of this experience is for students to combine their knowledge of aging and dementia and their interaction skills to design a meaningful activity session for an individual older adult based on the person's interests. Through planning this experience and individually interacting with the older adult, students may experience firsthand knowledge of an older adult as a person who has interests and a rich life story. Students also gain experience in organizing and setting up the activity and the environment for an older adult who has dementia. The students need to collaborate with the older adult throughout the session and adapt the activity as needed to maximize the individual's participation throughout the session. At the end of the session, students are responsible for cleaning up the environment and providing closure with the older adult. Faculty and/or staff should be available in the room to address any questions or concerns.

This activity is an example of a collaboration with an older adult day-care center. This collaboration may provide the opportunity for older adults with dementia to interact with undergraduate or graduate students while engaging in a meaningful activity that was designed based on their own interests. The students may bring a fresh approach as to how to structure those activities that were identified as meaningful for the older adults. In addition, the collaborative engagement of doing an activity together (such as making pudding and eating together) can provide social participation and interaction that might contribute to a person's quality of life.

Assessment

Students are provided with verbal feedback from their supervisor immediately following the session. They are also given an evaluation sheet ("Evaluation of Student Geriatric Experience"; see Appendix 3.2B) that provides feedback on their performance throughout the experience. Please see the supplemental materials. If two students worked with one older adult, peer feedback could be part of the assessment process.

An evaluation form is provided, but it may be modified to meet other individual or specific course/site objectives. This student assessment focuses on their performance related to planning, interpersonal interaction, communication, and clinical reasoning skills. This includes their preparation, organization, modification of the activity, and their overall ability to engage the older adult throughout this experience and reflect on the experience. The assessment also includes items related to managing time and addressing safety concerns while interacting with the older adult. The evaluator should recognize that students may encounter some unique challenges in working with individuals with dementia and understand that an individual's participation may be limited or vary throughout the session. Feedback should be constructive to promote more knowledge, skill development, and comfort regarding working with these clients.

As mentioned earlier, students may also elicit feedback from the older adult during the session by asking questions such as: "Do you like this activity?" "Are you having fun?" The staff at the adult day-care center may also be encouraged to provide pertinent feedback to the students and faculty regarding the interaction. Students may also complete a written self-reflection. Sample content for the self-reflection is included in Appendix 3.2C.

This experience may be completed one time per quarter, semester, or school year depending on when the course is offered.

ADDITIONAL CONSIDERATIONS

It is highly recommended that the course director meet with the facility in advance to develop a collaborative working relationship with their community partner and to understand the culture and climate of the facility and their clients. The expectations for students' professional conduct (e.g., professional dress, how to address staff and clients, safety policies, special diets) at the facility should be discussed in advance. It is important to be open to discussing any questions or concerns with students. It is beneficial to be specific and constructive in your feedback to students to enhance their comfort, skills, and understanding of working with this population.

It is extremely beneficial if the facility staff have positive relationships with the clients and their families in order to learn about the clients' interests and abilities. Since the facility staff are most familiar with the client, it is extremely helpful if staff can be available to either supervise or assist throughout the experience. As noted earlier, this assignment can be modified in various ways to be conducted with a number of different graduate and undergraduate student groups and at different types of facilities. As an example, in some settings it may be possible to conduct a similar activity with a higher student to supervisor ratio. Therefore, a number of modifications could be made to the structure and goals of this assignment to meet the needs of various educational programs who want to incorporate intergenerational learning experiences as part of their educational curriculum.

REFERENCES

Alzheimer's Association. (2013). 2013 Alzheimer's disease facts and figures. Retrieved from http://www.alz.org/downloads/facts_figures_2013.pdf

McGhee, J. (2011). Effective communication with people who have dementia. *Nursing Standard, 25*(25), 40–46.

Robinson, A., & Cubit, K. (2007). Caring for older people with dementia in residential care: Nursing students' experiences. *Journal of Advanced Nursing, 59*(3), 255–263.

RECOMMENDED RESOURCES

Alzheimer's Association. (2016). Adult day centers. Retrieved from https://www.alz.org/care/alzheimers-dementia-adult-day-centers.asp

National Adult Day Services Association. (2016). About adult day services. Retrieved from http://www.nadsa.org/learn-more/about-adult-day-services/

National Caregivers Library. (2016). What is adult day care? Retrieved from http://www.caregiverslibrary.org/caregivers-resources/grp-caring-for-yourself/hsgrp-support-systems/what-is-adult-day-care-article.aspx

APPENDIX 3.2A: SELF-REFLECTION: GERIATRIC EXPERIENCE

The purpose of this self-reflection is to analyze and critique your learning following your interaction with the older adult. This includes reflecting on your skills, interactions, and your comfort with working with your assigned individual. The reflection should include consideration of the role of planning and preparation for the activity and its contribution to the overall experience. It is as important to understand and discuss what went well during the experience as it is to reflect on any challenges.

1. What is your overall impression of this interaction?

   _____

2. How do I feel about my own interactions with the client?

   _____

3. What went well?

   _____

4. What did I do well?

   _____

5. What did not go as planned?

   _____

6. What would I change or do differently in the future?

   _____

7. What did I learn about working with older adults with dementia?

   _____

8. What did I learn about my own skills and abilities?

   _____

9. What is my comfort level with the prospect of working with individuals with dementia in the future?

   _____

APPENDIX 3.2B: EVALUATION OF STUDENT GERIATRIC EXPERIENCE

Activity	Below Expectations 1 Point	Meets Expectations 2 Points	Above Expectations 3 Points	No Opportunity
Planning				
Activity designed to address client interests with consideration of client's abilities				
Preparation, setup, and organization of materials is appropriate to environment and activity				
Interaction/ Communication				
Interacts with client respectfully				
Provides clear, simple directions				
Collaborates with client when possible or assists client as needed to enhance the experience				
Implementation/ Clinical Reasoning				
Responds (thinks/ acts) in the moment to enhance engagement in activity (e.g., modifies verbal, tactile, and/or visual cues;				

(continued)

(*continued*)

Activity	Below Expectations 1 Point	Meets Expectations 2 Points	Above Expectations 3 Points	No Opportunity
Implementation/ Clinical Reasoning				
upgrades or downgrades the activity; timely in providing necessary modifications; provides setup and/or assistance as appropriate)				
Time Management				
Manages time effectively to enhance meaningful engagement in the activity and end task on time				
Safety				
Addresses and prevents all safety concerns				
Self-Reflection of Experience				
Provides insight into what went well, challenges, and discusses learning that occurred as a result of experience				
Additional comments				
Total Score				

APPENDIX 3.2C: CASE EXAMPLE

(This example is not based on a specific individual situation, but based on a composite of different experiences to illustrate what this experience may entail.)

BACKGROUND

Jessica is completing her "geriatric interaction assignment" for this course. Jessica has had course content related to understanding and working with people with dementia. She has been provided with background information on her assigned older adult's interests and abilities. She learns that Mrs. Betty Smith used to love making doughnuts and decorating cakes. Mrs. Smith does not have any known food allergies, likes eating sweets, and is able to eat, move, and walk independently. She attends activities but takes prompting to initiate activities. She likes to be called "Betty" and lives with her daughter. She does not talk much but will usually ask questions. Betty also has short-term memory issues and some difficulty attending.

Jessica came up with the ideas of purchasing some plain doughnuts and bringing in premade frosting for Betty to decorate the doughnuts. She discussed the activity materials, organization, setup, and cleanup with her instructor.

MATERIALS

Jessica decided she would bring in four doughnuts (one for each of them to eat and two for later). She also decided to bring a container for the doughnuts that Mrs. Smith could decorate if they had time. Other materials included three tubes of frosting in different colors (to provide a limited choice), edible sprinkles, paper towels, stickers to decorate the container, a marker, and hand sanitizer wipes. Jessica also verified that there was a sink and paper towels available if needed.

EXPERIENCE AT SITE

Jessica arrived at the site with seven other students who were also assigned to individual clients. There were four faculty members from the school at the site, and each faculty member supervised two students at a time. The students and faculty were split into two rooms, and there was a staff member in each room. The staff member brought Betty into the room and introduced her to the student and faculty member. Betty sat down at a table next to Jessica, who had paper towels on the table covering the work surface.

Jessica asked Betty if she liked doughnuts and would like to decorate them. Betty said, "That sounds good." Jessica asked what colors of frosting she would like and showed her the choices. Betty pointed to the white and red. Jessica asked if she could open the tube or if she needed help. When Betty appeared to struggle, Jessica assisted her. Jessica then demonstrated how she used the tube frosting to decorate her own doughnut. Betty had difficulty and seemed frustrated. Eventually, Jessica started squeezing the frosting tube, and Betty was able to squeeze the tube and started decorating her own doughnut. It was messy, but Jessica encouraged her and continued to offer her assistance. Betty decided to start eating her doughnut after they used one color of frosting. Jessica said she would also eat her doughnut. Jessica attempted to make small talk with Betty, but Betty focused on eating her doughnut.

When she was finished, Jessica asked if it was good. Betty replied, "Very good." Jessica asked if she would like to decorate the rest of the doughnuts and bring them home to her daughter. Betty nodded yes.

Jessica suggested they wipe their hands before starting and handed Betty a wipe. Betty wiped her hands. Jessica waited for Betty to start decorating the next doughnut, but Betty did not initiate. After a few minutes, Jessica's faculty supervisor cued Jessica to ask Betty if she wanted help. Betty said yes. Jessica then asked if she wanted the same color. The tubes were hard for Betty to squeeze, so Jessica's supervisor suggested cutting the nozzle of the tube to make the opening larger. This worked, and Betty was able to complete frosting the doughnut with minimal assistance. Betty was able to add some sprinkles on top of the doughnut once Jessica opened the container. After the doughnuts were decorated, Jessica asked if Betty wanted to put stickers on the container for the doughnuts. Betty said yes. Jessica asked which stickers. Betty tried but could not get the sticker off the page. Jessica did this for her and asked Betty to point to the sticker and where she wanted to place it. When this was completed, Jessica suggested they put her name on the container and asked Betty to write it. Betty was able to write her name on the container. There was about 5 minutes left, so Jessica asked if Betty wanted to wipe her hands and explained she was going to clean up the table. She asked Betty if she liked making the doughnuts, and Betty said yes. She said they were good. Jessica asked the staff member if Betty could have another one. The staff member indicated that she would have lunch soon, so maybe later. Jessica thanked Betty for working with her and said good bye. Betty said, "Come back some-time."

FEEDBACK

The staff member said that Jessica did a nice job of engaging Betty. Jessica thought the experience went well but recognized that some of the tasks were difficult for Betty. The faculty supervisor agreed, and they discussed other ways to modify the tasks (e.g., spreading canned frosting, initially cutting the opening of the tube so more frosting came out, starting the corner of the sticker for Betty and/or larger stickers, stamps or other ways to decorate the container). The faculty supervisor also asked if Jessica tried the activity herself before doing it at the facility. Jessica had not, so she was not aware of how difficult some of the tasks may be. They also discussed the positive ways that Jessica was able to be flexible and adapt in the moment (e.g., assisting Betty, adjusting the plan and eating the doughnut when Betty wanted to eat the doughnut, and opening the sprinkle bottle for Betty based on observations that this would be difficult for Betty). The faculty supervisor asked if Jessica thought it may have been better to intervene earlier when Betty was getting frustrated, and they discussed this situation. Her faculty supervisor also suggested that both Jessica and Betty wash their hands before starting the activity. These comments were recorded on the assessment form. Jessica's self-reflection indicated that she liked the experience because she thought Betty enjoyed the experience. Also, she felt a little more comfortable working with individuals with dementia.

Several students conducted activities with various clients throughout the day. The staff indicated they were pleased with the activities and how they were conducted. They felt the students were professional, creative, and respectful of the clients. They were able to engage some clients that often have difficulty participating. The majority of clients were interested in doing this experience with another group of students. The faculty supervisors indicated they were able to easily supervise two students at a time.

CHAPTER 4

DEMOGRAPHY

Hallie E. Baker

WHAT IS DEMOGRAPHY?

Have you ever listened to a news story about the change in the "face" of the United States? How about the prediction you've seen in this book that by 2050, one in every five Americans will be over the age of 65? Where do all these numbers and predictions come from? Furthermore, have you ever looked at the world population clock? Where do those numbers come from? Demography provides answers to those questions and so much more in the scientific study of human population, including the causes and consequences of changes in the human population (Weeks, 2012). Demography studies include examining how many people are in a given geographic location; population growth or decline resulting from trends in fertility, mortality, and migration; where people are located and why; and characteristics of the population. Characteristics of interest within populations include sex, age, education level, income, occupation, belief systems (religious, moral, political), family relationships, and many other areas of interest. One key to remember is that demography is very much a macro perspective, looking at societies, countries, and the world as a whole, not individuals or groups. When looking at populations, demographers both look to the past for trends and seek to predict future trends.

FORCES THAT CHANGE POPULATIONS

Populations change over time because of specific forces, including fertility, mortality, and migration, and that is ultimately why the United States and many other countries are facing an aging population. The three main forces are fertility (additions to the population due to births), mortality (loss of population members due to death), and migration (loss and gains in members due to movements in and out of the population) (Weeks, 2012).

What Influences Fertility?

- The addition of new members of a population due to births and the rates of these births influence population sizes and composition (Weeks, 2012).
- *Birth rates* report the number of live births per every 1,000 members of a population during a given time, often a year. However, this is not the most accurate count.
- *Fertility rates*, or the number of live births per a single woman in their lifetime of fertility (usually from age 15 to 44), provide a better understanding of how much population growth or decline is driving changes in overall population numbers.
- High birth or fertility rates lead to larger numbers of younger members of a population, and thus a younger population overall.
- Populations need to maintain a *replacement rate*, or the number of births needed to maintain a zero growth population. The rate is usually somewhere over two births on average per woman so that one child can "replace" each parent, and another to replace a peer who dies before reproducing or who never has children. If a population does not maintain this rate, the population declines.

What Influences Mortality?

- The loss of new members of a population due to deaths and the rates of these deaths with the ages they occur influence population sizes and composition (Weeks, 2012).
- *Death rates* represent the number of people who die each year in each age group.
- *Life span* states the maximum number of years an organism could live if no disease, environmental factors, or medical conditions cause damage or death to it.
- *Life expectancy* results from demographers examining death rates and defines how long a member of a group is expected to live after a certain age. For example, life expectancy from birth is approximately 78.8 years in 2017 (Centers for Disease Control and Prevention, 2017), but in 1900 it was 47.3 years.
- Life expectancy is influenced by infant mortality, childhood disease and accidents, chronic or acute medical conditions, and other factors that shorten the lives of some members of a population. Countries with lower infant mortality rates, like the United States, have longer life expectancies than countries with high infant mortality rates, wars, or even AIDS. If life expectancy is higher, then the country will be older or aging.

What Influences Migration?

- The number of people moving into and out of a geographic area and/or population changes a population, but not to the extent of fertility and mortality (Weeks, 2012).

- Generally, immigrants tend to be younger or of a different ethnicity or racial group and can cause shifts in those areas. However, the overall impact remains smaller on the larger population characteristics.

For demographers, all three forces change populations and can have definitive impacts on population growth or decline. Human populations can also be stable or stationary (Weeks, 2012). A *stable population* presents no change over time. A stable population may be growing, declining, or remaining the same size, but the rates remain constant. In contrast, a population not growing or declining is a *stationary population*. Within a stationary population, fertility and mortality rates remain constant, and even with migration the population growth is zero. Therefore, a population can be stable and stationary, but stability can apply to decline and growth. Overall, demography tracks changes or trends in populations over time, including population aging.

DEMOGRAPHY EDUCATION EXERCISES

The two activities in this chapter offer students opportunities to apply demography and demographic ideas to our aging world and their own hometowns. From a global to local level, these activities explore the implications for policy, healthy aging, and our living environment through the use of a discipline students may not be familiar with.

In Activity 4.1, Applying the Demography of Aging to Countries Around the World, students can learn how countries have changed over time and can become more savvy about the information they are exposed to regarding trends in populations. The activity takes a global aging perspective and promotes critical thinking skills, encouraging students to bring economic, historical, and political contexts into their analysis of why a country's population appears the way it does. The "boring" numbers take on a life of their own when placed in such context and challenge students to broaden their ways of thinking.

In contrast, Activity 4.2, Hometown Age Demographics, moves the focus to the student's local area, making the information more personal and contextualizing the data in a different manner. The activity seeks to challenge students to examine their own communities to discern whether their hometowns are experiencing population aging or not. Further, how are population changes influencing the living environments of those communities? Do they live in age-friendly living environments? By moving the focus from national or international numbers or figures, the activity allows students to make personal connections and learn where to find information for themselves at the local level.

REFERENCES

Centers for Disease Control and Prevention. (2017). Life expectancy. Retrieved from https://www.cdc.gov/nchs/fastats/life-expectancy.htm

Weeks, J. R. (2012). *Population: An introduction to concepts and issues* (11th ed.). Belmont, CA: Wadsworth/Cengage.

ACTIVITY 4.1 APPLYING THE DEMOGRAPHY OF AGING TO COUNTRIES AROUND THE WORLD

Hallie E. Baker

ACTIVITY INFORMATION

Type

____X____   In class

_____   Online

_____   Take home

_____   In community

Difficulty

____X____   Introductory

_____   Intermediate

_____   Advanced

OVERVIEW

Demography provides a way to understand how populations have changed over time and will change in the future. By teaching students to understand what the trends are, how to interpret the terms, and statistics used in demography, we promote more savvy consumers of information. Sadly, many students tend to find the topic dry, so the current activity was created as a way to engage students in an activity that provides a practical application of class discussions of demographic terms and trends to current countries around the world.

The selection of the countries allows the professor/instructor to bring in how historical contexts impact countries as well as individuals. For example, the population pyramid for France in the 1950s shows the population decline caused by the two world wars and then the post war booms. The U.S. population pyramids over time allow one to track the aging of the Baby Boomers. The use of such historical contexts in addition to discussions of the demographic transition in developed versus under- or nondeveloped countries can promote critical thinking in students about what forces shape populations or countries. Further, the activity promotes critical thinking of the forces that lead to a country being categorized as young, aging, or aged. Overall, the activity can bring the "boring" terms to life and provide greater insight into why policies and programs, such as national pensions or health care plans, may or may not work in certain countries based on their population makeup.

ACTIVITY LEARNING GOALS

Following this activity, students should be able to . . .

- Apply demographic terms and concepts to determine a country's or area's status in terms of population aging now and in the future.
- Discuss changes in populations and what those changes might mean in the future for the governments, economies, and policies of those areas.
- Identify the diversity of population profiles across the globe in relation to the areas of population aging and growth.

ASSOCIATION FOR GERONTOLOGY IN HIGHER EDUCATION COMPETENCIES

- Relate social theories and science of aging to understanding heterogeneity, inequality, and context of aging.

MINIMUM/MAXIMUM NUMBER OF PARTICIPANTS

- 10 to 50

TIME NEEDED TO IMPLEMENT ACTIVITY

- 20 to 30 minutes

SETTING

- General classroom setting

MATERIALS
Required

- At least 15 country profiles drawn from the UN: Profiles for over 100 countries can be found at: www.un.org/esa/population/publications/worldageing19502050/countriesorareas.htm
  - Key is to choose a variety of countries from the developed and nondeveloped world, for example, at least one each from Europe, Asia, Africa, the Arabic world, North America, South America.
  - Also look for countries with odd or different shaped population pyramids, such as the United Arab Emirates versus Japan or Sweden, or a very "old" country like Italy versus a "young" one like Mexico.
  - Worksheet to guide students as they examine the country profiles (see Appendix 4.1A).

Optional

- PowerPoint presentation of the selected countries to facilitate class-wide discussion of the different countries as each group reports on its chosen country.
- Two readings written by Dr. Baker, Demographic Transition (Appendix 4.1B) and Demographics of Aging in the United States and World (Appendix 4.1C) as supplemental readings.

PROCEDURE

Preparation

- The students need to have had an introduction to demography including the demography of aging.
- The fundamentals of population growth, decline, and aging must have been covered before they can complete this activity. (Ideally the Demographic Transition and population pyramids will also have been covered.)

  ○ The introduction to this section also provides key definitions for the activity.

Introduction

- After the basic information on demography is taught, review one country profile with the students. You may want to use the United States for familiarity purposes. Once the students are oriented to the profile form, you may begin the activities.

Activity

1. Arrange students in groups of three to four members.
2. Instruct students to pick a scribe (someone to do the writing) and someone to come up and get their exercise sheet and select their country profile.
3. Remind students that we will be gathering back together to discuss profiles so their group will be "reporting" to the rest of the class.
4. Allow about 10 to 15 minutes for them to work through the questions.
5. As the instructor, you will need to move around and speak with each group, engaging them about how historical, economic, or other factors might impact their country. Challenge them to think about how that country compares to the United States (a familiar point of reference for most).

Discussion/Reflection

- Once all the groups are done, gather the class back together and have each group report on its country including: whether it is a "young," "aging," or "old" country with what evidence they used to come to that conclusion; what might be odd about their country with their theory to explain that difference; and any surprises they may have had.

- Encourage the class to ask questions of each group and add their own theories about the findings of the group.

Wrap-Up

- For the facilitator, it is important to validate and reflect on themes you hear emerging from the student comments.
- Collect the worksheets at the end of the time.

Follow-Up

- If the class seems to be missing a concept or term, correct them, using it as a teachable moment to apply what you have previously covered to a real life example.

Assessment

- Collect the worksheets. Credit can be given for the assignment, but the worksheet provides an opportunity to assess how well the students have completed and comprehended the lesson(s) on population aging and demography.
- You can also add an essay question to the next exam specifically asking the students to examine a country profile (one none of them have seen before and with the country name removed) and answer questions about the country of an applied nature, such as, "Is the country 'old' or 'young,' and why?"
  - Students who participated in the activity historically have done better on the exam questions than those who did not participate.
  - For extra credit, you may ask students to try to identify the country for fun.

CONTENT SOURCE

The country profiles come from the electronic copy of "World Population Ageing 1950–2050" published by the Population Division, DESA, United Nations. Retrieved from http://www.un.org/esa/population/publications/worldageing19502050

APPENDIX 4.1A: DEMOGRAPHY OF AGING ACTIVITY WORKSHEET

Group members:

1. _____

2. _____

3. _____

4. _____

1. What country did you get? _____

2. What story do the:
   a. Fertility rates tell
   b. Life expectancy rates tell
   c. Dependency ratios tell
   d. Population pyramids tell

3. How is this population aging? Are they "old" now, or will they be "aging" from here on out? Justify your response.

4. When compared to the United States, what story does this country have about its population?

5. What other interesting facts caught your eye?

6. What other facts or events might be impacting your country's population? For example, France's population in 1950 showed the effects of World War II.

APPENDIX 4.1B: DEMOGRAPHIC TRANSITION OR "HOW DO YOU GO FROM A YOUNG TO AN OLD COUNTRY?"

Hallie E. Baker

HOW DO YOU GO FROM A YOUNG TO AN OLD COUNTRY?

Populations around the world are aging (Weeks, 2012). For Western Europe, the United States, and Canada, the aging of the population occurred over hundreds of years. In contrast, Japan, South Korea, and other countries transitioned from "young" to "old" within three generations, a significantly faster rate than other industrialized countries.

Populations age through three fundamental processes. Fertility rates, morality rates, and migration combine to change the population age (Weeks, 2012). Fertility and mortality rates impact population age more than migration. Falling fertility rates age a population as do falling mortality rates, which result in increased life expectancies. Immigrants do tend to be younger and thus lower a population's age, but migration rarely reaches a rate that tops the forces of birth and death.

So how do birth and death cause countries to age? Simple, they go through the demographic transition. The *demographic transition* is a theory that describes population aging as a process during which, as countries develop/advance, the birth and death rates change from being very high to low birth and death rates resulting in an increase in the average age of a population. The transition includes a three stage shift—pretransition, transition, and posttransition—during which birth and death rates change from high to low. Economics, culture, and technology influence each stage. Figure 4.1 demonstrates how the birth and death rates change through each stage. Now let's look at each stage in turn.

Pretransition

Societies or populations in the pretransition stage rely upon agricultural economies in which women marry young and have many children (Weeks, 2012). The graph in Figure 4.1 shows a relatively steady and high birth rate with fluctuations in death or mortality rates. Due to disease (particularly epidemics), famine, accidents, and so forth, mortality rates are high for all ages. However, a lack of knowledge or technology to prevent disease and store food for future use results in periods where large portions of the population die off at higher rates. Remember history and the Black Death of Middle Age Europe? Between 1346 and 1350, an estimated one third of the population of Europe died. While the plague remained a threat through the 19th century, the 4-year period between 1346 and 1350 demonstrates a large increase or flux in mortality rates. Wars, famines, and other natural disasters also contribute to higher death rates in pretransition societies.

As a result, in order to have security later in life, parents need to have a large number of children to increase the odds that at least one child will live to adulthood and provide for their parents. Further, children provide labor for the

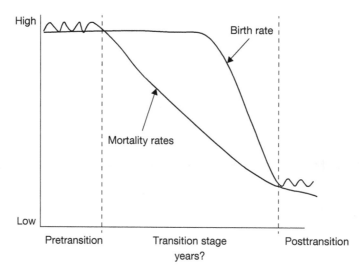

Figure 4.1   Demographic Transition.

agriculture; thus, the more children in a family, the more crops can be grown and harvested. Overall, birth rates remain stable, though high, during the pretransition stage. Despite the high birth rates, populations do not show significant growth during this stage because the high death rates balance out the high birth rates.

Transition

The second stage of the demographic transition occurs when death rates begin to decline (Weeks, 2012). During the transition stage, as shown in Figure 4.1, death or mortality rates decline first, followed by a decline in birth rates at a slower pace at first. Improvements in technology including better health care to prevent some illnesses and provide treatments or cures for other conditions allow individuals to live longer. One reason the plague of the Middle Ages continued to kill was due to the rats and fleas who carried the disease. Once sanitation improved and the carriers were kept away from food and water sources, the rates of infection of the plague declined. The development of antibiotics decreased mortality for other illnesses and injuries. Advances in manufacturing allow for the storage of food for longer periods of time, thus lessening the impact of one bad harvest on farms. Over time, infant mortality also declines with the improvements as well. Finally, life expectancies begin to increase, which in turn impacts birth rates.

In the beginning of the transition stage, birth rates remain high as families required many children to assure that one or more survive to adulthood. Before the decline in births a population increase often occurs. As death rates decline, families begin to realize they don't need as many children to assure the future and slowly begin to decrease the number of children born. Additionally, increased technology and health care provides alternative and often more effective forms of birth control, allowing for women to exercise more control over their fertility. As economies evolve and industrialize, opportunities also open for women to work outside the home and obtain more education. The increase in opportunities contributes to women waiting to marry and/or start their families, thus decreasing the number of years a woman does bear children and resulting in a lower fertility rate. Eventually, the birth rate decline catches up with the death rate and by the end of the transition stage both are significantly lower than at the beginning of the stage.

Posttransition Stage

The final stage of the demographic transition results in the population aging as birth and death rates remain low (Weeks, 2012). Figure 4.1 demonstrates the final lower state of birth and death rates. The posttransition stage characteristics include more deaths caused by chronic ailments and fluctuations in birth rates. Once a population reaches the posttransition stage, life expectancy continues to increase as technology and health care decrease the mortality in acute illnesses such as the flu. Epidemics result in fewer deaths as technology and record keeping provide better tracking opportunities and health care provides preventive measures, treatments, or cures. However, as individuals reach ever older ages, chronic conditions such as arthritis and heart disease begin to emerge as primary causes of death.

In contrast to the pretransition stage when death rates fluctuated, in the posttransition stage birth rates fluctuate. Examples of such booms in births include the famous, or infamous, Baby Boom of the late 1940s and 1950s and the mini-boom that occurred once Baby Boomers began having children of their own. Populations continue to grow in the posttransition phase unless the fertility rate falls below the replacement rate.

SO WHAT DETERMINES THE PACE OF CHANGE?

For Western Europe, the United States, and Canada, the demographic transition took centuries to complete. The Industrial Revolution of the 1800s resulted in the transition stage for these three populations. After World War II, Western Europe, the United States, and Canada settled into the posttransition phase. However, other populations experienced a condensed or abbreviated demographic transition. For example, when the United States occupied Japan after World War II, the occupation force shared technology, specifically medical technology. Therefore, when added to the effort put forth prior to World War II to expand Japan's holdings and military, Japan underwent the transition within two generations from an agricultural based economy to an industrial power. Colonization or occupation by industrialized countries may speed up the demographic transition in other populations as they benefit from the advances of others instead of having to develop them on their own. Japan and South Korea are facing a rapidly aging population and the challenges it brings.

CONCLUSION

The demographic transition continues to be a widely accepted theory of how populations age. Regardless of how it occurs, the United Nations and other bodies have predicted the aging of the world's population and the challenges that accompany the change. As birth rates and death rates continue to decline, the question becomes where will populations go from here?

REFERENCE

Weeks, J. R. (2012). *Population: An introduction to concepts and issues* (11th ed.). Belmont, CA: Wadsworth/Cengage.

REVIEW QUESTIONS

1. What is the demographic transition?
2. Describe the three stages of the demographic transition.
3. What forces influence the three stages?

APPENDIX 4.1C: DEMOGRAPHICS OF AGING IN THE UNITED STATES AND WORLD

Hallie E. Baker

In 2008, the global population of individuals over the age of 65 was estimated to be 506 million (Kinsella & Wan, 2009). Within the next decade the number of adults 65 and older will outnumber children under the age of 5. By 2050 the older population will triple to one and a half (1.5) billion outnumbering the total number of children in the world for the first time in human history. In this reading, we discuss the demography of aging, implications of population for the world, challenges of tracking aging populations, and other emerging demographic trends.

DEMOGRAPHY OF AGING

While the numbers mentioned in the opening of this reading indicate that the entire human population appears to be aging, how do demographers measure aging within specific populations or countries? Three measures provide descriptions of the relative aging of a population. Absolute number of older adults, median age of population, and proportion of older people in a population provide different descriptions, but each presents its own challenges and strengths.

Absolute Number of Older People in a Population

The very first sentence for the module reflects the absolute number of older people in a population (Weeks, 2012). The *absolute number of older people in a population* provides a count of how many adults over the age of 65 are living in the country. The count provides a crude number and gives an idea of how many, but can mislead because it does not allow for comparison. For example, the United States' older population has increased from 3.1 million in 1900 to 35 million in 2000, an impressive 10 times the previous size over the century. However, what does it mean? Did the rest of the U.S. population grow at that rate as well, or at a slower rate? In fact, the U.S. population grew from 76 million in 1900 to 281 million in 2000. Thus, while the total U.S. population almost quadrupled, the older population grew at twice that rate. The absolute number of older people in a population also does not allow for comparisons between countries or populations. How does the United States' 35 million older adults compare to France whose total population is 42 million? Therefore, while comparisons are possible within a population over time, other measures are needed to compare countries and populations.

Median Age of Population

In contrast to the absolute number of older people in a population, the median age of a population provides a mid-point of the population's age (Novak, 2009). *Median age of population* represents the mid-point or the exact age at which half the population is younger and half the population is older than that age. The median age of a population reflects changes in populations as the population ages or becomes younger. The median age is a more sensitive measure as the number will move in the direction of the shift; for example, if the country ages the median age will move higher (e.g., 50), or if the country becomes younger it will move lower (e.g., 30). The United States' median age in 2008 was 36, while Japan's median age was 43 (Kinsella & Wan, 2009). Therefore, one could conclude that Japan's population is older even though the crude number of individuals over the age of 65 is much smaller than their peers in the United States. The median age allows for comparisons between countries and within countries. However, a median age tells us nothing about the size of different age groups. For example, is there a large number of 5-year-olds and 85-year-olds or an even distribution across all ages? The median age also does not inform us about how the age groups' sizes have changed over time. The result is an inability to compare changes in a population's age groups over time and an inability to compare how the relative sizes of those age groups compare to other countries. So let's move on to the method most used by gerontologists.

Proportion of Older People in a Population

Gerontologists use the proportion of older people in a population more than the other two measures (Novak, 2009). A *proportion of older people in a population* takes the number of individuals over 65 and divides it by the total population. The resulting number, always less than one, provides the proportion. Easily converted into a percentage by multiplying by 100, the proportion allows for comparisons between countries or populations of different sizes by standardizing the groups by how much each is represented within the whole population. The United States has over 49 million adults over the age of 65 or 15.25% of its population while Monaco has 9,580 adults over 65 yet they make up 31.33% of that country's population. The proportion confirms the median age statistic that Monaco with a median age of 52.4 years is an older country than the United States which has a median age of 37.9. In fact, Monaco is the oldest country in the world as of 2013 (Central Intelligence Agency, 2013).

Additionally, the proportion allows for comparisons between groups. Such comparisons between groups within a population can have serious policy impacts in addition to impacts on society as a whole. For example, by 2050 it is estimated that 21.2% of the U.S. population will be over the age of 65 compared to 18.6% under the age of 14 (United Nations, Department of Economic and Social Affairs, Population Division, 2011). What policy implications do these numbers have? Perhaps more money should go toward elder services than schools because the older adult population makes up more of the U.S. population than children? In business, if you were an entrepreneur would you rather go after a market of individuals age 65 and older or younger than 14? How might the shift impact what TV shows or media trends emerge over the next 40 years? By using the proportion of older people in a population, researchers, demographers, politicians, and others (ideally) make decisions in a more rational manner with a clear idea of what a population's age structure is instead of just going by the crude numbers.

IMPLICATIONS OF POPULATION FOR THE WORLD

Economic, social, and cultural implications result from the aging of our populations as different challenges present themselves for different countries within the world.

Changes in population compositions include increasing numbers of the oldest old, migration within countries, changing sex-ratios, and changing dependency ratios. Each trend in turn needs closer examination.

Even as the world population ages, the older population itself is aging (Kinsella & Wan, 2009). Individuals within the older population are reaching ever higher ages, with the category of the oldest old experiencing the fastest growth. The aging population is split into the young-old, individuals between the ages of 65 and 74; the middle-old, people aged 75 to 84; and the oldest old, individuals at or over the age of 85. The oldest old population represents the fastest growing proportion of the older population; its projected growth over the next 30 years is more than a 233% increase compared to a 160% increase for those over the age of 65 and 33% for the total global population. While most see reaching ever older ages as a bonus, economically the growth presents a problem. This is because the oldest of the old account for a disproportionate share of a society's resources (Zhou, Norton, & Stearns, 2003). Since the United States spends the most money on the oldest old, particularly in the health care arena, a jump in that part of the population could mean higher health care costs in the future. Besides health care, longer life spans result in more money spent on pensions and more time spent in retirement. The longer retirement periods also result in the next trend, new migration patterns within the United States.

Not surprisingly, most elders live within cities, not rural areas, but a three-stage pattern of migration of retirees has evolved within the United States (Novak, 2009). Initially after retirement, retirees often move to places with the amenities or a comfortable lifestyle they want. For example, the move to Florida, cliché as it is, allows retirees to enjoy warm winters and many recreational opportunities. Years later, sometimes up to 20 years or more, as the retirees begin to develop more chronic conditions, disabilities, or lose a spouse to death, a second move occurs back to where their families are in search of assistance. The second move focuses on being near friends and family members who can provide companionship and care as needed. The final move occurs when the elder can no longer remain independent in the community and must move to a facility for support. Historically, the final move was to a nursing home, but now long-term care options have expanded to include assisted living, retirement communities and other options. As the baby boomers begin to retire, the three-stage pattern may remain or change as they seek to be different from their parents. As with where they live, older women in the future may not only change where they live, but who they live with.

Women live longer than men, which resulted in 62 million more women than men in 2008 among the population 65 years and older worldwide (Kinsella & Wan, 2009). *Sex ratios*, the number of men divided by the number of women (usually multiplied by 100), tracks the proportion of women to men in a population (Weeks, 2012). Generally, men have higher mortality rates from birth onward than women do (Kinsella & Wan, 2009). The only exception is maternal deaths during childbirth in less developed countries. Male mortality rates in the future are projected to improve faster than their female peers. Some epidemiologists question if a change in mortality might occur as more women enter the workforce and begin to pursue more traditionally male occupations. A result of this change might be an increase in women's mortality to more masculine levels. Further, some health choices such as smoking or high-fat food may increase female mortality as male mortality declines.

As both genders live longer, marriage and remarriage may evolve as a result. Currently, health facilities in the United States such as nursing homes are 90% or more female; more males might lead to changes in room configurations and activities offered to appeal to more male customers. What other changes might more men in the older population lead to?

Changing dependency ratios, or who pays the bills, place more pressure on populations over time (Kinsella & Wan, 2009). *A dependency ratio* defines how many individuals are dependent, both old and young, on individuals who economically provide for them (Weeks, 2012). *Youth dependency ratio* measures how many children (usually from the ages of 0 to 14) per 100 workers in the country, while *older dependency ratio* measures the number of individuals 65 and older per 100 workers (usually individuals aged 15 to 64). The dependency ratio adds both youth and older. In countries with larger older populations, the older dependency ratio is higher. For example, the U.S. Census Bureau calculated Japan's older dependency ratio at 36 per 100 people aged 20 to 64 compared to the U.S. ratio of 21 (Kinsella & Wan, 2009). In the United States, the older dependency ratio will grow through 2050 while the youth dependency ratio remains consistent. At the same time the number of working adults in the United States will be decreasing over the next century. The result is more people dependent upon fewer workers; therefore, there will be more economic strain to support dependents. Dependency ratios are not without critics. Some argue against the fundamental assumption that anyone over the age of 65 does not contribute to the economy. Elders also bring economic advantages through continuing to work past retirement age, volunteering, or providing child care services for workers. Others argue that elders may simply increase social costs, but also lead to a better use of resources (Novak, 2009). The change in dependency ratio represents the primary reason an aging population brings strains to countries now and in the future.

CONCLUSION

Population aging affects more than just the United States, Western Europe, and Japan. As the worldwide population shifts and the older population triples by 2050, some argue the change is a triumph for medical, social, and economic advances while others note the challenges to current policies, programs, and institutions (Kinsella & Wan, 2009). Another outcome is an ever expanding need for individuals to provide services for and research about older adults. The challenge each society will face is to first determine if the aging population is a problem or a benefit. Next, countries need to decide how to address the challenges and build upon the strengths provided by having more older adults around. The change can also have impacts upon policy and program implications, but the lesson for now is that population aging is not something to fear into the future, but needs to be addressed in the here and now.

REFERENCES

Central Intelligence Agency. (2013). *The World Factbook 2013–14*. Washington, DC: Author. Retrieved from https://www.cia.gov/library/publications/the-world-factbook/index.html

Kinsella, K., & Wan, H. (2009). *An aging world: 2008*. International Population Reports, U.S Census Bureau. Washington, DC: U.S. Government Printing Office.

Novak, M. (2009). *Issues in aging* (2nd ed.). Boston, MA: Pearson.

United Nations, Department of Economic and Social Affairs, Population Division. (2011). World population prospects: The 2010 revision, ST/ESA/SER.A/313. Retrieved from https://esa.un.org/unpd/wpp

Weeks, J. R. (2012). *Population: An introduction to concepts and issues* (11th ed.). Belmont, CA: Wadsworth/Cengage.

Zhou, Y., Norton, E. C., & Stearns, S. C. (2003). Longevity and health care expenditures: The real reasons older people spend more. *Journals of Gerontology Series B: Psychological Sciences and Social Sciences, 58*(1), S2–S10.

REVIEW QUESTIONS

1. What three ways do scholars measure the age of populations? What are each one's strengths and weaknesses?
2. What are the four big changes/implications of each?

ACTIVITY 4.2 HOMETOWN AGE DEMOGRAPHICS

Joann M. Montepare and Kimberly S. Farah

ACTIVITY INFORMATION

Type

__X__   In class

__X__   Online (Note: Could be adapted; students submit presentations to be viewed by others, who respond in online discussions about things they noticed, questions they had, and so on, about the different communities featured.)

_____   Take home

_____   In community

Difficulty

__X__   Introductory

__X__   Intermediate (Note: Could be adapted with more focused questions related to particular course content, or by including assigned readings about evaluating and planning age-friendly communities.)

_____   Advanced

OVERVIEW

The Hometown Age Demographics activity was designed to introduce undergraduate students to age demographics and their implications in their social and physical worlds as part of a multidisciplinary course that focused on healthy living spaces and age-friendly communities. It may be adapted and used in any course that addresses shifting age demographics, such as aging and adult development or social gerontology.

Discussions of age demographics are common at the onset of aging-related courses; however, they are typically presented at the national level. As such, students often do not see their immediate relevance. The present activity was crafted as a way to connect students more directly with population information by having them explore the age demographics of their own hometowns. This activity also prompts students to examine their communities through an age lens and to begin to see challenges and opportunities that make for age-friendly living environments. It also gives them an opportunity to hone their research skills by locating and evaluating demographic data, and evaluating it in light of associated community factors.

ACTIVITY LEARNING GOALS

Following this activity, students should be able to . . .

- Collect age demographic information from various sources.
- Describe local age demographics.
- Evaluate how age demographics may impact local communities.
- Provide information about age-friendly community issues.

ASSOCIATION FOR GERONTOLOGY IN HIGHER EDUCATION COMPETENCIES

- Relate social theories and science of aging to understanding heterogeneity, inequality, and context of aging.
- Distinguish factors related to aging outcomes, both intrinsic and contextual, through critical thinking and empirical research.

MINIMUM/MAXIMUM NUMBER OF PARTICIPANTS

- Unlimited

TIME NEEDED TO IMPLEMENT ACTIVITY

- Student fact finding, content development, slide design (approximately 3 hours)
- Individual presentations (10–15 minutes each)

SETTING

- Typical classroom

MATERIALS
Required

- Recommended resources from the list at the end of this activity.

Optional

- Final slides "with comments" in the PPT notes section may be presented as an assignment in place of the class presentation.

PROCEDURES
Preparation

Prior to completing this activity, instructors should prepare one to two orienting lectures to introduce students to information about shifting age demographics at the national level, along with questions about their implications and the extent to which communities are prepared to support an aging population.

The activity works well if completed early in the course (within the first several weeks) as it is geared toward getting students to work with age data and ask age-related questions about their environments. It also serves as a way to identify gaps in information and preconceptions students may have about aging, which informs ongoing course work and discussions.

Introduction

The Hometown Age Demographics activity is described to students as an opportunity for them to learn "up close and personal" about age demographics and their implications by exploring the population of their hometown (or a selected town of interest with which they are personally familiar) and their age-friendly components. Students should be given approximately 2 weeks to complete the activity. Final work is ideally submitted as an in-class presentation during designated class times.

Activity

The goal of this activity is to learn more about age demographics and their implications for communities and individuals. It may be adapted to different courses at different levels. Students will explore the age-related demographics along with related aging population issues and community characteristics of their hometowns. To this end, it is recommended that students work with data sources such as Census Explorer (www.census.gov/censusexplorer) and ePodunk (www .epodunk.com/about.html) to begin exploring age demographics and related information about their hometowns. If students cannot find sufficient information from these sources and/or want to consult additional sources, they should see whether their town or state has a website with local demographics. In the event that a student cannot find ample information about a particular town, another town may be selected. Students may also consult online resources such as Walkscore (www.walkscore.com), AARP Livability Index (livabilityindex.aarp .org), and state resources such as the Massachusetts Healthy Aging Data Report (mahealthyagingcollaborative.org) to gain information about community characteristics and aging issues. Students may also use other relevant community sources.

Students prepare five slides with specific information: (a) *title slide*, with information about location and other relevant background information (such as year established, reputation, brief history); (b) *demographic slide* with age distribution of the population and related characteristics such as gender, race, ethnicity, income, and educational level of the community; (c) *community slide* with several examples of age-related physical, social, health, and related issues observed in the community; (d) *community slide* with several examples of aging-friendly community characteristics and/or areas to consider for improving the community as a good place for aging (see World Health Organization [WHO] guidelines); and (e) *sources slide*.

The number and content of the slides may be adapted to the unique aims of the course. However, it has been found that giving students a specific number of slides with requirements for basic information greatly helps them focus their attention better on evaluating the data and their implications. A similar format also makes it easier to make comparisons across hometown evaluations.

Students should *not* be told what specific age-related components to consider, as it is instructive in their presentations to reflect on what they identified as key issues and to reflect on the similarities and differences that emerged across presentations. It is also likely that some students will identify age-related components within a narrow perspective (e.g., if their town has a nursing home or senior center) which will offer the instructor a valuable opportunity to explore age biases and what the broader view of an age-friendly community entails.

Students should be given the opportunity to infuse their own perspective and "personal touch" in the activity. To this end, students should be encouraged to work at making their slides visually informative and appealing, but not overly dense with text. During presentations, they may be advised to be prepared to walk the class through their observations using their slides as visual aids.

Discussion/Reflection

Students should submit their presentations to the instructor or course website several days in advance of the designated presentation period, as it is useful for the instructor to know in advance what communities will be discussed so that presentations may be grouped or ordered to highlight certain issues and/or make particular comparisons. As well, this offers the instructor time to develop questions for discussion and reflection based on students' observations.

Interesting topics for discussion include the extent to which students did or did not present age group breakdowns in the "65 and above" category and the implications of using one 65-plus category to describe older adults; the extent to which age demographics were connected to other demographic information (gender, race, etc.) and the implications of these linkages; the extent to which aging issues focused on declining health concerns versus opportunities for growth and engagement; and the extent to which age-friendly factors included intergenerational relations.

Wrap-Up

Following presentations, time may be given to reviewing key observations that emerged and how they will connect to other information to be explored in the course. The instructor may also conclude with an overview of the WHO guidelines for age-friendly communities to inform students about national hometown efforts.

Follow-Up

During the semester, the instructor may wish to connect back to information or questions that emerged during the Hometown Age Demographics presentations. Although this is not always a simple task to achieve, when connections can be made they reinforce for students the value of their work and the personal importance of learning about aging in their local communities.

Assessment

Instructors may evaluate the activity in a number of ways. For example, a rubric framework may be used (1/poor-2/good-3/excellent) that reflects the extent to which students (a) made use of relevant sources, (b) organized their presentation within the five-slide guideline, (c) identified appropriate age-related issues, and (d) offered apt assessments of age-friendly elements.

ADDITIONAL CONSIDERATIONS

Adjustments to the format of this activity may be made for a large class or if there is limited class time for presentations. For example, students may work in teams to examine select towns, such as communities in which they might consider living when they are older, or communities identified as age-friendly by the WHO, or "good places to retire" by other sources. Teams may also work collaboratively. For example, one team may be (randomly) chosen to present an overview of a particular town and its demographics, with other teams offering information based on their independent assessment of different age-related community characteristics (housing, transportation, education, etc.). An advantage of the latter method is that different information and interpretations will likely emerge, giving students an example of the variability of assessments even when a similar age lens is used—which often prompts discussions about how age-related information can be further evaluated, validated, and integrated.

Another option is for students to complete the activity without the final presentation component. In this case, students can be asked to comment on their observations described in each slide in the "notes" section. If this option is selected, the instructor may nevertheless wish to share particular findings and observations with the class to bring the work full circle and "back home" in the pedagogical spirit of the Hometown Age Demographics activity.

RECOMMENDED RESOURCES

In addition to the information sources noted in the activity section, some general online resources that are useful for both instructors and students include the following:

AARP Public Policy Institute Livable Communities. Retrieved from http://www .aarp.org/ppi/issues/livable-communities. Resources to learn more about the benefits of livable communities, and access to publications on reports on housing, transportation, aging in place, universal design, and other issues.

CDC Healthy Aging & the Built Environment. Retrieved from http://www.cdc .gov/healthyplaces/healthtopics/healthyaging.htm. Centers for Disease Control information, reports, guides, and links to other health issue sites and resources.

CDC Healthy Aging Research Network & Creating Aging-Friendly Communities. Retrieved from http://agingfriendly.org. Centers for Disease Control online resources, as well as online modules with recorded presentations, interactive discussion areas, and tools on key topics.

Dannenber, A., Frumkin, H., & Jackson, R. (2011). *Making healthy places: Designing and building for health, well-being, and sustainability.* Washington, DC: Island Press. An excellent overview of information regarding healthy living spaces that can be used in an undergraduate course that focuses on age-friendly communities.

WHO Global Network of Age-Friendly Cities and Communities. Retrieved from http://www.who.int/ageing/age-friendly-world/en. Resources, activity guides, and information about cities and communities in different parts of the world working at being age-friendly.

CHAPTER 5

HEALTH CARE

Hallie E. Baker

Health care covers a broad spectrum of services, professions, equipment, and businesses. In 2014, the United States spent over $3.0 trillion on health expenditures, which equals $9,523 per person, or 17.5% of the gross domestic product (National Center for Health Statistics, 2016). Beyond the growing costs of the health care industry, defining just what is covered by health care is complicated. In the broadest sense, health care seeks to maintain or restore health to individuals by professionals. Some define this as trained and licensed professionals, while others expand it to include alternative medicine. The World Health Organization adds services such as "prevention, promotion, treatment, rehabilitation and palliation" (World Health Organization, 2013, p. xi). The health care system within the United States is a diverse and complex system. Often elders and their families enter the system with no background or preparation to deal with the choices and challenges they will face. The result can lead patients to feeling confused and lost no matter what age they are. Adding to the issue, the impacts of ageism also influence and hinder the care older adults receive.

Within the United States, older adults interface with the health care system in several different ways. First is their *primary care* provider (for example, doctor or nurse practitioner) who provides treatment for common health problems, such as acute or chronic diseases, or prevention services (Bodenheimer & Grumbach, 2012). *Acute disease* processes include the common cold or the flu and present with quick onset and short duration. In contrast, *chronic disease* develops over long periods of time and lasts for months or years (for example, diabetes or heart disease).

Preventative services include mammograms, vaccines, and other screening tests with the goal of avoiding both acute and chronic illnesses.

For many patients, the primary care provider is someone they are comfortable with and have confidence in. The primary care provider often acts as the gatekeeper for referrals to other aspects of the health care system or as the coordinator of services as needed (Bodenheimer & Grumbach, 2012). When a patient displays symptoms or requires more intensive or specialized care, the primary care provider most frequently is the one to both identify the issue and make the referral to a specialist or secondary care provider. Thus, for older adults, their primary care provider often acts as a guide or source of referrals.

When an individual has a health issue that requires more intensive or specialized care, the person often goes to *secondary care*, which includes hospitals, specialist doctors, or other intensive care providers (Bodenheimer & Grumbach, 2012). An example with older adults is a fall, which could lead to a trip to a secondary care setting such as a hospital emergency room, leading to surgery to repair a broken bone, such as a hip, and a stay in the acute care hospital. For older adults and their families, entering secondary care due to trauma or chronic disease can be a challenge because the pace of services can vary. Referrals to specialists could result in long waiting periods to see such specialists due to limited available times for appointments. In contrast, a trauma such as a hip fracture could result in the fast-paced hospital stay due to health insurance (e.g., Medicare) guidelines that encourage short hospital stays as a cost control measure. The result is that a patient is often facing questions about aftercare or rehabilitation the day after surgery or being admitted to the hospital.

Often the hospital stay is followed by a stay in another setting for rehabilitation or home care for older adults (Huded & Heitor, 2016). Choices, including nursing homes, home health care, assisted living, and other options, add further options for secondary care. The result is even more options and potential confusion for elders and their families. Enhanced discharge planning has been recommended for older adults after hospital stays; however, this remains something that is not commonly done (Altfeld et al., 2013).

Beyond primary and secondary care providers, another network exists to provide ancillary services (Bodenheimer & Grumbach, 2012). Pharmacies, durable medical supplies, and alternative medicine play important roles in providing comprehensive health care to individuals. Primary care providers often make referrals or place orders with the ancillary service network to meet the needs of a patient. However, often the primary or even secondary care provider may not be aware of the financial costs or insurance coverage of those services. One outcome can be hard choices for families who have limited resources. The addition of ancillary services to the network of health care services expands the options and confusion that an older adult and their family can find themselves in.

A final issue within the health care system for older adults was summarized by Chrisler, Barney, and Palatino in 2016, which is ageism among health care workers. Ageist stereotypes often frame older adults as "rigid, religious, irritable, boring, lonely, isolated, asexual, easily confused, depressed and depressing, needy, frustrating, and nonproductive" among health care workers (Chrisler et al., 2016, p. 91). Further issues include a drive by doctors who view success as being able to cure their patients. This is something that is often not possible with both chronic conditions and normal physical aging effects. Thus, doctors can shy away from older adults as a result. While nurses tend to have more positive attitudes toward older adults, they and other professionals have been found to have more benevolent ageism, which leads to less explanation to their patients about what is going on. Instead, the providers focus on reassuring the older adult or using simple sentences, baby talk, or language more commonly used with children. Thus, instead of being informed and understanding what is going on, older adults are marginalized, increasing a sense of powerlessness. The result is a need to educate students, professionals, and even the elders themselves about health care in an effort to take the confusion out of the system and improve understanding.

HEALTH CARE EDUCATION EXERCISES

The following activities provide students the opportunity to engage with various aspects of the health care system and for future health care professionals to engage with elders to minimize potential ageist attitudes. Activity 5.1, An Evidence-Based Team Approach: Benefits of a Gerontological Interdisciplinary Team, helps to encourage nursing students and other future health care workers to interact with other disciplines in order to provide the best possible care for older adults and their families. Activity 5.2, Bingocize®: An Intergenerational Service-Learning Initiative to Improve Older Adults' Functional Fitness encourages students to interact with older adults through exercise programs, helping them see older adults as capable of being actively involved in prevention programs and their own health care. Activity 5.3, Medical Students, Community Engagement, offers medical students and other future health care providers a chance to practice much-needed skills while interacting with healthy elders as part of a preventative service project. Finally, Activity 5.4, What Would You Do? Getting Resources for Your Older Adult Activity, challenges participants to plan out care for a loved one based on available resources within the health care system, the limits of insurance, and the loved one's strengths/needs. By changing the dialog from just teaching about older adults in the abstract to encouraging interactions with older adults, the first three activities can decrease ageist attitudes, while the first and last activities can help participants begin to understand how to navigate the network of health care systems in the United States.

REFERENCES

Altfeld, S. J., Shier, G. E., Rooney, M., Johnson, T. J., Golden, R. L., Karavolos, K., . . . Perry, A. J. (2013). Effects of an enhanced discharge planning intervention for hospitalized older adults: A randomized trial. *The Gerontologist, 53*(3), 430–440.

Bodenheimer, T., & Grumbach, K. (2012). *Understanding health policy: A clinical approach.* New York, NY: McGraw-Hill.

Chrisler, J. C., Barney, A., & Palatino, B. (2016). Ageism can be hazardous to women's health: Ageism, sexism, and stereotypes of older women in the healthcare system. *Journal of Social Issues, 72*, 86–104. doi:10.1111/josi.12157

Huded, J., & Heitor, F. (2016). Skilled nursing facilities and post-hospitalization options for older adults. In L. A. Lindquist (Ed.), *New directions in geriatric medicine: Concepts, trends, and evidence-based practice* (pp. 127–145). Basel, Switzerland: Springer International. doi:10.1007/978-3-319-28137-7

National Center for Health Statistics. (2016). Health expenditures. Atlanta, GA: Centers for Disease Control. Retrieved from http://www.cdc.gov/nchs/fastats/health-expenditures.htm

World Health Organization. (2013). *Research for universal health coverage: World health report 2013.* Geneva, Switzerland: Author.

ACTIVITY 5.1 AN EVIDENCE-BASED TEAM APPROACH: BENEFITS OF A GERONTOLOGICAL INTERDISCIPLINARY TEAM

Colleen Steinhauser and Cheryl Bouckaert

ACTIVITY INFORMATION

Type

__X__	In class
__X__	Online
_____	Take home
_____	In community

Difficulty

_____	Introductory
__X__	Intermediate
_____	Advanced

OVERVIEW

The reason for creating this activity was to help students realize and understand the importance of collaboration and working within an interdisciplinary team to do the following: Provide holistic, patient-centered care; consider financial impacts of collaborative care; facilitate safe and effective transactions across levels of care for older adults and their families; and realize the nurse's role within the interdisciplinary team. Use of published articles supports student correlation of evidence to practice in the roles of nurse, social worker, prescribing provider, and/or case manager (hereafter referred to as health care provider).

ACTIVITY LEARNING GOALS

Following this activity, students should be able to . . .

- Discuss how interdisciplinary teams shorten the need for dependent self-care in the older adult.
- Discuss how collaborative care would shorten the hospital stay of the older adult.
- Discuss how collaborative care would lower health care costs for the older adult.
- Discuss the potential barriers with successful communication of the interdisciplinary team in the care of the older adult.

ASSOCIATION FOR GERONTOLOGY IN HIGHER EDUCATION COMPETENCIES

- Engage collaboratively with others to promote integrated approaches to aging.

MINIMUM/MAXIMUM NUMBER OF PARTICIPANTS

- 4 to 48 (no more than six students per group)

TIME NEEDED TO IMPLEMENT ACTIVITY

- 1 hour

SETTING(S)

- Classroom with chairs and tables or online

MATERIALS

Required

- Availability of at least one computer (or electronic device) with Internet access
- A textbook that has a chapter or references regarding collaboration and interdisciplinary teams
- Preferably access to scholarly journals (i.e., CINAHL, PubMed, MEDLINE, Health Source: Consumer Edition)

PROCEDURES

Preparation

Have students read chapter or reference regarding collaboration and interdisciplinary teams.

Example: Lange, J. W., & Tolson, D. (2012). An evidence-based team approach to optimal wellness. In *The nurse's role in promoting optimal health of older adults: Thriving in the wisdom years*. Philadelphia, PA: F. A. Davis.

Introduction

Review objectives with students: Discuss the health care provider as a member of the interprofessional team. Discuss the rationale for interprofessional teamwork. Give instructions to the groups of how to complete the learning activity.

Activity

Form groups of four to six students, with no more than six students per group. Complete the learning activity (see Appendix 5.1, Collaborative Team Assignment Worksheet). Students present findings in class via large group discussion and post written responses to an online shared forum set up in a Learning Management

System for further sharing and review. If done as an online class, groups may post replies in an online discussion board for peers and the instructor to comment on. Students are expected to comment on other groups' postings.

Discussion/Reflection

Students share their responses to questions provided by the activity either in class or via synchronous or asynchronous discussion boards. The instructor implementing this activity should be prepared to have their own guided questions to further this discussion and adjust questions based on the evidence-based research the students present. Some examples of instructor questions are the following:

- What is the health care provider's role in an interdisciplinary team?
- Why is the health care provider's role central to the interdisciplinary team?
- How can the health care provider better manage and coordinate the care of an older adult within an interdisciplinary team?
- What are the consequences of fragmented and poorly organized care to older adults?
- What is the value of effective teamwork?
- Why are we as health care providers challenged to promote wellness and maximize independence to help older adults successfully manage their chronic health problems?
- What does the Institute of Medicine say about collaborative care?

Wrap-Up

Faculty members submit a summary response to the shared discussion forum. This could also be done in class via PowerPoint or other preferred method.

Example: All of you did a really good job identifying the benefits and challenges of collaborative care of the gerontological patient and working with interdisciplinary teams!

According to Nagamine, Jiang, and Merrill (2006), "older adults account for more hospital stays than any other age group and comprise more than 35% of patients you will care for" (Lange, 2012, p. 75). Uncoordinated care and a fragmented, inadequately organized U.S. health care system has led to increased health care costs, poor patient outcomes, and squandered resources. In regards to patient care, nurses are in a position to recognize the unmet needs of their patients. Therefore, the nurse's role is central and it is the "primary responsibility of the nurse . . . to collaborate with other health professionals to care for older adults in a variety of residential settings as well as hospital, rehabilitative, and outpatient environments" (pp. 75–79). Nurses must work collaboratively using a team approach and evidence-based practice to help better coordinate care of older adults, which can lead to decreased cost, decreased lengths of stay, improved patient outcomes, and appropriate use of resources (p. 92).

Assessment

Students are assessed by active participation in the activity and short answer exam questions based on activity objectives. The expectation is that 75% of the class correctly answers the questions.

ADDITIONAL CONSIDERATIONS

This activity was first used with senior nursing students in a standalone gerontological nursing course. It can be adapted to have the instructor substitute any future role the student may have in the care of the older adult (nurse, social worker, prescribing provider, case manager).

REFERENCES

Lange, J. W. (2012). *The nurse's role in promoting optimal health of older adults: Thriving in the wisdom years.* Philadelphia, PA: F. A. Davis.

Nagamine, M., Jiang, H. J., & Merrill, C. T. (2006, October). *Trends in elderly hospitalizations, 1997–2004* (HCUP Statistical Brief #14). Rockville, MD: Agency for Healthcare Research and Quality. Retrieved from http://www.hcup-us.ahrq .gov/reports/statbriefs/sb14.pdf

APPENDIX 5.1: COLLABORATIVE TEAM ASSIGNMENT WORKSHEET

COLLABORATIVE TEAM ASSIGNMENT

The class will divide into groups of six. Each team will discuss one of the following assigned items and find one journal article to support the discussion. Each team will create a Word document summarizing the group's discussion incorporating findings from the journal article into the summary. The document should be no more than two paragraphs in length.

Use APA format to cite any in-text citations and cite the full reference of the journal article at the end of the document. Correct grammar, punctuation, and spelling are expected. Submit the document to the "Collaborative Team Assignment" forum in the online learning management system for shared learning.

OBJECTIVES

Identify the benefits and challenges of the collaborative interaction of a gerontological interdisciplinary team.

Each team will define interdisciplinary teams and the benefits of a comprehensive assessment.

- Discuss how the gerontological client's collaborative care with an interdisciplinary team shortens the need for dependent self-care. Support the discussion with one journal article (*Group 1*).

- Discuss how collaborative care by the interdisciplinary team would shorten the hospital stay of the gerontological client. Support the discussion with one journal article (*Group 2*).

- Discuss how collaborative care would lower health care costs for the gerontological client Support the discussion with one journal article (*Group 3*).

- Discuss the potential barriers faced in the achievement of successful communication of the interdisciplinary team in the care of the gerontological client. Support the discussion with one journal article (*Group 4*).

ACTIVITY 5.2 BINGOCIZE®: AN INTERGENERATIONAL SERVICE-LEARNING INITIATIVE TO IMPROVE OLDER ADULTS' FUNCTIONAL FITNESS

K. Jason Crandall

ACTIVITY INFORMATION

Type

___X___ In class

_____ Online

_____ Take home

___X___ In community

Difficulty

_____ Introductory

_____ Intermediate

___X___ Advanced

OVERVIEW

The population of older adults is increasing and the benefits of physical activity have been well documented. However, the majority of older adults reported no leisure time physical activity in the past month. To address this problem, there is a pressing need for fun, evidence-based, and cost-effective physical activity programs for older adults. Intergenerational service-learning initiatives like Bingocize® can provide valuable experiences for undergraduate students to meet course learning outcomes while meeting the needs of the older adult community.

ACTIVITY LEARNING GOALS

Following this activity, students should be able to . . .

- Understand the biological, physiological, and psychosocial aspects of aging.
- Understand the acute and chronic effects of exercise on older adults.
- Evaluate the efficacy of exercise programs for older adults.
- Apply relevant American College of Sports Medicine knowledge, skills, and abilities for older adults.
- Understand the personal perspectives of older adults.

ASSOCIATION FOR GERONTOLOGY IN HIGHER EDUCATION COMPETENCIES

- Relate biological theory and science to understanding senescence, longevity, and variation in aging.
- Relate psychological theories and science to understanding adaptation, stability, and change in aging.
- Develop a gerontological perspective through knowledge and self-reflection.
- Engage collaboratively with others to promote integrated approaches to aging.
- Promote older persons' strengths and adaptations to maximize well-being, physical health, and mental health.
- Promote quality of life and positive social environment for older persons.
- Engage in research to advance knowledge and improve interventions for older persons.

MINIMUM/MAXIMUM NUMBER OF PARTICIPANTS

- There is no minimum or maximum. The number of participants is determined by the number of senior facilities available and students enrolled in the course.

TIME NEEDED TO IMPLEMENT ACTIVITY

- One 45- to 60-minute session per week for 10 to 15 weeks. The number of sessions per week and the number of weeks may be increased based on the length of the semester.

SETTING(S)

- The program can be implemented in a large recreation area or office at any senior facility (e.g., independent living, nursing home, senior community center, and assisted living) with open space and access to tables/chairs.

MATERIALS

Required

- The required materials for this activity are minimal. Any type of table with sturdy chairs, preferably armless, is needed. Also, a standard bingo game, available at most senior facilities, is needed along with small prizes for game winners. Prizes can be supplied by the senior facilities or the university.

Optional

- The types of exercises performed are based on the ability levels of the participants. Less physically functional participants will not need any equipment. More physically functional participants may use graded resistance bands, 3 and 5 lb. hand weights, and/or balance pads. Playing participant-selected music adds another fun element to the program.

PROCEDURES

Preparation

Prior to the semester of implementation, service coordinators and activity directors from local senior facilities are invited to host a Bingocize® program. The number of facilities needed is determined by the course enrollment. The Bingocize® sessions are typically administered during the scheduled course time once per week. Additional sessions can be added at the instructor's discretion. The remaining weekly course sessions are used to present information related to the exercise and aging. Service coordinators and activity directors use flyers and word-of-mouth promotion to encourage participation in the program.

Introduction

The first day of the semester, groups of three to five students are formed. Each group is assigned to one senior facility. During the first 2 weeks of the semester, students are trained to conduct the program including leading safe and effective exercises. Students make an orientation visit prior to the first day of the program to meet the facility staff and the participants. The first day of the actual program is typically set for the third week of the semester. Exercise equipment is assigned to each group and prizes for the games are distributed to the students.

Activity

The program integrates bingo with exercises to keep the sessions interesting and enjoyable. Each 60-minute session consists of between 35 to 40 minutes of exercise and 15 to 20 minutes of bingo. One student demonstrates the exercises while the remaining students are positioned around the room to assist the participants in performing the exercises. A session begins with the senior participants sitting at tables with their bingo cards and optional exercise equipment. Warm-up exercises consisting of stepping in place and stretching exercises precede the start of the game. Participants perform three exercises followed by calling a bingo letter/number combination. This pattern is continued until a participant wins the bingo game. Incentive prizes to encourage continued participation are awarded to the winner of each bingo game. Prizes (<$2.00 each) can be donated by local businesses, purchased with university funds, or supplied by the senior facility. Examples of past prizes include lotion, crossword puzzles, dish towels, toilet paper, and so forth. Additional games of bingo can be played to allow for completion of the exercise protocol and to keep the participants interested in the program.

Participants complete 12 to 15 different exercises each session. The selected exercises should focus on improving cardiovascular (CV) fitness, muscular strength and endurance, flexibility, and balance using the American College of Sports Medicine guidelines for older adults. Beginning with one set of eight repetitions for each exercise, participants progress until capable of completing three sets of 15 repetitions by the end of the semester. The CV activities include walking and stepping in place or walking within the facility. Each CV bout lasts between 30 and 60 seconds. Participants complete a minimum of 20 minutes of CV exercise during each session.

Discussion/Reflection

During the class session following a Bingocize® session, the instructor provides opportunities for students to discuss their experiences. This is an opportunity to make connections with the course material, solve problems, and allow students to share ideas/best practices with one another. Students also submit weekly reflections online using the course's management software.

Wrap-Up

During the final week of the course, each group of students presents a 5- to 7-minute video showcasing their senior facility program. The video is modeled after a TED talk. See the iMovie Rubric for evaluation criteria.

Assessment

The students' peers (see Group Evaluation Form), the senior facility supervisor (see Service-Learning Community Partner Rubric), and the instructor use rubrics to evaluate the individual Bingocize® programs at each facility.

ADDITIONAL CONSIDERATIONS

Replicating the program is not difficult. First, there is minimal equipment needed to start the program. Many older adult facilities already have a bingo game and the optional exercise equipment is inexpensive. Second, stakeholders have much to gain from participating. The students are in need of experience, the older adults are interested in socializing and improving their health, the university likes community partnerships, and, finally, the community sites appreciate help implementing new and innovative programs. Please view this video (youtu.be/qXMZ0KJoPhg) for an overview of the activity.

RECOMMENDED RESOURCES

Chodzko-Zajko, W. J., Proctor, D. N., Fiatarone Singh, M. A., Minson, C. T., Nigg, C. R., Salem, G. J., & Skinner, J. S. (2009). Exercise and physical activity for older adults. *Medicine and Science in Sports and Exercise, 41*(7), 1510–1530. doi:10.1249/MSS.0b013e3181a0c95c

Crandall, K. J., Fairman, C., & Anderson, D. (2015). Functional performance in older adults after a combination multicomponent exercise program and bingo game. *International Journal of Exercise Science, 8*(1), 38–48.

Crandall, K. J., & Steenbergen, K. I. (2015). Older adults' functional performance and health knowledge after a combination exercise, health education, and bingo game. *Gerontology and Geriatric Medicine, 1.* doi:10.1177/2333721415613201

APPENDIX 5.2A: SYLLABUS

INTERGENERATIONAL SERVICE-LEARNING PROJECT

One of the primary objectives of this course is to apply what we are learning in the classroom for older adult facilities in the community. We will utilize the five principles of service-learning to answer a central question: What can I do to enhance the quality of life of older adults? Service-learning teaches you to ask what you can do rather than just assuming. The five principles of service-learning are the following:

- Reciprocity
- Partnership
- Capacity
- Sustainability
- Reflection

Focused on these five principles, you and your group members (four to five students per group) will plan, implement, and evaluate an evidence-based physical activity program at an older adult facility. You will attend your community site during our scheduled class time starting week 3 of the semester and ending the week before finals.

The program you will be implementing is called Bingocize®. It has been implemented in over 25 facilities in eight different states over the past 4 years. The program focuses on improving cardiorespiratory fitness, muscular strength, flexibility, mobility, and balance. Each 60-minute session begins with the participants sitting at tables with bingo cards and exercise equipment (balance pads, exercise tubing). After every two to three exercises, a letter and number combination is announced for the game. This pattern is continued until a participant wins the game. Household products are awarded to the winners of each bingo game (funds allowing). The combination of exercise and bingo significantly improved adherence and measures of functional physical fitness in three groups of older adults (Crandall, Fairman, & Anderson, 2015; Crandall & Shake, 2016; Crandall, Shake, & Xing, 2015; Crandall & Steenbergen, 2015). As a result, the Department of Health and Human Service Administration on Aging (AoA) found the Bingocize® program to meet AoA's minimal level criteria for evidence-based disease prevention and health promotion programs. Bingocize® was also added as a Promising Practice to the Healthy Communities Institute database.

The first couple of weeks of the semester will be used to train you to implement this program. Much of the planning for the program is complete, but you will need to plan for other things such as safety, equipment needs, prizes, and so forth. It is important, however, to implement the activity as instructed to maintain fidelity of the program.

REQUIREMENTS FOR SERVICE-LEARNING PROJECT

Reflections (individual written assignment): Reflection is one of the key principles of service-learning. You will reflect on the following: (a) community site experience (e.g., reflect on any aspect of diversity that you can relate to your site experience, your recognition of stereotypes, barriers, anything you are learning related to diversity and your site participants, how you are similar/different to the participants and how this impacts your experience), (b) required reading assignments (e.g., what stood out to you in each reading, any critiques, how you personally relate), and (c) class discussions (e.g., reflect on others' comments, activities that were done, whether your perspective changed. You do not need to address every aspect of class discussion/presentations). The reflective log should tie these three areas together whenever possible. Please do not simply describe the activities you did at your site or that were done in class, or summarize the readings. This portion of your grade will reflect the depth with which you reflect upon these areas, in addition to the quality of the writing. These are some questions/topics that may help guide your reflections. This is not an all-inclusive list and you do not have to address every question in each reflection.

1. Describe your feelings, thinking, and response to your time in the community.
2. What changes occurred for you as a result of your community participation?
3. What disturbs you when you reflect on your community experience?
4. Describe the connections you found between our readings and your community experience.
5. Identify barriers (i.e., culture, physical surroundings, and economic constraints) to health promoting behaviors, which are specific to your community site.
6. Describe the problem-solving and collaboration with your site partners as well as other students.
7. How is the experience preparing you for your future career? Be specific.
8. Look back on today. What struck you most strongly? What happened?
9. What images stand out in your mind? What sights and sounds and smells? What experiences and conversations? What was it about those things that made you remember?
10. What did you find most frustrating? Most hopeful? Why?
11. Look back on today. Who did you meet and work with during the day? Who did you relate to most easily? Who did you find it hardest to talk with? Why?
12. What did you learn about the people you met? How are their experiences most like yours?
13. What did you learn about yourself today? What do you like about what you learned? What do you dislike and most what to change?
14. What was happening in your head? How did the experience change or challenge your convictions and beliefs?
15. What needs did your service involvement try to meet? Why did or didn't it succeed?
16. What information or skills did you learn today?
17. How did you apply knowledge and information you had learned before this project?
18. What hopes and expectations do you have for those you served? For yourself?

iMovie (group assignment): The purpose of this assignment is to describe your experiences at the community site in a creative and captivating way. The requirements for this project are simple. You will use iMovie or another video application to compile images/video into a 5- to 7-minute video. Your group will capture photos, videos, and other images (tables, graphs, etc.) that help to describe the experiences at your community site. Obtain permission from both participants and the site supervisor before taking pictures/video. You must include at least 60 images (pictures, tables, figures, etc.) and at least two video clips. Once compiled, you will add voice to the iMovie describing your experiences. The iMovie will be graded using the rubric provided later in this syllabus. You have the freedom to be as creative as you like! In fact, a large part of your grade will be based on how creatively you present your information. With that said, you must address the following questions during your iMovie. Do not just present the questions and then answer during the iMovie. That would be boring. *It is critical you use information presented in class to address these questions!!*

1. What was the purpose of your service-learning project?
2. What was the community site like?
3. What were your older adults like?
4. What did you do to achieve your purpose/objectives?
5. What did you accomplish? What did you not accomplish?
6. What did you get out of this project?
7. What did your participants get out of this project?
8. What would you do differently?
9. What is the take-home message you want to leave with your audience?

Group Evaluation: Along with the completed movie, each student will complete a Group Evaluation Form that will provide an evaluation of self and group member(s).

REFERENCE

Crandall, K. J., Fairman, C., & Anderson, D. (2015). Functional performance in older adults after a combination multicomponent exercise program and bingo game. *International Journal of Exercise Science, 8*(1), 38–48.

Crandall, K. J., & Shake, M. (2016). A mobile application for improving functional performance and health education in older adults: A pilot study. *Journal of Aging Science, 4*(151). doi:10.4172/2329-8847.1000151

Crandall, K. J., & Steenbergen, K. I. (2015). Older adults' functional performance and health knowledge after a combination exercise, health education, and bingo game. *Gerontology and Geriatric Medicine, 1*, 1–7. doi:10.1177/2333721415613201

Crandall, K. J., Xing, G., & Shake, M. (2015). Bingocize 3.0: A game based platform for promoting wellness in older adults. In *Proceedings of the 6th annual ACM Conference on Bioinformatics, Computational Biology and Health Informatics* (pp. 478–479). doi:10.1145/2808719.2811416

APPENDIX 5.2B: IMOVIE RUBRIC

iMovie Rubric					
	4	3	2	1	Total
Purpose and content	Clearly relates to the learning objective or illustrates a concept. Thoroughly addresses all required questions.	Relates to the learning objective or illustrates a concept. Addresses required questions with little detail.	Some relation to the learning objective or concept. Minimally addresses required questions.	Does not relate to the learning objective or does not illustrate a concept. Does not address required questions sufficiently.	
Titles, transitions, and effects	Titles and/or transitions enhance the video.	Titles and/or transitions do not detract from the video.	Attempts to use titles and/or transitions, but they detract from the video.	No titles or transitions exist.	
Video/photos	Video and photos relate to the subject.	Videos and photos mostly relate to the subject.	Videos and photos are few and some are off topic.	No videos or photos relate to the subject.	
Audio	Movie includes voice and music. Audio levels are just right.	Movie includes voice and music. Audio levels are too low or too loud.	Movie has only music. Audio levels are too low or too loud.	Movie has no sound.	
Use of technology	Skilled operation of computer and program enhances presentation.	Satisfactory operation of computer and program during presentation.	Minimal operation of computer and program during presentation.	Incorrect operation of computer and program detracts from presentation.	

(continued)

iMovie Rubric

	4	3	2	1	Total
Presentation	Shared final product with audience, answered all questions in knowledgeable way.	Shared final product with audience, answered some questions in knowledgeable way.	Shared final product with audience and attempted to answer questions.	No final product to share.	
Mechanics	Presentation has no misspellings or grammatical errors.	Presentation has fewer than two misspellings and/or grammatical errors.	Presentation has three or more misspellings and/or grammatical errors.	Presentation has four or more misspellings and/or grammatical errors.	
Design	Clips and photos are appropriate to the content and communicate the information at a high level. Clips are long enough to convey meaning but without being too lengthy.	Clips and photos communicate the content information in an effective manner. Some clips are either too long or too short to be meaningful.	Clips and photos barely communicate the information intended. Most clips are too long or too short and confuse the content.	The clips and photos interfere with the communication of the content. The clips do not make sense and are randomly placed.	

APPENDIX 5.2C: SERVICE-LEARNING COMMUNITY PARTNER RUBRIC

(To be completed by community site supervisor and e-mailed directly to instructor)

Site: _____

	Excellent	Good	Fair	Poor	Unacceptable
	5	4	3	2	0
1. Teamwork					
Did the group work well together?					
2. Professionalism					
Did the team show up on time? Did they demonstrate a clear plan? Were they dressed appropriately?					
3. Activities					
Were the activities appropriate for older adults? Were the activities designed to accomplish the group's goals?					
4. Preparation					
Were the students prepared each day?					
5. Attitude					
Did all of the team members possess a positive attitude?					
6. Assessment					
Did the team members conduct appropriate assessments to determine the outcomes of the program?					
7. Effort					
Did the team members give every effort to make sure the program was done well?					

What could the students have done differently that would have produced a better outcome for the program?

Would you welcome this particular group of students back for another program if possible? Why or why not?

Would you welcome another group of students back next semester to continue our programming? Why or why not?

APPENDIX 5.2D: GROUP EVALUATION FORM

Write the name of each group member in a separate column. For each group member, indicate the degree to which you agree with the statements on the left, using a scale of 1 to 4 (1 = strongly disagree; 2 = disagree; 3 = agree; 4 = strongly agree). Total the numbers in each column.

Your Name:

Evaluation Criteria	Self-Evaluation	Group Member	Group Member	Group Member	Group Member	Group Member	Group Member
Effective in discussions, good listener, capable presenter, and proficient at diagramming, representing, and documenting work							
Attended group meetings regularly							
Displayed or tried to develop a wide range of skills in service of the project, and readily accepted changed approach or constructive criticism							
Was dependable and completed assignments well and on time							
Demonstrated cooperative and supportive attitude							
Contributed overall to the success of the project							
Carried a fair load of the group work							
Communicated effectively with other group members (and the group's teaching assistant)							
Totals:							

APPENDIX 5.2E: FEEDBACK QUESTIONS

(Answer on the back of this page or on a separate page, typed.)

1. Please comment about your specific contributions to this project. What tasks did you do that aided in its completion? What were your most important contributions? In what ways (if any) might you have contributed more? How effectively did your group work?

2. Please comment about each group member's contributions to this project. Be sure that you discuss each group member individually, by name. What tasks did each group member do that aided in the project's completion? What were their most important contributions? In what ways (if any) might each member have contributed more?

3. Identify any problems or disputes that occurred during your interactions.

4. How could disputes have been avoided and/or how were they resolved?

ACTIVITY 5.3 MEDICAL STUDENTS' COMMUNITY ENGAGEMENT

Jennifer Mendez, Sasha Stine, and Preeya Prakash

ACTIVITY INFORMATION

Type

X	In class
_____	Online
_____	Take home
_____	In community

Difficulty

_____	Introductory
_____	Intermediate
X	Advanced

OVERVIEW

Prior to the Affordable Care Act, student-run free clinics saw an average of 20 to 30 patients a week, who were screened for blood pressure and other basic health assessments. Currently, approximately five to six patients show up weekly, to address the drop in patients, a need arose for other venues for medical students. To continue to get experiences practicing their blood pressure screening skills.

During June through August, Detroit Medical Center's Rosa Parks Center of Excellence and Senior ER organizes a walking program for older adults every Tuesday and Thursday from 8:30. a.m. to 10:30 a.m. Each week, approximately 200 older adults attend.

A request was made to the administrators to allow six medical students to assess an average of 30 older adults' blood pressure prior to and after their walks. Students look forward to this opportunity and older adults are pleased that they can contribute to the medical students' educational experience.

ACTIVITY LEARNING GOALS

Following this activity, students should be able to . . .

- Monitor blood pressure.
- Experience how older adults stay active and healthy.
- Practice and improve communication skills with older adult patients.

ASSOCIATION FOR GERONTOLOGY IN HIGHER EDUCATION COMPETENCIES

- Relate biological theory and science to understanding senescence, longevity, and variation in aging.
- Relate psychological theories and science to understanding adaptation, stability, and change in aging.
- Promote older persons' strengths and adaptations to maximize well-being, health, and mental health.
- Promote quality of life and positive social environment for older persons.

MINIMUM/MAXIMUM NUMBER OF PARTICIPANTS

- 6 to 12 per week

TIME NEEDED TO IMPLEMENT ACTIVITY

- 2 hours each session, two sessions per week

SETTING

- Outdoor space with table and chairs

MATERIALS
Required

- Blood pressure cuffs and stethoscopes

Optional

- Storage space for assessment forms and required materials

PROCEDURES
Preparation

Teach health professional students how to take blood pressures; create blood pressure logs with explanations of the readings attained. An orientation–training should include proper blood pressure measurement techniques: selecting the correct size blood pressure cuff and directing the patient to sit comfortably—for example, rest elbow on a flat surface and plant both feet flat on the ground. Education and counseling information should be made available on nutrition and exercise—for example, instruct patients to reduce sodium intake, reduce high fat-containing foods, and add moderate exercise to daily routine.

Introduction

In most medical schools, students receive didactic lectures about taking blood pressures, but opportunities to practice are limited. Through service-learning opportunities, partnerships with community agencies that have older adults attending activities on regular bases could be sites for health care students to practice their communication and blood pressure monitoring skills.

Activity

Meeting with and monitoring blood pressure of engaged active older adults who participate in, for example, a walking program or other activities where older adults congregate on a regular basis.

Discussion/Reflection

Each time students volunteer, they should discuss the patients seen; since most of the older adults come regularly and bring the blood pressure logs, the students get an opportunity to communicate and suggest better health practices (e.g., lowering sodium intake). This could be done through journaling or in a class small group session.

Wrap-Up

In order to start becoming more confident in taking blood pressures, students should look for other opportunities for practicing this clinical skill, which is part of the competencies assessed in health career education.

Follow-Up

All older adults seen by medical students are advised to take the blood pressure log to their family physician to discuss further medical goals.

Assessment

Twice a year the medical students select one volunteer opportunity using a prescribed evaluation tool to provide feedback.

ADDITIONAL CONSIDERATIONS

Community agencies are often short staffed and welcome student volunteers; contact them when you have an idea.

CONTENT SOURCES

Centers for Disease Control and Prevention. (n.d.). High blood pressure educational materials for patients. Retrieved from https://www.cdc.gov/bloodpressure/materials_for_patients.htm

HealthinAging.org. (n.d.). Blood pressure targets are different for very old adults. Retrieved from http://www.healthinaging.org/aging-and-health-a-to-z/topic:high-blood-pressure/info:unique-to-older-adults

APPENDIX 5.3: BLOOD PRESSURE INFORMATION SHEET AND LOG

Blood Pressure	
What is blood pressure? Blood pressure is the force of the blood pushing against your blood vessels. The higher your blood pressure, the harder your heart works. Blood pressure is written as 120/80 mmHg. The top number, 120, is the force of blood when your heart beats. The bottom number, 80, is the force of blood between heartbeats. **What is prehypertension?** This is slightly high blood pressure. It will turn into high blood pressure if no changes are made to your lifestyle. These changes can be eating healthier and exercising as little as 20 to 30 minutes a day. **What is hypertension?** Hypertension is the name for high blood pressure. You can have this for years without feeling sick. You can work with your doctor to lower it. **Why is blood pressure important?** High blood pressure is when your heart works much harder than normal. It has to push blood to your whole body. You are at risk for many problems, such as: • stroke: where blood flow to your brain stops • heart attack: where blood stops going to part of your heart • kidney disease: where your kidneys are damaged and cannot keep you healthy You can get rid of these problems by lowering your blood pressure.	**What do the numbers mean?** **Under 120 and under 80.** This is normal. **120/80 to 139/89** Prehypertension **140/90 to 159/99** Stage 1 hypertension **160 or higher/100 or higher** Stage 2 hypertension **180/anything and higher** This is a hypertensive crisis. *Please go to the emergency room!*
Where can I get more information? Call 1-800-342-2383 Talk to your doctor. Ask for more information about blood pressure and what you can do to lower it. Go to www.cdc.gov/bloodpressure Go to www.mayoclinic.com/health/high-bloodpressure/DS00100	

VITALS LOG			
Date	Blood Pressure	Current Health Issues	Medications

ACTIVITY 5.4 WHAT WOULD YOU DO? GETTING RESOURCES FOR YOUR OLDER ADULT ACTIVITY

Hallie E. Baker

ACTIVITY INFORMATION

Type

__X__ In class

_____ Online

_____ Take home

_____ In community

Difficulty

_____ Introductory

__X__ Intermediate

_____ Advanced

OVERVIEW

Medicare and Medicaid both have complex and at times humorous coverage and gaps in their coverage. The author has, in the past, used this for laughs in her class and from those discussions the current activity emerged. The activity was created, to engage students in practical applications of class discussions of Medicare and Medicaid coverage. By engaging students in real-life scenarios, students utilize critical thinking skills about how families and elders have to interact with the health care system to get the services they need. Further, the students' understanding of the programs and macro structures is enhanced.

Medicare benefits vary by what part or section of the program the person is enrolled in (Friedland, 2005). Part A and B are the original aspects of the program with all eligible participants automatically being enrolled in Part A at the age of 65 or under other special circumstances. Part A covers hospitalization, skilled nursing home care, some home health services, and other major health costs (Medicare, 2016c). Part B is an optional portion of the program that participants pay into on a sliding scale. Benefits include coverage for doctor's visits, lab work, medical supplies, preventive services, and much more (Medicare, 2016d). Under Medicare part D, or the Prescription Drug Plan, participants choose the plan; thus, the medications or drugs covered vary between plans along with the costs. However, it will be less than paying for the drugs on your own (Medicare, 2016b).

In contrast to Medicare, which is more of an age-based program, Medicaid is a need or financial-based program (Center on Budget and Policy Priorities, 2015). A joint program between the federal government and states, Medicaid is funded by both with basic mandatory coverage set by the federal government with options available to the states to extend coverage options. Thus, benefits can vary from state to state (Medicaid.gov, 2016). Since Medicaid covers low-income individuals or those with financial needs due to high health care costs, individuals of all ages can qualify for the program. Once an individual meets the financial and other qualifications, then that person is covered by the program. Mandatory benefits, or those that are universal to all states, include hospital services, nursing home services, home health care, physician services, lab services, transportation, and medical equipment, to name a few. Optional services that states can add include hospice care, eyeglasses, dental care/dentures, and many others. It is important for individuals to check with their state agency to verify what is covered by their state.

The end result is a tangled challenging system that often requires an experienced case manager, nurse manager, or social worker to help them work through. The activity gives students a chance to get a feel for what families often face before facing it in a real-life situation; this often involves many emotions besides the financial burden and confusion of dealing with the health care system, which can be complex in and of itself.

The activity is not for beginners and does require an instructor or professor to provide background information on both health care and aging, as well as Medicare and Medicaid. Resources for the activity provided include suggested readings, resources for the instructor to use as one facilitates the activity, and PowerPoint slides from the author on lectures she gives on the previous topics. When set up and executed properly, students will be challenged and have a greater understanding of the health care system, Medicare, and Medicaid while improving their critical thinking skills.

ACTIVITY LEARNING GOALS

Following this activity, students should be able to . . .

- Identify and discuss practical differences between Medicare and Medicaid program coverages.
- Identify what factors might put elders at risk because of gaps in different social programs.
- Demonstrate improvement in skills to engage others to problem solve for a solution to a mutual problem.

ASSOCIATION FOR GERONTOLOGY IN HIGHER EDUCATION COMPETENCIES

- Develop a gerontological perspective through knowledge and self-reflection.
- Promote older persons' strengths and adaptations to maximize well-being, health, and mental health.
- Address the roles of older persons as workers and consumers in business and finance.

MINIMUM/MAXIMUM NUMBER OF PARTICIPANTS

- 10 to 50

TIME NEEDED TO IMPLEMENT ACTIVITY

- 20 to 30 minutes

SETTING

- Classroom

MATERIALS

Required

- Exercise worksheet
- Instructor resources to help facilitate activity:
  - Instructor reference sheet
  - Medicare coverage information
  - Medicaid benefits information
  - PowerPoints on the following topics for references or use in class
    - Characteristics of the U.S. Health Care System
    - Health Care and Aging
    - Medicare
    - Medicaid
- Suggested readings, but not required
  - Center on Budget and Policy Priorities. (2015). Policy basics: Introduction to Medicaid. Retrieved from www.cbpp.org/cms/index.cfm?fa=view&id=2223
  - Friedland, R. B. (2005a). How medicaid works. *Generations, 29*(1), 35–38.
  - Friedland, R. B. (2005b). How Medicare works. *Generations, 29*(1), 30–34.

PROCEDURES

Preparation

The activity should take place after a solid introduction to Medicare, Medicaid, and the health care system. Information is provided for the instructor along with suggested readings.

Introduction

Introduce the activity as a chance to apply what students have learned and explore the role of caseworkers.

Arrange students into groups of three to four per group, either by allowing students to self-select groups, have them count off numbers, or other methods.

Activity

1. Instruct students to pick a scribe (someone to do the writing) and someone to come up and get their exercise sheet.
   a. There are six different scenarios, so you may have to make more copies to cover the whole class.
2. Allow about 10 minutes for them to work through the exercise sheet.
3. The instructor/professor should walk about playing the role of case manager/ resource for the groups as they work out what will pay for different types of care and different strategies.
   a. As the instructor/professor moves from group to group, ask each group questions about what would maximize the elder's independence, if there is a creative way to deal with the issue, or how they would handle it if it was their grandmother/father or relative.

Discussion/Reflection

The worksheet will ask for student reflections on the assignment, but the wrap-up will allow for larger group discussion.

Wrap-Up

- Gather the class back together.
- Have each group (or, if more than one group is working on a scenario go by scenario) report on the scenario and what they did.
  ○ Ask others in the class to give further suggestions or options that the group(s) may not have thought about.
  ○ Ask if there was anything that surprised them, or if anything made them change their plan as they worked through the scenario.
- Ask the group, as a whole, what other reactions they had.
- Validate and reflect back any themes or comments the students provide.
- Collect the worksheets at the end of the time.

Follow-Up

- When returning the worksheets, take the time to make comments and suggestions to the students to make it more of a conversation.
- When covering caregiving, refer back to the activity as students will remember it and can, upon reflection, show more insight on how informal caregivers can be impacted by gaps in Medicare and Medicaid coverage.

Assessment

- The worksheet is handed in and can provide insight into how the students did.
- The rubric in Appendix 5.4E, What Would You Do? Getting Resources for Your Older Adult—Rubric, can help assess the student's achievement of basic skills and insight into the tasks of the activity.
- Credit can be provided for participation or a grade assigned along with using the feedback to assess the activity's effectiveness.

ADDITIONAL CONSIDERATIONS

- Look for the theme of how economic status impacts the options available for families and elders.
- The instructor needs to be comfortable in the role of case manager/facilitator with a good knowledge of Medicare/Medicaid coverage for services.

REFERENCES

Center on Budget and Policy Priorities. (2015, June). Policy basics: Introduction to Medicaid. Retrieved from http://www.cbpp.org/research/health/policy -basics-introduction-to-medicaid?fa=view&id=2223

Friedland, R. B. (2005a). How Medicare works. *Generations, 29*(1), 35–38.

Friedland, R. B. (2005b). How Medicare works. *Generations, 29*(1), 30–34.

Medicaid.gov. (2016). Benefits. Retrieved from https://www.medicaid.gov/ medicaid-chip-program-information/by-topics/benefits/medicaid-benefits .html

Medicare. (2016a, April). Preventive & screening services. Retrieved from https:// www.medicare.gov/coverage/preventive-and-screening-services.html

Medicare. (2016b, April). What drug plans cover. Retrieved from https://www .medicare.gov/part-d/coverage/part-d-coverage.html

Medicare. (2016c, April). What Part A covers. Retrieved from https://www .medicare.gov/what-medicare-covers/part-a/what-part-a-covers.html

Medicare. (2016d, April). What Part B covers. Retrieved from https://www .medicare.gov/what-medicare-covers/part-b/what-medicare-part-b-covers .html

RECOMMENDED RESOURCES

There are some good sources to help with this assignment.

- For Medicare coverage, this website is helpful: www.medicare.gov/coverage/ is-your-test-item-or-service-covered.html
- For Medicaid coverage, a place to start is here: www.medicaid.gov/medicaid/ benefits/index.html and/or www.medicaid.gov/medicaid/benefits/list-of -benefits/index.html. However, checking with the state Medicaid office website will provide more information.

APPENDIX 5.4A: ACTIVITY WORKSHEETS WITH SCENARIOS

Group members:

1. _____

2. _____

3. _____

4. _____

5. _____

You are the family members of an elder who has recently fallen. . . . Your task is to meet the needs of your family member under the following circumstances:

1. The individual will need a hip replacement: 3- to 4-day hospital stay.
2. Postsurgery rehabilitation will take place in a nursing home for 2 to 3 weeks.
3. When the individual returns home their physical therapy will need to continue and someone will need to be with them at night.
4. The individual will need a walker, wheelchair (temporarily), and bedside commode.
5. The individual is covered by Medicare Parts A and B and has Medigap insurance.

1. Is the individual covered by Medicare?
2. Is the individual covered by Medicaid?
3. How will you pay for each of the care needs listed earlier?
4. What will the family have to provide?
5. What other concerns do you have?
6. What is your reaction to this exercise?

Group members:

1. _____

2. _____

3. _____

4. _____

5. _____

You are the family members of an elder who has recently fallen. . . . Your task is to meet the needs of your family member under the following circumstances:

1. The individual will need a hip replacement: 3- to 4-day hospital stay.
2. Postsurgery rehabilitation will take place in a nursing home for 2 to 3 weeks.
   a. Medicare will pay 100% of the stay for the first 20 days; after that, it will only pay 80%.

3. When the individual returns home their physical therapy will need to continue and someone will need to be with them at night.
4. The individual will need a walker, wheelchair (temporarily), and bedside commode.
5. The individual is covered by Medicare Parts A and B and has limited savings/income.

1. Is the individual covered by Medicare?
2. Is the individual covered by Medicaid?
3. How will you pay for each of the care needs listed earlier?
4. What will the family have to provide?
5. What other concerns do you have?
6. What is your reaction to this exercise?

Group members:

1. _____

2. _____

3. _____

4. _____

5. _____

You are the family members of an elder who has been diagnosed with Alzheimer's disease and is now needing more care. . . . Your task is to meet the needs of your family member under the following circumstances:

1. The individual needs someone to:
   a. cook for them
   b. monitor their medications
   c. do all instrumental activities of daily living (IADLs)
   d. monitor the individual's location because they are now wandering
2. The individual does not qualify for skilled nursing care in a nursing home; therefore, Medicare will not pay for their care.
3. You have been told that due to increasing frailty, the individual needs a walker and bedside commode.
4. The individual is covered by Medicare Parts A and B and has extensive savings.

1. Is the individual covered by Medicare?
2. Is the individual covered by Medicaid?
3. How will you pay for each of the care needs listed earlier?
4. What will the family have to provide?
5. What other concerns do you have?
6. What is your reaction to this exercise?

Group members:

1. _____

2. _____

3. _____

4. _____

5. _____

You are the family members of an elder who has been diagnosed with Alzheimer's disease and is now needing more care. . . . Your task is to meet the needs of your family member under the following circumstances:

1. The individual needs someone to:
   a. cook for them
   b. monitor the individual's medications
   c. do all IADLs
   d. monitor the indivdual's location because they are now wandering
2. The individual does not qualify for skilled nursing care in a nursing home; therefore, Medicare will not pay for their care.
3. You have been told that due to increasing frailty, the individual needs a walker and bedside commode.
4. The individual is covered by Medicare Parts A and B, has no savings, and has only $2,500 a month in income.

1. Is the individual covered by Medicare?
2. Is the individual covered by Medicaid?
3. How will you pay for each of the care needs listed earlier?
4. What will the family have to provide?
5. What other concerns do you have?
6. What is your reaction to this exercise?

Group members:

1. _____

2. _____

3. _____

4. _____

5. _____

You are the family members of an elder who has advanced diabetes and needs an amputation. . . . Your task is to meet the needs of your family member under the following circumstances:
So now . . .

1. The individual will need an amputation: 3- to 4-day hospital stay.
2. Postsurgery rehabilitation will take place in a nursing home for 2 to 3 months.
   a. Medicare will pay 100% of the stay for the first 20 days; after that, it will pay only 80% for days 21 to 100 or as long as the individual requires skilled care.
   b. Will receive a prosthesis.

3. When the individual returns home their physical therapy will need to continue, and someone will need to be with them at night and most of the day.
4. The individual will need a walker, wheelchair (temporarily), and bedside commode.
5. The individual is covered by Medicare Parts A and B and has limited savings and income.

1. Is the individual covered by Medicare?
2. Is the individual covered by Medicaid?
3. How will you pay for each of the care needs listed earlier?
4. What will the family have to provide?
5. What other concerns do you have?
6. What is your reaction to this exercise?

Group members:

1. _____
2. _____
3. _____
4. _____
5. _____

You are the family members of an elder who has advanced diabetes and needs an amputation. . . . Your task is to meet the needs of your family member under the following circumstances:
So now . . .

1. The individual will need an amputation: 3- to 4-day hospital stay.
2. Postsurgery rehabilitation will take place in a nursing home for 2 to 3 months.
   a. Medicare will pay 100% of the stay for the first 20 days; after that, it will only pay 80% for days 21 to 100 or as long as the individual requires skilled care.
   b. Will receive a prosthesis.
3. When the individual returns home their physical therapy will need to continue and someone will need to be with them at night and most of the day.
4. The indiviual will need a walker, wheelchair (temporarily), and bedside commode.
5. The individual is covered by Medicare Parts A and B and is on Medicaid as well.

1. Is the individual covered by Medicare?
2. Is the individual covered by Medicaid?
3. How will you pay for each of the care needs listed earlier?
4. What will the family have to provide?
5. What other concerns do you have?
6. What is your reaction to this exercise?

APPENDIX 5.4B: INSTRUCTOR REFERENCE SHEET

MEDICARE COVERAGE

- Part A helps pay for medically necessary inpatient care in a hospital, inpatient acute care in a skilled nursing facility, or treatment in a psychiatric hospital; for hospice care; for medically necessary home health care; and for wheelchairs, hospital beds, and other durable medical equipment supplied under a home health care benefit.
  - Set benefit times, eligibility, and periods for various parts of care
  - Often includes co-pays or deductibles
- Part B also covers outpatient hospital services, certain vaccinations, x-rays and laboratory tests, certain ambulance services, durable medical equipment such as wheelchairs and hospital beds used at home, mammograms, Pap smears, and pelvic exams.
- Part D covers prescription drugs.

MEDICAID COVERAGE

- Coverage includes inpatient hospital, laboratory and x-ray, nursing facility services for beneficiaries age 21 and older, family planning services and supplies, physicians' services, medical and surgical services of a dentist, and home health services for beneficiaries who are entitled to nursing facility services under the state's Medicaid plan.
- Home health services to beneficiaries who are entitled to receive nursing facility services under the state's Medicaid plan.
- States may include any other services described under Medicaid law subject to any limits based on comparability of services.
- Optional Medicaid state plan services
  - Passport, assisted living waiver programs

GENERAL LIST OF SERVICES, INCLUDING WHO PAYS FOR THEM: MEDICARE, MEDICAID, OR BOTH

- Hospital stays—Both pay.
- Prescription drugs—Both pay.
- Home health care—Both pay.
- Nursing home care—Both pay.
- Assisted living—Medicaid waiver only.
- Continuing care retirement communities (CCRCs)—Neither pay.

- Wheelchairs or walkers—Medicare will pay for one or the other, not both; Medicaid pays for them as well.
- Lift chairs—Medicare will pay for the motor only, not the chair.
- Electric wheelchairs/scooters—Medicare and Medicaid will pay except for the replacement battery.
- Home oxygen—Both pay.
- Housekeeping help—Neither pay.
- Adult day-care—Only Medicaid waiver programs pay.

APPENDIX 5.4C: MEDICAID BENEFITS INFORMATION

MEDICAID BENEFITS

States establish and administer their own Medicaid programs and determine the type, amount, duration, and scope of services within broad federal guidelines. States are required to cover certain "mandatory benefits," and can choose to provide other "optional benefits" through the Medicaid program.

This includes services furnished in a religious nonmedical health care institution, emergency hospital services by a non-Medicare certified hospital, and services in a critical access hospital (CAH).

Check your state by going to this link: www.medicaid.gov/about-us/contact-us/contact-state-page.html

RECOMMENDED RESOURCES

- Medicare.gov: Benefits. Retrieved from https://www.medicaid.gov/medicaid/benefits/index.html; List of Medicaid benefits. Retrieved from https://www.medicaid.gov/medicaid/benefits/list-of-benefits/index.html

APPENDIX 5.4D: MEDICARE COVERAGE INFORMATION

MEDICARE COVERAGE

The following websites provide information about what Medicare covers:

www.medicare.gov/what-medicare-covers/part-a/what-part-a-covers.html

www.medicare.gov/what-medicare-covers/part-b/what-medicare-part-b-covers.html

www.medicare.gov/what-medicare-covers/not-covered/item-and-services-not-covered-by-part-a-and-b.html

www.medicare.gov/part-d/coverage/part-d-coverage.html

www.medicare.gov/coverage/preventive-and-screening-services.html

www.medicare.gov/coverage/durable-medical-equipment-coverage.html

APPENDIX 5.4E: WHAT WOULD YOU DO? GETTING RESOURCES FOR YOUR OLDER ADULT—RUBRIC

Area	Points				Points
	0	**1**	**2**	**3**	
Did the student(s) correctly identify if the elder qualified for Medicare?	No	Yes			
Did the student(s) correctly identify if the elder qualified for Medicaid?	No	Yes			
Did the student(s) correctly identify the resources needed?	No	In one or two areas, but failed to realize the full needs of the elder	Successfully realized the needs, and met them, but did not maximize the elder's independence	Successfully realized the needs, met the needs, and maximized the elder's independence	
Did the student(s) identify what the family might have to provide?	No	Yes			
Did the student(s) identify any other concerns or issues that might arise?	No	Yes			
				Total:	

CHAPTER

HOUSING

Rona J. Karasik

"Home" is a term laden with multiple meanings and personal associations, encompassing factors such as independence, family, personal identity, safety, privacy, and socioeconomic status. It should not be surprising, therefore, that many elders indicate a preference to "**age in place**"—choosing to remain in their current homes for as long as possible (Golant, 2015). In fact, the vast majority of adults 65 and older live independently in the community. Relatively few (3.1%) reside in institutional settings (U.S. Department of Health and Human Services, 2016).

Significant life changes (e.g., retirement, widowhood, emptying-nests), however, can affect how well people "fit" with the living situation where they are currently aging in place. Potential threats to one's person-environment fit can include affordability (e.g., rising costs and/or fixed incomes), declines in safety and/or available services in one's surrounding areas, and physical or cognitive challenges that impact one's activities of daily living.

For better or worse, many approach poor environmental fit by simply "making do" as best they can. Others may modify their existing housing (e.g., adding ramps, better lighting) and/or bring in community-based services (e.g., housekeepers, meals on wheels) as needed. Still others may consider (or be cajoled by concerned others to consider) moving to a different living arrangement. Numerous factors, including personality, social support, and income, can have a strong impact on later-life housing decisions.

Widely held perceptions and stereotypes about the availability and/or quality of housing alternatives can also influence housing decisions. Many in the United States view housing for older adults as a dichotomy—it's either your own home or a nursing home. A broad continuum of housing options exists, however, including at one end a variety of housing options for independent, healthy older adults, and at the other end a number of "housing with services" models designed to provide a greater level of care (physical, cognitive, or both) for more frail elders.

Distinguishing between specific categories of housing along the continuum can be slightly challenging given the somewhat fluid, nuanced, and often unregulated definitions applied to particular types of living arrangements (Folts & Muir, 2002; Howe, Jones, & Tilse, 2013). In part, this fluidity may reflect regional differences, as well as between professional and lay uses of the specific name designations. Definitional ambiguity may also result from the providers attempting to disassociate their facilities with any negative connotations that may become attached to a particular housing type (e.g., the shift from "nursing home" to, among other names, "care communities"). Finally, some confusion may also arise from agency "*mission creep*" when housing providers adjust their service offerings to accommodate changing needs of residents aging in place.

HOUSING OPTIONS FOR "INDEPENDENT" OLDER ADULTS

In addition to all the traditional housing options available for all ages (e.g., house, apartment, condo), some other options for elders who do not require high levels of formal assistance include:

- *Senior Housing*: The term *senior housing* can have several meanings, including any housing where older adults live; age-segregated housing designed for older adults; and most specifically, age-segregated housing that provides limited to no additional support services. Often, the term will be applied to apartments (either market rate or subsidized) designed for independent older adults.

- *Retirement Communities*: Age-segregated campuses or residential areas designed and equipped with amenities specifically for the interests and needs (e.g., leisure, socialization) of healthy older adults. May be comprised of a single housing complex, or, as in Del Webb's Sun City, AZ, an entire town (McHugh & Larson-Keagy, 2005).

- *Ancillary Dwelling Units (Antoninetti, 2008)*:

    ◦ *ECHO Units (Elderly Cottage Housing Opportunity; a.k.a. "Granny Flats")*: Small, temporary, separate (i.e., not attached to or within an existing house) housing unit that can be installed in a backyard.

    ◦ *Accessory Apartment (a.k.a. "mother in law" apartment)*: Unit added to or created within a single family dwelling *(e.g., attached)* with provision for independent cooking, living, bathroom facilities, and sleeping occupying no more than 30% of the gross floor area of the principal structure.

- *Home-Sharing (a.k.a. "share-a-home")*: A living arrangement in which two or more people live together in a private apartment or a house for mutual benefit (e.g., companionship, support, cost-sharing). Arrangements may be either formal (through a share-a-home program or agency) or informal. Often, but not always, the older person's own home is the one shared as a way to support their ability to age in place.

HOUSING OPTIONS WITH "*FORMAL*" SUPPORT

With the increasing number of older adults and the long-term impact of state Certificate of Need (C.O.N.) programs limiting new nursing home capacity (Rahman, Galarraga, Zinn, Grabowski, & Mor, 2016), the range of supportive housing, also known as "housing with services," for older adults continues to expand. As indicated previously, exactly what constitutes a particular type of supportive housing varies considerably, and facilities with similar labels may leave consumers comparing apples to oranges (not to mention a few pickles and rotten tomatoes). With this caveat, broad definitions of a few of the more common options include:

- *Adult Foster Care*: Typically offers family-style housing and support services to a small number of older adults. Available services vary considerably depending on a home's license. May be run by a license holder who lives in the home as a primary caregiver (family adult foster care) or by an agency where the license holder does not live in the home and care is provided by hired staff (corporate adult foster care).

- *Assisted Living Facilities* (ALFs): An extremely diverse category of housing offering services ranging from minimal to comprehensive. ALFs range in size from small home-like environments to complexes serving upwards of 600–800 residents. At minimum, services typically include housing, meals, assistance with one or more activities of daily living, and 24/7 emergency monitoring (which should not be confused with the availability of 24/7 skilled nursing care; Allen, 2004).

- *Multi-Level Care*: Facility or campus environment providing more than one type of housing option (e.g., independent apartments, assisted living, and skilled nursing care) on site.

- *Continuing Care Retirement Communities* (CCRCs): A form of multi-level care typically requiring significant entrance fees in addition to monthly maintenance fees, depending on level of care needed. May also be known as "*Life Care Communities.*"

- *Skilled Nursing Facility* (SNF): Known by a growing number of names (e.g., *nursing home, convalescent home, care community*), SNFs are highly regulated, licensed residential facilities providing 24/7 on-site skilled medical care. While typically providing long-term care, they may also offer short-term rehabilitation services under a variety of names (e.g., *subacute care, restorative care, short-stay care*).

HOUSING EDUCATION ACTIVITIES

The following activities offer several unique perspectives on understanding issues of housing for older adults. For example, Activity 6.1, Find a Nursing Home, simulates some of the challenges older adults and their families face by actively engaging participants in the process of evaluating nursing home quality. Activity 6.2, Field Trips to Senior Facilities, provides hands-on context to understanding the diverse housing options in the senior housing continuum. Activity 6.3, Household Disaster Planning Kits, addresses an often overlooked concern for persons aging in place.

In addition to introducing the participants to the importance of planning for the unexpected and providing instruction for how to create practical planning kits, the end result of the experience is to provide the tailored kits to elders who need them. Activity 6.4, Long-Term Care Residence Disaster Planning, similarly addresses the issue of emergency preparedness, this time in the context of conducting research and a focus on institutional rather than individual planning. Finally, Activity 6.5, Applying Anti-Racist Pedagogy to the Exploration of Senior Housing, provides the opportunity to step back from the day-to-day practices of senior housing to look more broadly at how both historical and contemporary social policies and context continue to influence the housing opportunities and decisions of ethnic minority elders currently.

REFERENCES

Allen, J. (2004). *Assisted living administration: The knowledge base.* New York, NY: Springer Publishing.

Antoninetti, M. (2008). The difficult history of ancillary units: The obstacles and potential opportunities to increase the heterogeneity of neighborhoods and the flexibility of households in the United States. *Journal of Housing for the Elderly, 22*(4), 348–375.

Folts, W. E., & Muir, K. B. (2002). Housing for older adults: New lessons from the past. *Research on Aging, 24*(1), 10–28.

Golant, S. M. (2015). *Aging in the right place.* Baltimore, MD: Health Professions Press.

Howe, A. L., Jones, A. E., & Tilse, C. (2013). What's in a name? Similarities and differences in international terms and meanings for older peoples' housing with services. *Ageing and Society, 33*(4), 547–578.

McHugh, K. E., & Larson-Keagy, E. M. (2005). These white walls: The dialectic of retirement communities. *Journal of Aging Studies, 19*(2), 241–256.

Rahman, M., Galarraga, O., Zinn, J. S., Grabowski, D. C., & Mor, V. (2016). The impact of certificate-of-need laws on nursing home and home health care expenditures. *Medical Care Research and Review, 73*(1), 85–105. doi: 10.1177/1077558715597161

U.S. Department of Health and Human Services. (2016). *A profile of older Americans: 2016.* Washington, DC: Author. Retrieved from https://www.acl.gov/sites/default/files/Aging%20and%20Disability%20in%20America/2016-Profile.pdf

ACTIVITY 6.1 FIND A NURSING HOME

Carrie Andreoletti

ACTIVITY INFORMATION

Type

   X   In class (in a computer lab or with laptops)

   X   Online

   X   Take home

_____ In community

Difficulty

   X   Introductory (can be made more challenging for more advanced students)

_____ Intermediate

_____ Advanced

OVERVIEW

The Find a Nursing Home activity was designed to familiarize undergraduate or graduate level students with resources on the Medicare website and factors that should be considered when choosing a nursing home. This activity makes students aware of the Nursing Home Compare tool on the Medicare website and gives them an opportunity to learn about the quality measures that are currently used to evaluate nursing homes. This activity promotes more meaningful engagement with the material by asking students to imagine they are choosing a nursing home for a family member and giving them the opportunity to consider nursing homes in their own communities. This activity is appropriate for any course that covers long-term care.

ACTIVITY LEARNING GOALS

Following this activity, students should be able to . . .

- Use the Nursing Home Compare tool on the Medicare website as a resource for evaluating nursing home quality.
- Describe the quality measures and other information provided by the Nursing Home Compare tool.
- Discuss the limitations of the Nursing Home Compare tool.
- Discuss factors that should be considered when choosing a nursing home or other long-term care facility.

ASSOCIATION FOR GERONTOLOGY IN HIGHER EDUCATION COMPETENCIES

- Relate social theories and science of aging to understanding heterogeneity, inequality, and context of aging.
- Adhere to ethical principles to guide work with and on behalf of older persons.
- Promote older persons' strengths and adaptations to maximize well-being, health, and mental health.
- Engage in research to advance knowledge and improve interventions for older persons.

MINIMUM/MAXIMUM NUMBER OF PARTICIPANTS

- No limit as this is typically done as an individual assignment. Could be adapted for use in small groups.

TIME NEEDED TO IMPLEMENT ACTIVITY

- 45 to 60 minutes (Depends whether it is done as a take home assignment or in class. Students should be able to complete in an hour. It could be introduced and demonstrated in class in about 20 minutes.)

SETTING(S)

- Home/online, classroom

MATERIALS

Required

- Computer with Internet access

PROCEDURES

Preparation

In preparation for the activity, instructors should introduce the topic of long-term care and the legislative issues associated with the long-term care of older adults. For example, instructors may wish to cover the history of legislation related to the regulation of nursing homes and the failure of such legislation to prevent nursing home abuse (for a good summary, see Chapter 12 in Whitbourne & Whitbourne, 2014). Discussion of the 2002 Nursing Home Quality Initiative is recommended as it involved efforts to make more information about nursing home quality available to consumers, which led to Medicare's development of the Nursing Home Compare tool. If Internet access is available in the classroom, it may be helpful for instructors to show students the Medicare website and features of the Nursing Home Compare tool prior to assigning the activity.

Prior to the activity, instructors should check the Medicare website (www .medicare.gov) to ensure that the Nursing Home Compare tool link is still available in the same location and revise the handout instructions (see Appendix 6.1) as needed.

Activity

Students are asked to imagine that they need to find a nursing home for an aging relative (see Appendix 6.1 for complete instructions). This activity can be easily adapted to make it more or less difficult depending on the number of nursing homes and quality measures students are asked to compare. The tool will allow you to compare up to three nursing homes at a time. As an introductory assignment, it is recommended that the instructor choose one high-quality nursing home with which the person is familiar and ask students to choose another for comparison. This is helpful for several reasons. First, it ensures that students will have the opportunity to learn about a reputable nursing home. Second, it provides a point of reference for the instructor for class discussions and when assessing assignments related to the activity.

When reviewing the instructions with students, instructors should emphasize that the quality measures are separate from the other information provided about the nursing homes such as number of beds, type of ownership, and staffing information. Furthermore, there are separate quality measures for short versus long stay residents so the instructor may wish to have students focus only on one or the other. Overall, there are currently 24 quality measures. Although some instructors may wish to have students focus on specific quality measures depending on their learning objectives, allowing students to pick any two encourages them to read about a variety of measures. As the Nursing Home Compare tool explains *why* each quality measure is important, students should be able to both describe and explain the importance of the quality measures they choose.

Discussion/Reflection

After students do the activity, have them share with the class which nursing home they chose and why. This allows for further discussion of nursing home characteristics, the quality measures, and also provides a good opportunity to discuss some of the limitations of the Nursing Home Compare tool such that it only includes nursing homes that are Medicare or Medicaid Certified and that the information is self-reported by the nursing homes.

Wrap-Up

Instructors should emphasize that while the Nursing Home Compare tool is a good resource for consumers, it should not be the only resource consumers rely on when choosing a nursing home. Instructors can wrap-up the activity by providing additional guidelines for choosing a nursing home such as visiting the facilities at different times of day and observing and talking with a variety of staff. Toward this end it may be helpful to discuss the Nursing Home Checklist that can be downloaded from the Medicare website (see the link that follows).

Assessment

Instructors may evaluate the activity by asking students to write a short paper that compares and contrasts the two nursing homes. Papers can be evaluated based on the extent to which students (1) include basic information on each nursing home such as number of beds, type of ownership, and staffing information; (2) describe and explain the importance of each quality measure they chose; and (3) make appropriate use of the information provided by the Nursing Home Compare tool to make their decision about where to send their loved one. Alternatively, instructors may choose to assess the activity using oral or poster presentations. This may be particularly useful if students present on different quality measures.

ADDITIONAL CONSIDERATIONS

Although designed as an individual homework assignment, this activity could be adapted for small groups or used as an in-class activity for an entire class. Depending on Internet access and availability of computers/tablets, small groups could work together on the assignment either inside or outside of the classroom. If a classroom is equipped with the appropriate technology, the activity could also be conducted with an entire class by asking students to suggest local nursing homes they would like to compare and having them choose different quality measures to examine. Finally, if time permits, this activity could be paired with a visit to a nursing home or expanded to include visits to the nursing homes compared.

REFERENCE

Whitbourne, S. K., & Whitbourne, S. B. (2014). *Adult development & aging: Biopsychosocial perspectives* (5th ed.). Hoboken, NJ: Wiley.

RECOMMENDED RESOURCES

Centers for Medicare & Medicaid Services—Your Guide to Choosing a Nursing Home or Other Long-Term Care. Retrieved from https://www.medicare.gov/Pubs/pdf/02174.pdf

Information and Resources About the Nursing Home Quality Initiative (NHQI) From the Centers for Medicare & Medicaid Services (CMS). Retrieved from https://www.cms.gov/Medicare/Quality-Initiatives-Patient-Assessment-Instruments/NursingHomeQualityInits/index.html?redirect=/nursinghomequalityinits/45_nhqimds30trainingmaterials.asp

Nursing Home Checklist. Retrieved from https://www.medicare.gov/NursingHomeCompare/checklist.pdf

Nursing Home Quality: CMS Should Continue to Improve Data and Oversight. GAO-16-33: Published: Oct 30, 2015. Publicly Released: Nov 30, 2015. Retrieved from http://www.gao.gov/products/GAO-16-33

Nursing Home Quality Initiative Overview. Retrieved from https://www.cms.gov/Medicare/Quality-Initiatives-Patient-Assessment-Instruments/NursingHomeQualityInits/Downloads/NHQIOverView20030731.pdf

Senate Special Committee on Aging Report. (2000). *Nursing home initiative: A two-year progress report.* Retrieved from http://www.aging.senate.gov/imo/media/doc/publications/9282000.pdf

APPENDIX 6.1: ACTIVITY INSTRUCTION SHEET

FIND A NURSING HOME

Imagine that you need to find a nursing home for an aging relative. The purpose of this assignment is for you to become familiar with the Medicare website and the Nursing Home Compare tool that allows you to compare nursing homes on the quality measures used to assess nursing homes. Your task is to go to the Medicare website and compare [INSTRUCTOR INSERT NURSING HOME NAME] to one other nursing home in your community. Write a short paper (2–3 pages typed, double-spaced) that compares and contrasts the two nursing homes. You should include basic information on each home such as number of beds, type of ownership, and staffing information. **In addition, discuss at least two different quality measures**. Be sure to explain the purpose and importance of each quality measure you choose. Which nursing home would you choose for your loved one and why?

Go to www.Medicare.gov.

Click on "Find nursing homes," which is under the heading "Find doctors, providers, hospitals, plans & suppliers." Follow instructions for finding and comparing nursing homes. You will be able to access the quality measures information once you have selected at least two nursing homes to compare. Prior to comparing your nursing homes, you should spend some time reading about the Nursing Home Compare tool, the different information provided, and the meaning of the quality ratings and measures. This information can be found by selecting the "About Nursing Home Compare" tab at the top of the Nursing Home Compare page.

ACTIVITY 6.2 FIELD TRIPS TO SENIOR FACILITIES

Sharon A. DeVaney

ACTIVITY INFORMATION

Type

_____ In class

_____ Online

_____ Take home

__X__ In community

Difficulty

__X__ Introductory

__X__ Intermediate

_____ Advanced

OVERVIEW

While teaching the graduate course on Social Policy and the Economics of Aging, it was apparent that many students had never visited a senior facility such as low-income housing, independent living, or assisted living and/or memory care facility. At least half of the graduate students were from other countries and the idea of older adults living independently was hard for them to understand. Also, many American students had negative impressions of nursing homes.

ACTIVITY LEARNING GOALS

Following this activity, students should be able to . . .

- Describe the residential options available to older adults in many locations in the United States.
- Explain that residential options for older adults could vary by income level, physical need, and cognitive need.
- Understand that the quality of life of older adults could be enhanced by the social activities and companionship available in the senior facilities.

ASSOCIATION FOR GERONTOLOGY IN HIGHER EDUCATION COMPETENCIES

- Utilize gerontological frameworks to examine human development and aging.
- Relate biological theory and science to understanding senescence, longevity, and variation in aging.

- Relate psychological theories and science to understanding adaptation, stability, and change in aging.
- Relate social theories and science of aging to understanding heterogeneity, inequality, and context of aging.
- Engage collaboratively with others to promote integrated approaches to aging.
- Promote older persons' strengths and adaptations to maximize well-being, health, and mental health.
- Promote quality of life and positive social environment for older persons.
- Encourage older persons to engage in life-long learning opportunities.

MINIMUM/MAXIMUM NUMBER OF PARTICIPANTS

- 20

TIME NEEDED TO IMPLEMENT ACTIVITY

- 1½ to 2 hours

SETTING(S)

- Field trips

MATERIALS

Required

- Transportation to visit two senior facilities at two different class meetings.

PROCEDURES

Preparation

- Prior to beginning of the course, the instructor should contact senior facilities for permission to visit.
- Instructor should consider the students' capability to travel to the senior facilities and help students make plans for travel, if needed.

Introduction

- Help students prepare questions to ask residents about their satisfaction with meals, activities, and other needs, such as managing travel to medical appointments, essential shopping, church services, and other appointments.

Activity

- Meet with director. Separate into small groups to tour facility, see a resident's apartment, and visit with residents.

Discussion/Reflection

- After touring the facility and visiting with residents, students should write a summary and reflect on their impressions before and after the visit.

Wrap-Up

- Students should relate their assigned readings for the course and their previous impressions to the impressions gained during the visit.

Follow-Up

- Some students returned to conduct individual research projects after writing a proposal and obtaining Institutional Review Board permission for their study.
- Other students included their impressions and evaluations in term papers for this course and other courses in the gerontology major or minor.

Assessment

- Essay question(s) on a final exam such as comparison to living arrangements for older adults in other countries or other locations in the United States and how residents are included in activities to stimulate social engagement and cognitive and physical activity.

ADDITIONAL CONSIDERATIONS

- Students said that it helped them understand the economics of aging when they were able to compare their visits to a low income independent senior facility and an upscale senior facility with several levels of care.
- It is important to visit facilities that represent different economic settings and levels of care.

CONTENT SOURCES

- The instructor should visit each senior facility in advance of class visits. It is helpful if the instructor is able to establish relationships with the director of each facility.
- Visits to senior facilities should take place about one-third or halfway through the course. This allows time for students to learn how economic status affects the lifestyle of older adults.

ACTIVITY 6.3 HOUSEHOLD DISASTER PLANNING KITS

Elizabeth Fugate-Whitlock and Eleanor Krassen Covan

ACTIVITY INFORMATION

Type

__X__	In class
__X__	Online
__X__	Take home
__X__	In community

Difficulty

_____	Introductory
__X__	Intermediate
__X__	Advanced

OVERVIEW

The impact of disasters can be particularly severe for older adults who may have minimal resources and lack the infrastructures that they need to survive (Rudowitz, Rowland, & Shartzer, 2006). For example, despite the fact that only 15% of New Orleans residents were older than 65, 74% of hurricane-related deaths occurred to people in that age group (Hyer, Brown, Berman, & Polivka-West, 2006). Stress related to inadequate resources can be compounded by limited physical mobility, diminished sensory awareness, chronic health conditions, and both social and economic problems (Fernandez, Byard, Lin, Benson, & Barbera, 2002).These conditions can prevent elders from taking appropriate actions. Furthermore, those over 60 years old and their families received far less aid from most sources after a disaster than did younger victims (Kilijanek & Drabek, 1979). Older adults impacted by disasters did receive slightly more help from religious organizations and governmental agencies, yet these differences were not statistically significant and almost one out of five received no aid from any source (Kilijanek & Drabek, 1979). Kilijanek and Drabek labeled these findings a "pattern of neglect." Other researchers (Bell, 1978; Fugate-Whitlock, 2011) found informal support structures are consistently valued more by older adults and are more effective for them in disaster circumstances. Working with older adults to create their own disaster planning kits to respond to a natural disaster will aid in identifying resources they have on hand and those that they must obtain to be best prepared for events of this kind in the future. Moreover, when students review the written plans that are included in these kits, comparing them to others prepared by older adults with the assistance of their classmates, the students begin to understand how personal attributes and social differentiation contribute to disaster preparation.

The activity described in the following text is well-suited to courses whose primary focus is on current issues in gerontology. In every location, the potential for natural disaster exists, be it a nuclear accident, hurricane, fire, flood, or earthquake. Faculty implementing a service-learning project of this kind should create a reading list about responding to natural disasters in general and in particular addressing the type(s) of disasters that have the greatest potential for occurrence in their community.

In the project described in the following text, we used a template to gather information for written individual household disaster management plans. The template was created by the U.S. Department of Health and Human Services and was published with very minor variations on a website provided by our home state to encourage citizens to plan for natural disasters. A copy of this template is available at https://ncdhhs.s3.amazonaws.com/s3fs-public/documents/files/family_disaster_plan.pdf. We introduce the work to be required of students with course lectures and readings related to natural disasters, living arrangements for older adults, demography, research ethics, and data collection techniques (Appendix 6.3A). While this activity is not primarily employed in a research course, students must handle confidential information in helping older adults to create their plans. They need to learn not only what information is needed in a household disaster management plan, but also how to protect that information so that it is accessible only to those who need it. Students collect and report information in the context of an interview and record the information on a template that is similar in design to a research instrument. Much private information is required including names and addresses of family members, Social Security numbers, lists of prescriptions, bank account numbers, and the like. Students are prepared for this activity initially by completing the NIH online training on research ethics. Students are taught that household disaster management plans are personal documents that should be stored with other personal documents that older adults will take with them if they need to evacuate their homes quickly. They are also taught what items must be collected by older adults and stored in an accessible kit so they can be taken with them in the event of evacuation following a natural emergency.

ACTIVITY LEARNING GOALS

Following this activity, students should be able to . . .

- Conduct interviews with older adults, record their responses, and apply the information to the creation of household disaster plans.
- Understand how older adults define "natural disaster."
- Demonstrate rudimentary understanding of challenges of aging that may be a consequence of the distribution of wealth, power, prestige, or racial, ethnic, and gender diversity, especially with regard to planning an appropriate response to a natural disaster.
- Demonstrate competence in the area of research ethics by completing an online tutorial on the protection of human subjects.
- Debate the utility of disaster planning kits for older adults.

ASSOCIATION FOR GERONTOLOGY IN HIGHER EDUCATION COMPETENCIES

- Relate social theories and science of aging to understanding heterogeneity, inequality, and context of aging.
- Distinguish factors related to aging outcomes, both intrinsic and contextual, through critical thinking and empirical research.
- Identify and explain research methodologies, interpretations, and applications used by different disciplines to study aging.
- Use critical thinking to evaluate information and its source (popular media and research publications).
- Respect the person's autonomy and right to real and meaningful self-determination.
- Respect interdependence of individuals of all ages and abilities.
- Recognize ethical standards and professional practices in all phases of work and research with and on behalf of older persons including informed consent.

MINIMUM/MAXIMUM NUMBER OF PARTICIPANTS

The maximum number of older adult participants is equal to the number of students enrolled in the class multiplied by two. The maximum number of students is equal to the number of students who enroll in the course and who also pass the NIH tutorial.

TIME NEEDED TO IMPLEMENT ACTIVITY

8 to 10 hours. Time is needed to identify older adults, explain the project, conduct the interviews, complete the template with and without confidential data, and make follow-up visits as necessary to ensure accuracy and completion and to assist in gathering items for the older adults' household disaster kits.

SETTING(S)

The course content leading up to this activity can be done in a classroom (virtual or face to face) and then moves to the community. For the comfort of the older adult, an initial meeting may be scheduled in a public space such as a library or senior center. However, students do the majority of the work with older adults in their homes because it is in the home that older adults have most of what is needed to create the written household disaster plan and to create the household disaster kit. Once the activity is complete, educational discussion returns to the classroom (virtual or face to face) where students share reflections about their service-learning projects.

MATERIALS

Required

Faculty must gather initial materials including instructions for students, an informed consent document, a short list of open-ended avenues of inquiry, and a template for recording information needed in a written household disaster plan. Faculty create the first three items while the latter is available on a state website.

To create a household disaster kit an older adult will eventually require both a written plan and a box to store items that they must access in the event of a natural emergency. The disaster kit includes items such as a flashlight, batteries, first aid kit, whistle to signal for help, a 3- to 7-day supply of nonperishable food and medications, and personal items unique to the individual. An older adult who has a pet, for example, might need to include a 3-day supply of pet food and other items for the animal. The student is not expected to supply the materials for the kit, but they may assist in gathering the necessary items.

Although experts know that older adults have their own methods for storing information and items required in a disaster planning kit, students nevertheless assist them in preparing a fill-in-the-blank template on which the information needed is accessible in a single location. Likewise they help older adults to store all of the items needed in an emergency in one location.

PROCEDURES

Preparation

This service-learning project is unique in that it works well in classes with an online format as well as those that meet face to face. Regardless of a student's geographic location they have access to older adults. Teaching online requires the instructor to prepare very detailed instructions before the course begins. These detailed instructions would, of course, be given to students as a handout in courses that meet face to face. For an example of instructions for students see Appendix 6.3B. Along with project directions, a related reading list must also be developed that includes web addresses for geographically specific disaster planning as well as academic sources.

A data gathering template must be selected for use in this project. It is suggested that a generic template suitable for any locale be used. Most if not all states have a template available on emergency planning websites. It is suggested that faculty use a template created by the state in which your campus is located. It is recommended that faculty consult with local planning officials to ensure the template meets current needs.

Activity

1. Faculty create instructions for students, an informed consent document, and avenues of inquiry used to introduce disaster planning to older adults (see Appendix 6.3B).
2. Faculty select a template for recording and reporting personal information necessary in a household emergency management plan.
3. Faculty develop lectures, educational modules, reading lists, and so on, on natural disasters, living arrangements for older adults, demography, research ethics, and data collection techniques.
4. Faculty teach students about data collection, demography, housing arrangements, and disaster management.
5. Students complete NIH training on research ethics.

6. Each student selects two interviewees—one between the ages of 65 and 74 and one 75 or older—to complete the assignment.

7. Students contact interviewees, explain the project, and arrange to meet.

8. Students meet with interviewees, obtain signed informed consent, and complete the written household disaster management plan, including responses to avenues of inquiry. Often one or more follow-up meetings is necessary as students help the interviewee obtain what is needed in the disaster kit.

9. Students present a complete written household disaster management plan, leaving it with an older interviewee with instructions to store the plan with important personal documents. When possible, they also view the older adult's disaster plan kit.

10. Students reflect on their role as service-learning participants.

11. Students submit four items to faculty for grading: (a) two signed consent forms, (b) transcripts of responses to avenues of inquiry, (c) two completed household disaster plans with confidential data redacted, and (d) a service-learning report.

Discussion/Reflection

The educational aspect of a service-learning project requires reflection. Students reflect on the ease or difficulty in initiating conversations with older adults, the ease or difficulty of gathering and recording personal information for an older adult's household disaster plan, and on how what they learn experientially complements or differs from what they learn from class readings and discussion. In their reflections they are asked to consider how ethical issues may impact the difficulty of obtaining the information on the household disaster template. They also speculate about whether or not older adults will use the household disaster plans and kits. To this end, students are required to prepare a service-learning report in which they reflect on their service-learning experiences. In particular, students are expected to discuss the service-learning assignment with regard to the following:

a. Challenges of aging that may be a consequence of the distribution of wealth, power, or prestige

b. Racial, ethnic, and gender diversity and their impact on experience in later years

c. Research ethics including how ethical considerations may impact the difficulty of obtaining the information on the template

Wrap-Up

Deliverables for this service-learning project include written emergency plans given to older adults, plus documents submitted to faculty for grading. The latter include two signed informed consent documents, interview responses to avenues of inquiry on the meaning of natural disaster from two older adults, two completed household disaster plans with private information redacted, and one service-learning report. In the service-learning reports, students are asked to comment on their service-learning project with regard to three considerations: (a) challenges of aging that may be a consequence of the distribution of wealth, power, or prestige; (b) racial, ethnic, and gender diversity and their impact on experience in later years; and (c) research ethics including how ethical considerations may impact the difficulty of obtaining the information required to assist an older adult in completing a household disaster plan and/or in putting together a disaster kit.

ASSESSMENT

This project was designed to meet two overall goals: applying foundational knowledge of gerontology to understand how heterogeneity may contribute to challenges of aging and to understand why conducting oneself ethically is essential when offering advice to vulnerable populations. The service-learning project was the avenue chosen to teach these competencies. With regard to foundational knowledge, we expected students to apply knowledge of the distribution of wealth, power, prestige, and racial, ethnic, and gender diversity to the challenges of aging, demonstrating that they understood the material that was presented to them in lectures and reading assignments. With regard to conducting oneself ethically, we expected students to protect the privacy of older adults.

The first competency may be measured using a reflection assignment and is assessed using the following rubric.

We suggest that students be required to complete the NIH online training on research ethics and that a student's score be reported for assessment. A second assessment of research proficiency may be based on analyzing the service project

Aspect Being Assessed	Novice	Competent	Proficient
Synthesis With Course Materials	No connection between the project and course materials was made.	The project (responses to avenues of inquiry interview and template data) were directly related to class activities, discussions, and readings implicitly—that is, course materials were referred to but not cited.	The project (responses to avenues of inquiry interview and template data) were directly related to class activities, discussions, and readings explicitly by referring to and citing course materials.
Challenges of Aging	The potential consequences of *limited* wealth, power, or prestige on disaster planning were not discussed.	Challenges of aging that may be a consequence of the distribution of wealth, power, or prestige were discussed, with examples that were limited to personal anecdotes.	Challenges of aging that may be a consequence of the distribution of wealth, power, or prestige were discussed, with examples from interviewees and examples from course readings and lectures.

(continued)

(continued)

Aspect Being Assessed	Novice	Competent	Proficient
Impact of Diversity	Racial, ethnic, and gender diversity and their impact on experience in later years in regards to a disaster kit was not discussed.	Racial, ethnic, and gender diversity and their impact on experience in later years in regards to creating a disaster kit was discussed with examples that were limited to personal anecdotes.	Racial, ethnic, and gender diversity and their impact on experience in later years in regards to creating a disaster kit was discussed with direct references to academic material and quotes from interviewees.
Research Ethics	NIH was not taken. Student was not allowed to participate in project and earns a grade of "0."	NIH passing score	NIH exemplary score
Completion of Data and Timeliness	Template was submitted late with unexplained missing data.	Either template was late OR missing data was not explained.	Either all items on the template were reported with data and/or missing data were adequately explained.
Privacy	Template turned in to instructor for grading without redacting private information.	Student removed private data from template submitted for grading, but did not explain the importance of doing so.	Student removed private data from template submitted for grading, and provided an explanation for doing so.

itself in a service-learning report in consideration of academic course material. A final assessment may be used to examine the extent to which templates are submitted by students in a timely manner and whether they have protected the privacy of older adults by removing personal data from the copy submitted to the faculty for grading. They are also assessed on the extent to which they explain why some items on the template may be missing.

REFERENCES

Bell, B. D. (1978). Disaster impact and response: Overcoming the thousand natural shocks. *The Gerontologist, 18*(6), 531–540.

Fernandez, L. S., Byard, D., Lin, C. C., Benson, S., & Barbera, J. A. (2002). Frail elderly as disaster victims: Emergency management strategies. *Prehospital and Disaster Medicine, 17*(2), 67–74.

Fugate-Whitlock, E. I. (2011). *Natural disasters and older adults: The social construction of disaster planning.* Doctoral Dissertation, Virginia Commonwealth University Archives, Richmond, Virginia.

Hyer, K., Brown, L. M., Berman, A., & Polivka-West, L. (2006). Establishing and refining hurricane response systems for long-term care facilities. *Health Affairs, 25,* w407–w411.

Kilijanek, T. S., & Drabek, T. E. (1979). Assessing long-term impacts of a natural disaster: A focus on the elderly. *The Gerontologist, 19*(6), 555–566.

Rudowitz, R., Rowland, D., & Shartzer, A. (2006). Health care in New Orleans before and after Katrina. *Health Affairs* [Web exclusive], *25,* w393–w406

APPENDIX 6.3A: SUGGESTED READINGS

The following are suggested readings for students engaging in this long-term care residence disaster planning project. Note that readings should cover research methods as well as the impact of disasters on older adults. The research methods readings are different for undergraduate and graduate students as they will have different levels of past research experience and knowledge but all students read the same disaster articles.

RESEARCH METHODS: FOCUS ON INTERVIEWING

Undergraduates

Quadango, J. (2018). *Aging and the life course: An introduction to social gerontology* (7th ed.). New York, NY: McGraw-Hill*

Graduates

Lawton, M. P., & Herzog, A. R. (Eds.). (1989). *Special research methods for gerontology.* Amityville, NY: Baywood.

*Can also be used for demography and broad living arrangements

DISASTERS (WITH EMPHASIS ON DIVERSITY AND LIVING ARRANGEMENTS)

Covan, E. K., & Fugate-Whitlock, E. I. (2010). Emergency planning and long-term care: Least paid, least powerful, most responsible. *Health Care for Women International, 31*(11), 1028–1043.

Enarson, E. (1999). Women and housing issues in two U.S. disasters: Hurricane Andrew and the Red River Valley flood. *International Journal of Mass Emergencies and Disasters, 17*(1), 39–63.

Kilijanek, T. S., & Drabek, T. E. (1979). Assessing long-term impacts of a natural disaster: A focus on the elderly. *The Gerontologist, 19*(6), 555–566.

Sanders, S., Bowie, S. L., & Bowie, Y. D. (2003). Lessons learned on forced relocation of older adults: The impact of Hurricane Andrew on health, mental health, and social support of public housing residents. *Journal of Gerontological Social Work, 40*(4), 23–35.

APPENDIX 6.3B: SAMPLE INSTRUCTIONS FOR STUDENTS

Each student must select two interviewees: one between the ages of 65 and 74 and one 75 or older to complete the following assignment. For each interview you will ask a series of questions concerning disasters, complete the disaster plan template, and submit a service-learning report. It is permissible to interview older adults that you know, such as family members or friends, but not required.

Interview avenues of inquiry (you must ask these questions, but you may also ask others that may come up in conversation):

- What is the meaning of disaster to you?
- According to your definition, what would happen in a disaster?
- Can you do anything to prepare for such a disaster?
- Do you have an emergency supply kit that you would use in a disaster? If the answer is yes, ask "What is in it?" Ask also whether anything is missing from their kit. If the answer is no, ask the respondent if they had such a kit, what the respondent would put in it.

After completing the interview you should complete the disaster plan template with your interviewee. You should print the following and take it with you to the interview: two copies of the informed consent document and two copies of the template. The first thing you should do when you meet face to face is ask the participant to read and sign the consent forms. The participant keeps one copy and you submit the second copy to the instructor. Without informed consent you may not conduct this project. Note that again two copies of the template are necessary: one goes to the participant and the second is submitted to the instructor. All personal financial information (such as insurance specifics) should be left blank on the instructor copy. On the instructor copy, just note if the participant has or does not have the information (e.g., the individual has insurance and identified the policy number and agent contact in the previous example). You should make this clear to the participant (it is also explained on the consent form) that we are not gathering this sort of personal information for ourselves. Our goal is to find out what plans are in place for a particular household and what resources are not in place.

On the top of the copy of the template and informed consent document that you submit to the instructor, please enter your initials followed by either <75 for your younger respondent or >75 for your older respondent. This is important as it will serve as the identifier for confidential data.

Remember that you will need to prepare a service-learning report later in the semester. Then you will be reflecting on your service-learning experiences with specific regard to course material. In particular it will help you to write this report if you take notes as you are working about the following:

a. Challenges of planning that may be a consequence of the distribution of wealth, power, or prestige
b. Racial, ethnic, and gender diversity and their impact on disaster experiences and planning

c. Research ethics including how ethical considerations may impact the difficulty of obtaining the information on the template.

You will eventually be asked to submit: (a) two signed consent forms (one for each participant), (b) your interview questions and transcripts of answers for each participant, (c) the completed emergency templates (without any personal identifiers) for each participant, and (d) your service-learning report.

ACTIVITY 6.4 LONG-TERM CARE RESIDENCE DISASTER PLANNING

Eleanor Krassen Covan and Elizabeth Fugate-Whitlock

ACTIVITY INFORMATION

Type

   X   In class

   X   Online

         Take home

   X   In community

Difficulty

         Introductory

   X   Intermediate

   X   Advanced

OVERVIEW

Faculty often have minimal resources to complete university mandates for research, teaching, and community service. Gerontology faculty may address minimal resources by designing research/service-learning projects that employ their students as research assistants. Although some campuses provide only a minor in gerontology in which no research methods course is offered in the gerontology curriculum, it is necessary to teach students about data collection and how data are used on behalf of older adults. In such cases, research and service may be infused throughout the gerontology curriculum to meet AGHE standards at the undergraduate level. Indeed, infusing research and service throughout the curriculum is helpful at both the undergraduate and graduate level even when a separate research course exists. In the particular course for which this service/research project has been designed, students are taught research ethics, interviewing and observational techniques, and data entry on a template. The activity described in the text that follows has not been used in a course that has a primary research focus but rather a substantive course for which applied research becomes a heuristic learning tool for students while simultaneously providing a service to those who engage on planning on behalf of older adults.

Academia is not the only context in which resources are minimal. Minimal resources and difficulty accessing infrastructure necessary for survival can make the impact of a disaster particularly severe for older adults (Rudowitz, Rowland, & Shartzer, 2006). In fact, the first casualties reported in Louisiana related to Katrina were those of three elderly nursing home residents being evacuated (Jacobson, 2006). The *New York Times* reported, "at least 91 patients died in hospitals and 63 in nursing homes not fully evacuated until five days after the storm" (Jacobson, 2006, p. 19). Comfort (2006) notes that this type of experience certainly emphasized the need for preparation on the part of public health and emergency officials, as well as health care providers, to avoid death, injury, infectious disease, and psychological, social, as well as economic distress, especially for the vulnerable elderly. Older adult residents of long-term care and adult care facilities have even fewer resources and are totally dependent on their facilities to provide safety during natural disasters.

In the project that we describe in detail in the text that follows, we designed a research/service-learning activity to efficiently collect data needed by emergency management personnel, in the hope of sparing some of the time that those employed in long-term care would otherwise be asked to provide to this end. It is understood by faculty that emergency personnel with these data in hand would be better prepared to assist older adults and long-term care residence staff in the event of a natural disaster. While government units understand the value of collecting these data, long-term care administrators may not see data collection as their priority. They may or may not see student assistance as beneficial. We introduce the work to be required of students with course lectures and readings related to research ethics, data collection, demography, structure of long-term care, and disaster management literature (see Recommended Resources). We prepare students for engagement in research/service projects by having them complete the NIH online training on research ethics and by teaching them about collecting data in an environment where the collection of data is not the primary concern of employees.

ACTIVITY LEARNING GOALS

Following this activity, students should be able to . . .

- Demonstrate competence in the area of research ethics by completing an online tutorial on the protection of human subjects.
- Conduct an interview/administer a survey with persons who are employed in long-term care management and to record responses that are complete and accurate.
- Understand the challenges of aging, with regard to planning an appropriate response to a natural disaster by those in the government sector as well as by administrators and residents of long-term care residences.
- Debate the utility of data collected to prepare a response to a natural disaster on behalf of frail older adults (graduate students only).

ASSOCIATION FOR GERONTOLOGY IN HIGHER EDUCATION COMPETENCIES

- Identify and explain research methodologies, interpretations, and applications used by different disciplines to study aging.
- Engage, through effective communication, older persons, their families, and the community in personal and public issues in aging.

MINIMUM/MAXIMUM NUMBER OF PARTICIPANTS

The maximum number of students is equal to the number of long-term care residences in a particular community multiplied by two, as students should be assigned to work on the project in teams of two. Larger student teams are not advised as they may be viewed as intrusive to long-term care administrators. Of course, larger teams are sometimes necessary when creating mentoring teams. That is, there might be more undergraduate students enrolled than there are graduate students. In a large city where many long-term care residences exist, this project could accommodate a large class of students. Faculty, however, should be prepared to create a representative sample of facilities if their number exceeds pairs of students registered in the course. The minimum number of participants would be two students, but in that instance only one facility would be providing data. The authors designed this activity to be used in a course that was the capstone for undergraduate gerontology minors and the introductory course for graduate students. The formation of the team allowed for collaboration and mentoring in both directions. While the authors assigned student participant teams of one graduate student and one undergraduate student, faculty elsewhere might assign participant groups differently.

TIME NEEDED TO IMPLEMENT ACTIVITY

8 to 10 hours. Time is needed for gaining entry to the long-term care facility by the students, observing the structure of a particular facility to identify staff with necessary information, conducting interviews to gather necessary data, entering the data on the template, and for participant team meetings to review the completed template before submission to the instructor for grading.

SETTING(S)

The course content leading up to this activity can be done in a classroom (virtual or face to face) and then moves to the community to the specific long-term care settings. Once the activity is complete, the discussion again moves back to the classroom (virtual or face to face). While the activity may be assigned in a virtual classroom, it works best when students who reside in the same locale are collaborating online. Students who reside a great distance from the location in which long-term care residences are located would have a difficult time collaborating with a team member.

MATERIALS

Required

A disaster template is needed on which students will record data given to them by long-term care employees. Often times a template exists, but does not meet the needs of all parties involved. It must be user friendly for personnel in long-term care to gather information. The template must present the material in a uniform manner for officials who need to compile statistical data. If an existing template meets these needs it should be used. If it does not, faculty can aid in creating an instrument in which data can be recorded for statistical and qualitative analysis.

Although gerontologists know that each facility has its own method of storing the information requested by emergency management personnel, a common fill-in-the-blank formatted template was created in the hope that uniformity would facilitate use and access to this information by county emergency response teams. The template included six broad categories of information: (a) basic facility information; (b) emergency status information; (c) resident and employee records; (d) sheltering in place, including sheltering residents from other facilities; (e) evacuation procedures; and (f) employee training. Basic facility information covered items such as facility name, contact information, owner information, building construction type, and number and type of beds. Organizational charts for normal operations as well as emergency operations were also requested in this category.

PROCEDURES

Preparation

As with all service-learning projects, preparation proceeds long before students enroll in gerontology coursework. Liaisons must be established between gerontology faculty in academic institutions and those who work on behalf of older adults. For this project faculty must establish a connection with both emergency management personnel and with administrators of long-term care residences. It is helpful in doing so to create a reading list for students in consultation with personnel in these organizations.

Once relationships have been established, a data gathering template can be designed to assist emergency management personnel and long-term care residence staff with disaster planning. Faculty may help to design an efficient template that contains all items outlined by the U.S. Department of Health and Human Services. The template we created appears as Appendix 6.4. It required collecting information regarding planning responses to potential hurricanes, yet templates can be modified to deal with other kinds of natural disasters.

Our faculty created this project to be part of their academic research agenda involving both community partners and their students as research assistants. In this instance, in preparation, faculty had to prepare an IRB protocol for review and approval by the university IRB Committee before initiation. The project, however, could be construed by faculty on other campuses to be purely service in which case an IRB protocol would not be required, but faculty elsewhere should still recognize that it is imperative that students learn how to handle sensitive information.

Preparation requires a division of labor. We suggest it is beneficial to have emergency management personnel explain the research/service project to long-term residence staff while faculty should provide the explanation to their students. This is because emergency management personnel must ultimately judge the adequacy of long-term care residence disaster management plans, and it is faculty who assess student performance. It is emergency management personnel who should send a copy of the emergency planning data gathering template to long-term care residence administrators before the latter have any contact with students. It is advantageous for a joint meeting to be held with emergency management personnel, long-term care residence administrators, and faculty before the project begins. This meeting should be facilitated by emergency management personnel.

As in any course, faculty lectures and reading lists are created before the course begins. Substantive content should include units on data collection, long-term care, and disaster management planning on behalf of older adults. Although this project is designed to be appropriate for undergraduate and graduate students who will work in teams, reading lists for undergraduate and graduate students should differ with more research articles disseminated for analysis by graduate students.

Student teams should be assigned by faculty to maximize opportunities for bilateral mentorship. Our structure was such that the course was offered as the capstone course for undergraduate students and the first course in our program for graduate students. In preparation for this project, student teams could be created with different parameters. In a course with enrollment of both gerontology and nongerontology students, teams may be so organized to foster opportunities for students in other disciplines to mentor one another.

Activity

Faculty establish a working relationship with both government agencies responsible for planning a response to a natural disaster emergency and administrators of area long-term care residences.

1. Faculty design a template for recording and reporting long-term care residence disaster management plans.
2. (Optional) Faculty design a research project and IRB protocol that will involve their students as research assistants to gather emergency planning data required by state and county departments of emergency management.
3. Faculty develop lectures, educational modules, reading lists, and so on, on data collection, demography, long-term care, and disaster management.
4. Faculty teach students data collection, demography, long-term care, and disaster management.
5. Students complete NIH training on research ethics.
6. Students contact administrators of long-term care residences and interview the administrator or designee(s) to complete information requested on the template. Follow up as necessary.
7. Students reflect on their role as service-learning research assistants.
8. Students turn in completed template to faculty for grading.
9. Administrators turn in plans to emergency management officials.

Discussion/Reflection

The educational aspect of a service-learning project requires reflection. As this project proceeds, students reflect on their different roles as students, service providers, and research assistants. In particular they consider the ease or difficulty in obtaining each particular piece of information requested by governmental personnel from administrators of long-term care residences. They also speculate about who will use the data they help to collect. Other reflections consider the ease or difficulty of working as a member of a team to collect data and to produce a research report. Graduate students are asked to delve deeper and to consider if and why some information requested by governmental staff seems consistently to be difficult for administrators to report.

Specifically it is suggested that students reflect on this service-learning project by providing an analysis of the goodness of fit between what is learned in the class and through service-learning. Using their experiences with the template and conducting their interview(s) combined with the readings on natural disasters students should consider the question of *whose* current issue is in the forefront of this service-learning research assignment. Is it that of governmental officials, the long-term care residence administrator or staff, the residents, or their families? In doing this, students should support their answers using course materials (discussions, lectures, and readings) and they should examine the different perspectives related to the issue of disaster planning. Students may either identify one perspective that they believe to be in the forefront or discuss the differing perspectives and how they are or are not at odds depending on student experiences and opinions.

Wrap-Up

Deliverables for this research service-learning project are twofold. After reviewing data recorded on a template, and after consideration and reflection about the data gathering process, students turn in completed templates to long-term care residence administrators for their review. Students also submit a copy to faculty for grading. The long-term residence administrators, not the students and not the faculty, submit the templates and an optional narrative plan to emergency management officials.

Assessment

This project was designed to meet two overall goals: competency in research and communication with community on behalf of older adults.

Students are required to complete the NIH online training on research ethics. To be eligible to participate in the project on the authors' campus a student must earn a passing score. For this assignment, a student's score is reported for assessment. A second assessment of research proficiency is based on analyzing the research project itself in terms of academic course material. A final assessment based on research methods was to examine the extent to which templates were submitted by students in a timely manner and whether they were complete in the sense that either all items on the template were reported with data and/or missing data were adequately explained.

To assess the second competency the student's reflection is used in concert with the following rubric.

Aspect Being Assessed	Novice	Competent	Proficient
Research Ethics	NIH was not taken. Student was not allowed to participate in the project and earns a grade of "0."	NIH passing score	NIH exemplary score

Goodness of Fit	Student did not analyze the goodness of fit between academic course material and experiences with project. No specific connections were made nor were references included.	Student analyzed the goodness of fit between academic course material and experiences with project but either specific connections were not made or references were not included.	Student analyzed the goodness of fit between academic course material and experiences with project. Specific connections were made. References were included.
Completion of Data and Timeliness	Template was submitted late with unexplained missing data.	Either template was late OR missing data was not explained.	Either all items on the template were reported with data and/or missing data were adequately explained.

Criteria	Novice	Competent	Proficient
Formatting Weight	Sources were not referenced. Many spelling and grammar errors. Paper was less than four pages.	One of the three conditions was present: missing sources, minor spelling/grammar errors, paper was less than three pages.	All sources were referenced. No spelling and grammar errors. Four to six pages in length.
Whose Issue? Weight	Student did not identify one or more perspectives nor identify factors such as who benefits, who creates the issue, or who cares about the issue.	Student identified one or more perspectives but did not identify factors such as who benefits, who creates the issue, or who cares about the issue.	Student identified one or more perspectives identifying factors such as who benefits, who creates the issue, or who cares about the issue.
Position Supported Weight	Student's position of whose issue is not supported explicitly or implicitly using course materials.	Student's position of whose issue is supported implicitly using course materials (no discussions, lectures, and readings were cited).	Student's position of whose issue is supported explicitly using course materials (cited discussions, lectures, and readings).

(*continued*)

(continued)

Criteria	Novice	Competent	Proficient
Different Perspectives Considered	Different perspectives related to the issue were not examined.	Two different perspectives, those of government officials and long-term care administrators, were examined.	Three or more different perspectives, including those in published literature, were examined.

REFERENCES

Comfort, L. K. (2006). Cities at risk: Hurricane Katrina and the drowning of New Orleans. *Urban Affairs Review, 41*(4), 501–516.

Jacobson, J. (2006). "Negligent homicide" charges for nursing home owners: The frailest residents paid the highest price when Katrina struck. *American Journal of Nursing, 105*(11), 19.

Rudowitz, R., Rowland, D., & Shartzer, A. (2006). Health care in New Orleans before and after Katrina. *Health Affairs* [Web Exclusive], 25, w393–w406.

RECOMMENDED RESOURCES

The following are suggested readings for students engaging in this long-term care residence disaster planning project. Note that readings should cover research methods as well as the impact of disasters on older adults. The research methods readings are different for undergraduate and graduate students as they will have different levels of past research experience and knowledge but all students read the same disaster articles.

Undergraduates

Quadango, J. (2018). *Aging and the life course: An introduction to social gerontology* (7th ed.). New York, NY: McGraw Hill.*

Graduates

Lawton, M. P., & Herzog, A. R. (Eds.). (1989). *Special research methods for gerontology.* Amityville, NY: Baywood.

*Can also be used for demography

Disasters

Covan, E. K., & Fugate-Whitlock, E. I. (2010). Emergency planning and long-term care: Least paid, least powerful, most responsible. *Health Care for Women International, 31*(11), 1028–1043.

Kilijanek, T. S., & Drabek, T. E. (1979). Assessing long-term impacts of a natural disaster: A focus on the elderly. *The Gerontologist, 19*(6), 555–566.

APPENDIX 6.4: TEMPLATE FOR LONG-TERM CARE EMERGENCY MANAGEMENT PLANS

1. Basic information concerning the facility:
   a. Name, address, telephone numbers, emergency contact numbers, fax numbers, email addresses
   b. Owner name(s), address, contact numbers
   c. Year facility was built, types of construction, date of any subsequent construction
   d. Number of beds
   e. Maximum number of clients on site
   f. Average number of clients on site
   g. Type of residents served
   h. Percentage of patients with Alzheimer's disease
   i. Percentage of patients requiring oxygen, dialysis, or other special equipment
   j. Number of patients who are self-sufficient
   k. Identify flood zone from Rate Maps
   l. Indicate how many miles/feet to a railroad or other major transportation route (for hazardous materials spills)
   m. Identify if facility is located within the 10 mile or 50 mile Emergency Planning Zone of the Brunswick Nuclear Power Plant or the Sunny Point Arsenal.
2. Statement indicating conditions under which facility will move to emergency operations:
   a. State procedures for timely activation and notification of staff.
   b. Note how timing varies by emergency and in the process of responding to emergency conditions.
3. Explanation of notification process:
   a. How does the facility receive warnings?
   b. Does notification change on weekends or holidays?
   c. List 24-hour contact number, if different from the number listed in the introduction.
   d. Procedure for notifying key staff.
   e. Procedures and policy for reporting to work for key workers.
   f. How will residents (patients) be alerted?
   g. What precautionary measures will be taken?
   h. Is there a back-up notification system, should the primary system fail? If so, explain.
   i. Procedures for notifying those facilities to which facility residents will be evacuated.

j. Procedures for notifying families of residents that the facility is being evacuated. Note any provisions that have been made for emergency workers' families.

4. Describe record keeping system for tracking residents and employees.
   a. Where are records stored?
   b. Do you have employee manuals that address emergency actions?
   c. Where are they kept?

5. Identify the hierarchy of authority in place during emergencies. Attach a regular organizational chart as well as an emergency organizational chart, if different from the usual organizational chart.
   a. Identify by name and title of who is in charge and one alternate.
   b. Identify the chain of command, identifying all key positions and responsibilities in the event of an emergency.

6. Place a check next to the disasters that are most likely to affect your facility:
   _____ Bioterrorism
   _____ Workplace violence
   _____ Chemical spill
   _____ Earthquake
   _____ Fire
   _____ Flood
   _____ Hurricane/wind
   _____ Ice/snow storm
   _____ Utility outages
   Other _____

7. Emergency operating plan
   a. Procedures for supplying food, water, and sleeping arrangements.
   b. Procedures for obtaining emergency power, natural gas, or diesel. (What is the back-up power system?)
   c. Transportation procedures (may be covered in evacuation system).
   d. List of all essential supplies that need to be on hand for a 72-hour period. (Note that many of these are listed on NHCEM website.)
   e. Transportation arrangements for residents including agreements or understandings that will be used to evacuate residents.
   f. Attach copies of transportation agreements.
   g. Arrangements to move records.
   h. Arrangements to move medications.
   i. Arrangements to move/provide food, water, and other necessities.

8. Emergency evacuation plan:
   a. Identify evacuation locations.
   b. Note the expected time needed to evacuate all residents to the receiving facility.
   c. Identify evacuation routes and secondary routes should the primary routes be impassable (attach map of route if possible using Mapquest.com).
   d. Attach copies of mutual aid agreements with facilities that will receive your residents.

    e. Develop procedures for ensuring all residents are accounted for and are out of the facility.

    f. Note what point in time you will prepare necessary supplies for evacuation.

    g. Indicate procedures for facility staff to accompany evacuating residents/ patients.

    h. Develop log system to track residents once they have been evacuated.

    i. Institute procedures for responding to family inquiries about residents who have been evacuated.

    j. Who is responsible for authorizing reentry to occur?

    k. Initiate procedures for inspecting the facility to ensure it is structurally sound.

    l. How will residents be transported from the host facility back to their home facility?

    m. How will you receive accurate and timely data on reentry operations?

    n. What are your plans to conduct salvage operations if your facility has been damaged? Consider who will take detailed inventory including pictures, video, and/or pocket tape recordings of the condition of the facility.

    o. Note who is responsible for documenting every action taken in order to reopen the facility.

9. Complete this section if your facility will shelter others in the event of an emergency:

    a. Describe receiving procedures for arriving residents/patients from evacuating facility.

    b. Identify where additional residents will be housed.

    c. Provide a floor plan that identifies the space allocated for additional residents or patients.

    d. Identify provisions of additional food, water, and medical needs of the hosted residents/patients for a minimum of 72 hours.

    e. Initiate procedures for ensuring 24-hour operations.

    f. Initiate procedures for providing sheltering for family members of critical workers.

    g. When will the facility notify NC DFS that the facility is exceeding its operating capacity due to the receipt of hosted patients?

    h. Initiate procedures for tracking additional residents or patients sheltered within the facility.

10. Training:

    a. Identify how key workers will be instructed in their emergency roles during nonemergency times.

    b. Who provides training of new employees regarding disaster plans?

    c. Describe your training schedule for all employees.

    d. Identify the provisions for training new employees regarding their disaster related role(s).

    e. Identify a schedule for exercising all or portions of the disaster plan on at least an annual basis.

    f. Establish procedures for correcting deficiencies noted during training exercises.

11. Checklist of appendices:

    a. Roster of employees and companies with key disaster roles:

    i. Names, addresses, and telephone numbers of all staff.

    ii. Name of the company, contact person, and contact numbers of providers such as transportation, fuel, food, water.

b. Agreements and understandings:

    i. Copies of mutual aid agreements, including reciprocal host facility agreements, transportation agreements, current vendor agreements, or any other agreement needed to ensure the operational integrity of this plan.

c. Evacuate route map describing how to get to the receiving facility.

d. Support material:

    i. Any additional material needed to support the information provided in the plan.

    ii. Copy of the facility's fire safety plan that is approved by the local fire department.

ACTIVITY 6.5 APPLYING ANTI-RACIST PEDAGOGY TO THE EXPLORATION OF SENIOR HOUSING

Kyoko Kishimoto and Rona J. Karasik

ACTIVITY INFORMATION

Type

__X__	In class (activity)
_____	Online
__X__	Take home (preactivity homework assignment)
_____	In community

Difficulty

_____	Introductory
_____	Intermediate
__X__	Advanced

OVERVIEW

The continuum of housing options for older adults is multifaceted, encompassing a wide range of elements (e.g., affordability, design, location, ability, status, services, aging in place, sense of place, independence, safety and social support). Demographics, social policies, and historical context associated with senior housing are similarly complex, with disparities found between groups of elders (e.g., elders with fewer resources have fewer housing options) and that certain groups (e.g., women, 85+, elders of color) are more or less likely to use a particular option (e.g., long-term care). Classroom materials have begun to acknowledge these ongoing disparities and in some cases may even examine their practical implications. They are much less likely, however, to challenge students to consider how such disparities with regard to race came to be, why they continue to persist, and what can or should be done about them. Empowering students with the tools to investigate root causes of these disparities (e.g., power relations) is needed to move toward identifying ways to dismantle institutional racism and create more equitable systems. Anti-racist pedagogy, with its attention to historical/political context and fostering skills for critical analyses and social change, offers a framework from which to introduce and explore these issues. Essential to anti-racism is the understanding of power, privilege, knowledge production, and identities (Wagner, 2005). Anti-racist pedagogy attempts to provide students with the critical and analytical skills to understand the power relations behind racism and how race has been institutionalized in U.S. society to create inequalities (Kandaswamy, 2007).

The following activity uses an anti-racist pedagogical approach to engage students in analyzing housing opportunities and experiences in later life from within the context of racial inequities experienced over the life course. The activity module uses components of anti-racist pedagogy to help students learn the material in a way that helps them develop critical analytical skills and challenge their social locations, which is important for when these students become practitioners. Developing these skills is a process—one that cannot be achieved in a single class period or two. This activity, therefore, is designed to offer students a starting point from which to begin this process. In order to prepare students for this exploration, a preactivity homework assignment is included to help students familiarize themselves with some of the basics of housing for older adults. This assignment may be omitted for students who already have a strong background in senior housing. Two video clips are also recommended to provide students with an introduction to institutional racism and its historical impact on housing in the United States. The activity itself consists of students working in groups to consider various factors that have an impact on past and future housing trajectories. Each group is provided with an alternate version of a vignette regarding Samuel, who is in his mid-fifties. Each description of Samuel is identical with the exception of the racial identities and related historical experiences of Samuel's father. Until each group has completed their work, they will likely be unaware of the slight differences in their vignettes. These variations will become evident as each group presents their findings to the class. The differences that emerge and their specific influences on Samuel's housing trajectory offer a starting point for discussing root causes of racial inequity with regard to housing for older adults.

ACTIVITY LEARNING GOALS

Following this activity, students will be able to . . .

- Apply a life course perspective to analyzing housing options for older adults.
- Place senior housing options and experiences into historical context (how current policies and disparities are impacted by public policies and institutional racism past and present).
- Recognize the influence of social location on experience and perspective (re: housing options for older adults).
- Recognize power differentials and how race and racism operate in policies and research.
- Employ critical analytical skills to the further study of later life housing experiences and options.

ASSOCIATION FOR GERONTOLOGY IN HIGHER EDUCATION COMPETENCIES

- Relate social theories and science of aging to understanding heterogeneity, inequality, and context of aging.
- Distinguish factors related to aging outcomes, both intrinsic and contextual, through critical thinking and empirical research.

- Develop a gerontological perspective through knowledge and self-reflection.
- Employ and generate policy to equitably address the needs of older persons.

MINIMUM/MAXIMUM NUMBER OF PARTICIPANTS

- 8 to 20 (four groups, with two to five participants per group)

TIME NEEDED TO IMPLEMENT ACTIVITY

- Two to three class periods (2–3 hours total) plus take home preactivity assessment and homework assignment

SETTING

- Classroom with audio-visual equipment and sufficient space for students to work in small groups and to hang up posters created during activity.

MATERIALS
Required

- Educator's Introduction to Anti-Racist Pedagogy (Appendix 6.5A)
- Senior Housing Primer (Appendix 6.5B)
- Pre/Postactivity Assessments (Appendix 6.5C)
- Preactivity Homework Assignment (Appendix 6.5D)
- Video Clips (Available on YouTube or the following original sources):
  - "Race: The Power of an Illusion" (excerpts from Episode 3: "The House We Live In"), retrieved from www.youtube.com/watch?v=mW764dXEI_8 (6:04 minutes).

    Pounder, C. H., Adelman, L., Cheng, J., Herbes-Sommers, C., Strain, T. H., Smith, L., & Ragazzi, C. (2003). *Race: The power of an illusion [videorecording]*. San Francisco, CA: California Newsreel.
  - "Unnatural Causes" (excerpts from Episode 5: "Place Matters"), retrieved from www.unnaturalcauses.org/video_clips_detail.php?res_id=217 (3:35 minutes).

    Adelman, L. (2008). *Unnatural cause: Is inequality making us sick [videorecording]?* San Francisco, CA: California Newsreel.
- Activity Instructions and Vignette (alternate versions for Groups 1–4: Appendix 6.5E)
- Housing Policies and Race Relations: A Context for Life-Course Analysis (Appendix 6.5F)
- Factors That Impact Past, Current, and Future Housing (Appendix 6.5G)
- Blank poster sheets and tape or tacks to hang them

- Multiple sets of markers
- Desirable: Internet access so students may use personal devices (e.g., tablets, laptops, smartphones) to search for supplemental information as needed during the activity

PROCEDURES

Preparation

- Review Educator's Introduction to Anti-Racist Pedagogy (Appendix 6.5A).
- Print materials:
  - Senior Housing Primer (Appendix 6.5B): copy for each student.
  - Pre/Postactivity Assessments (Appendix 6.5C): copy for each student.
  - Preactivity Homework Assignment (Appendix 6.5D): copy for each student.
  - Activity Instructions and Vignette (Appendix 6.5E): *Important*: Each student should receive a copy *only* of the instructions/vignette associated with their *designated* group (e.g., Group 1, Group 2, Group 3, Group 4).
  - Housing Policies and Race Relations: A Context for Life-Course Analysis (Appendix 6.5F): copy for each student.
  - Factors That Impact Past, Current, and Future Housing (Appendix 6.5G): copy for each student.
- Download video clips.

Class Prior to Activity

- Administer preassessment survey (Appendix 6.5C) in class or as a take home assignment.
- Introduce topic of senior housing* (Senior Housing Primer: Appendix 6.5B).
- Assign Preactivity Homework* (Appendix 6.5D).

Note: Some may prefer to have students complete the homework the class prior to beginning the discussion of senior housing. Others may prefer to assign the homework after providing students with the "Senior Housing Primer" and/or other information on the topic.

Activity

Distribute copies of Housing Policies and Race Relations: A Context for Life-Course Analysis (Appendix 6.5F) and Factors That Impact Past, Current, and Future Housing (Appendix 6.5G) to each student.

- Show video clips.
- Divide students into four groups.
- Provide paper, markers, and corresponding Activity Instructions and Vignette (Appendix 6.5E) to each group (e.g., Group 1 vignette materials to Group 1,

Group 2 vignette materials to Group 2). Each member of the group should have their own copy of the group's assigned vignette to refer to. *Note*: Due to important differences in each group's version of the vignette, it is recommended that discussions across different groups be discouraged until after each group is ready to present their finalized product to the full class.

- Within each group, have students review the entire activity directions and vignette prior to starting:
  - Step 1 "Looking Back": Each group discusses and then draws visual representation as directed in the Activity Instructions and Vignette materials.
  - Step 2 "Looking Forward": Each group discusses and then draws visual representation as directed in the Activity Instructions and Vignette materials.
- When visual representations are complete, have each group present their results to the class. (Note: Up until this point, groups may not realize that their versions of the vignette are not completely identical. This may cause some confusion at first, but it may also become a good starting point for the discussion that follows.)

Discussion/Reflection

After all of the groups have presented their outcomes, use the following questions to facilitate a full group discussion of the findings:

- How are your group's results similar to and/or different from the outcomes of the other groups in the class?
- What factors might account for these differences?
- Why do these factors seem important to Samuel's outcomes?
- How did your own social location come into play in how you interpreted Samuel's housing past and future?
- As a practitioner, how might you use this information to assist clients?

Assessment

Following the activity (either in class, online, or as a take home), have students complete the Postactivity Assessment (Appendix 6.5C) to assess what, if any, impact the activity had on students' understanding of senior housing options from a life course perspective, the influence of social location on critical analysis, and the impact of institutional racism in public policies as root causes of racial inequities in senior housing.

REFERENCES

Kandaswamy, P. (2007). Beyond colorblindness and multiculturalism: Rethinking anti-racist pedagogy in the university classroom. *The Radical Teacher, 80*, 6–11.

Wagner, A. E. (2005). Unsettling the academy: Working through the challenges of anti-racist pedagogy. *Race Ethnicity and Education 8*(3), 261–275.

RECOMMENDED RESOURCES

Adelman, L. (2008). *Unnatural cause: Is inequality making us sick [videorecording]?* San Francisco, CA: California Newsreel.

Atchley, R. C. (1982). Retirement as a social institution. *Annual Review of Sociology, 8*, 263–287.

Atchley, R. C. (1987). *Aging: Continuity and change.* Belmont, CA: Wadsworth.

Blake, K. S., & Simic, A. (2005). *Elderly housing consumption: Historical patterns and projected trends.* Fairfax, VA: ICF Consulting. Retrieved from https://www.huduser.gov/portal/Publications/pdf/Elderly_Housing_Consumption.pdf

Bridges, B., & Choudhury, S. (2009). Examining social security benefits as a retirement resource for near-retirees, by race and ethnicity, nativity, and disability status. *Social Security Bulletin, 69*(1), 19–44.

Bureau of Labor Statistics. Retrieved from http://www.bls.gov/cps

Costa, D. L. (1998). *The evolution of retirement: An American economic history, 1880–1990* (pp. 6–31). Chicago, IL: University of Chicago Press.

Davies, G., & Derthick, M. (1997). Race and social welfare policy: The Social Security Act of 1935. *Political Science Quarterly, 112*(2), 217–235.

ElderWeb. (2016). History of long term care (ElderWeb). Retrieved from http://www.elderweb.com/book/export/html/2806

Kailin, J. (2002). *Antiracist education: From theory to practice.* Lanham, MD: Rowman & Littlefield.

Karasik, R. J., & Kishimoto, K. (2016). Is gerontology ready for anti-racist pedagogy? A survey of educators' practices and perspectives. *Gerontology and Geriatrics Education.* doi:10.1080/02701960.2015.1115984

Kastenberg, E. C., & Chasin, J. (2004). Elderly housing. Retrieved from https://www.irs.gov/pub/irs-tege/eotopicg04.pdf

Kishimoto, K. (2016). Anti-racist pedagogy: From faculty's self-reflection to organizing within and beyond the classroom. *Race Ethnicity and Education.* doi: 10.1080/13613324.2016.1248824

Lee, S. J., Parrott, K. R., & Ahn, M. (2014). Housing adequacy: A well-being indicator for elderly households in southern U.S. communities. *Family and Consumer Sciences Research Journal, 42*(3), 235–251.

McKernan, S. M., Ratcliffe, C., Steuerle, C. E., & Zhang, S. (2013). *Less than equal: Racial disparities in wealth accumulation.* Washington, DC: Urban Institute.

McNamara, T., & Williamson, J. (2004). Race, gender, and the retirement decisions of people ages 60 to 80: Prospects for age integration in employment. *International Journal of Aging and Human Development, 59*(3), 255–286.

Portacolone, E., & Halpern, J. (2014). "Move or suffer" Is age-segregation the new norm for older Americans living alone? *Journal of Applied Gerontology, 35*(8), 836–856. doi:10.1177/0733464814538118

Pounder, C. H., Adelman, L., Cheng, J., Herbes-Sommers, C., Strain, T. H., Smith, L., & Ragazzi, C. (2003). *Race: The power of an illusion [videorecording].* San Francisco, CA: California Newsreel.

Ransom, R. L., & Sutch, R. (1986). The labor of older Americans: Retirement of men on and off the job, 1870–1937. *The Journal of Economic History, 46*(01), 1–30.

Rodriguez, V., & Drew, E. (2014, May). *Anti-racist pedagogy across the curriculum.* Presented at the Anti-Racist Pedagogy Across the Curriculum Workshop. St. Cloud State University, St. Cloud, MN.

Seitles, M. (1998). The perpetuation of residential racial segregation in America: Historical discrimination, modern forms of exclusion, and inclusionary remedies. *Journal of Land Use & Environmental Law, 14*(1), 89–124.

Stoloff, J. A. (2004, August 14). *A brief history of public housing.* Paper presented at the annual meeting of the American Sociological Association. San Francisco, CA. Retrieved from http://citation.allacademic.com/meta/p_mla_apa_research_citation/1/0/8/8/5/p108852_index.html

Trotman, F. K. (2002). Historical, economic, and political contexts of aging in African America. *Journal of Women & Aging, 14*(3/4), 121–138.

U.S. Census. Retrieved from http://www.census.gov

Willamson, J. B. (1984). Old age relief policy prior to 1900: The trend toward restrictiveness. *American Journal of Economics and Sociology, 43*(3), 369–384.

Workplace Flexibility. (2010). *A timeline of the evolution of retirement in the United States.* Washington, DC: Georgetown University Law Center.

APPENDIX 6.5A: EDUCATOR'S INTRODUCTION TO ANTI-RACIST PEDAGOGY

Before beginning this activity, it is important to familiarize yourself with the basic principles of anti-racist pedagogy. While a brief description is offered in the text that follows, we strongly recommend also referring to the sources cited for a fuller understanding.

GOAL OF THIS ACTIVITY

The goal of this activity is to help students begin to understand issues of senior housing from an anti-racist perspective. According to Karasik and Kishimoto (2016), "Anti-racist pedagogy encompasses three interconnected components: racial content addressing institutional racism within historical and political contexts (e.g., analysis of power relations); educational method (e.g., focused on fostering critical analytical skills while empowering students); and application of anti-racist analysis within and beyond the classroom (e.g., strategic organizing for social change)" (Kailin, 2002; Kandaswamy, 2007; Kishimoto, 2016; Rodriguez & Drew, 2014).

KEY CONCEPTS

Anti-racist pedagogy (Karasik & Kishimoto, 2016): A teaching approach that seeks to:

- Confront and dismantle ideas of institutional racism by examining the theory, structure, and practice of racism and power relations embedded in history and knowledge production
- Raise students' self-awareness of their social locations
- Empower students by validating and acknowledging their everyday experiences
- Foster students' critical thinking
- Equip students with anti-racist language and discussion skills
- Create a sense of community in the classroom
- Develop skills for anti-racist organizing

Social Location: An individual's social position as determined by their membership in groups based on factors such as race, gender, class, sexuality, religion, age, ability, and geographical location. Such social positions hold different degrees and intersections of privilege and oppression which then shape an individual's perspectives and experiences in society.

Institutional Racism: Racial inequality stemming from the systematic, inequitable distribution of resources, power, and opportunity in society.

Power Relations: Recognizing that we hold different positions of power according to our race, gender, class, and other intersecting identities.

REFERENCES

Kailin, J. (2002). *Antiracist education: From theory to practice.* Lanham, MD: Rowman & Littlefield.

Kandaswamy, P. (2007). Beyond colorblindness and multiculturalism: Rethinking anti-racist pedagogy in the university classroom. *The Radical Teacher, 80,* 6–11.

Karasik, R. J., & Kishimoto, K. (2016). Is gerontology ready for anti-racist pedagogy? A survey of educators' practices and perspectives. *Gerontology and Geriatrics Education.* doi:10.1080/02701960.2015.1115984

Kishimoto, K. (2016). Anti-racist pedagogy: From faculty's social location to organizing within and beyond the classroom. *Race Ethnicity and Education.* doi:10.1080/13613324.2016.1248824

Rodriguez, V., & Drew, E. (2014, May). *Anti-racist pedagogy across the curriculum.* Presented at the Anti-Racist Pedagogy Across the Curriculum Workshop, St. Cloud State University, St. Cloud, MN.

RECOMMENDED RESOURCE

Wagner, A. E. (2005). Unsettling the academy: Working through the challenges of anti-racist pedagogy. *Race Ethnicity and Education 8*(3), 261–275.

APPENDIX 6.5B: SENIOR HOUSING PRIMER

MYTHS AND REALITIES

There are many myths and stereotypes about where older adults live. For example:
   Myth: Most older adults live in nursing homes.

Reality: Only about 3% to 4% of older adults (65+) in the United States live in a nursing home or long stay institution, although risk of ever living in a nursing home increases with age:

Older Adults Living in Institutional Settings (Nursing Homes)

Percent	Number	
65+ (overall)	3.1%	1.5 million (1.3 in NH)
65–74 ("Young Old")	1.0%	
75–84 ("Old Old")	3.0%	
85+ ("Oldest Old")	10.0%	

(*Source*: U.S. Department of Health and Human Services, 2016)

Myth: Housing options for older adults are limited primarily to either one's own home or a nursing home.

Reality: There exists a broad and expanding continuum of housing options for older adults, including on the more independent side:

- Own home
- Retirement communities
- Senior apartments (either market rate or subsidized)

Senior housing with a range of services is also available, including:

- Board and care
- Adult foster care
- Assisted living
- Skilled nursing facility

Myth: Most older adults move to warmer climates (e.g., Florida, Arizona) after they retire.

Reality: Older adults are less likely to change residence than other age groups, and while certain areas do have a higher percentage of older adults, the largest numbers of older adults are found where the largest numbers of persons of all ages are (e.g., California, Florida, Texas, New York, and Pennsylvania). In fact, most older adults prefer to "*age in place*," wanting to stay where they currently are living. The CDC defines aging in place as "the ability to live in one's own home and community safely, independently, and comfortably, regardless of age, income, or ability level" (n.p.).

Myth: Medicare pays for most housing and nursing home care for older adults.

Reality: Medicare is a health insurance plan for older adults. It does not pay for housing, although it might cover a limited amount of in-home health care services. Medicare does not pay for long-term care, although it might cover a limited amount of time for short-term rehabilitative care provided in a skilled nursing care facility (Centers for Medicare & Medicaid Services, 2015; see www.medicare.gov for additional information).

Myth: Senior housing options and outcomes are the same for all older adults in the United States.

Reality: Where an older adult lives and the housing opportunities they have is the product of the adult's lifelong experiences.

HOUSING, THE LIFE COURSE, AND RACIAL DISPARITIES

Housing is a lifelong experience affected by many intersecting factors including socioeconomic status, education, gender, and race. Many racial and ethnic differences have been documented with regard to senior housing, assisted living, home care use, and quality of care.

Racial Disparities Across the Life Course

Significant disparities have been documented with regard to:

- Income
- Home ownership
- Health

Assisted Living (Hernandez, 2012; medicareadvocacy.org):

- Increasing number of White elders moving into assisted living
- Ethnic minority elders less likely to live in ALFs
- Lower income residents have reduced access to ALFs
- Assisted living facilities where ethnic minority elders do live have been found to be typically:
  - Older buildings
  - Smaller in size
  - Less expensive
  - Less private (more shared bedrooms and bathrooms)

Skilled Nursing Facilities (Feng et al., 2011; medicareadvocacy.org; Smith, Feng, Fennel, Zinn, & Mor, 2007):

- Majority of nursing home residents in the United States are White.
- Percentage of White nursing home residents has decreased significantly from 1999 to 2008.
- Ethnic minority access/use of long-term care is increasing.

- Continued concerns for racial segregation and discrimination occur in nursing homes.
- Racial disparities in nursing home care quality exist for ethnic minority elders.

REFERENCES

Centers for Disease Control and Prevention. (n.d.). Healthy places terminology. Retrieved from http://www.cdc.gov/healthyplaces/terminology.htm

Centers for Medicare & Medicaid Services. (2015). *Medicare coverage of skilled nursing facility care*. Baltimore, MD: Author. Retrieved from https://www.medicare.gov/pubs/pdf/10153.pdf

Feng, Z., Fennell, M. L., Tyler, D. A., Clark, M., & Mor, V. (2011). Growth of racial and ethnic minorities in US nursing homes driven by demographics and possible disparities in options. *Health Affairs, 30*(7), 1358–1365.

Hernandez, M. (2012). Disparities in assisted living: Does it meet the HCBS test? Generations, 36(1), 118–124.

Smith, D. B., Feng, Z., Fennell, M. L., Zinn, J. S., & Mor, V. (2007). Separate and unequal: Racial segregation and disparities in quality across US. nursing homes. *Health Affairs, 26*(5), 1448–1458.

U.S. Department of Health and Human Services. (2016). *A profile of older Americans: 2016*. Washington, DC: Author. Retrieved from https://www.acl.gov/sites/default/files/Aging%20and%20Disability%20in%20America/2016-Profile.pdf

RECOMMENDED RESOURCES

Chisholm, L., Weech Maldonado, R., Laberge, A., Lin, F. C., & Hyer, K. (2013). Nursing home quality and financial performance: Does the racial composition of residents matter? *Health Services Research, 48*(6, Pt. 1), 2060–2080.

Harvard Joint Center for Housing Studies. (2014). *Housing America's older adults: Meeting the needs of an aging population*. Cambridge, MA: Harvard.

Kirby, J. B., & Lau, D. T. (2010). Community and individual race/ethnicity and home health care use among elderly persons in the United States. *Health Services Research, 45*(5 Pt. 1), 1251–1267.

Kuebler, M., & Rugh, J. S. (2013). New evidence on racial and ethnic disparities in homeownership in the United States from 2001 to 2010. *Social Science Research, 42*(5), 1357–1374.

Medicareadvocacy.org. (n.d.). The changing demographics of nursing home care: Greater minority access . . . Good news, bad news. Retrieved from http://www.medicareadvocacy.org/the-changing-demographics-of-nursing-home-care-greater-minority-access%E2%80%A6-good-news-bad-news

Mold, F., Fitzpatrick, J. M., & Roberts, J. D. (2005). Minority ethnic elders in care homes: A review of the literature. *Age and Ageing, 34*(2), 107–113.

APPENDIX 6.5C: PRE/POSTACTIVITY ASSESSMENTS

Please Rate the Level You Agree With the Following Statements:	Strongly Disagree	Disagree	Neither Agree nor Disagree	Somewhat Agree	Strongly Agree
I have a good understanding of the range of housing options available to older adults.					
Everyone has access to adequate housing and services.					
Owning a house is something that an individual has earned only through their hard work and merit.					
The geographical location of where one lives has an impact on their education, employment, and health opportunities.					
One's life history plays a significant role in one's current and future housing.					
Racism has a strong impact on an individual's current housing situation.					
I am uncomfortable talking about issues of race and racism.					

(continued)

(continued)

Please Rate the Level You Agree With the Following Statements:	Strongly Disagree	Disagree	Neither Agree nor Disagree	Somewhat Agree	Strongly Agree
Socioeconomic status has a strong impact on an older person's experience with housing.					
I am generally knowledgeable about issues of race and racism.					
I am familiar with my own social location.					
People who work with older adults need to acknowledge their own social location.					
Racism is a system of advantage and disadvantage.					
I have a good understanding of what institutional racism is.					
I have a good understanding of how institutional racism is embedded in public policies.					

APPENDIX 6.5D: PREACTIVITY HOMEWORK ASSIGNMENT

Goal: To explore and identify the continuum of housing for older adults in the United States.

1. Using whatever tools are available (e.g., textbooks, library, Internet), identify a clear and consistent definition for each of the following:
   - Adult foster care
   - Aging in place
   - Assisted living
   - Board and care
   - Continuing care retirement community
   - Institutional racism
   - Market rate housing
   - Multi-level care
   - Section 8 housing
   - Section 202 housing
   - Senior home sharing
   - Skilled nursing facility
   - Social location
   - Sub-acute care
   - Subsidized housing

2. Identify and locate which of the previously listed types of senior housing are available in your local area.
3. Which senior housing option do you personally find the most desirable? Why?
4. Which senior housing option do you personally find the least desirable? Why?
5. What aspects of your own life/experiences influence your choices for most and least desirable senior housing options? Why?
6. What factors might help you to live in your most desired senior housing option? Why?
7. What factors might create barriers to living in your most desired senior housing option? Why?

APPENDIX 6.5E: ACTIVITY INSTRUCTIONS AND VIGNETTE

GROUP 1

Instructions: Using the materials provided, read the vignette and consider, discuss, and then record your group's responses to the questions that follow.

Samuel is a 56-year-old science teacher who both lives and works in Robbinsdale, MN. He and Lisa have been married for 7 years—not long after they met at a support group for widowed spouses. After Lisa's son, now 23, moved away for college, Samuel and Lisa moved into a split-level condo so that there would be room for Samuel's father to come live with them some day. Samuel's father, once a Tuskegee Airman, is a quiet but fiercely independent man who has other ideas. His father's current memory lapses, however, have Samuel concerned that his father probably shouldn't live on his own much longer.

Step 1: Looking Back: How did he get there?

1. Based on his life story and the information in the "Housing Policies and Race Relations" historical chart, identify *which* policies/historical events likely influenced how Samuel arrived at his current housing situation. Be sure to also explain *how* and *why* these policies affected his trajectory to his current housing.

2. Based on his life story and the variables listed in "Factors That Impact Past, Current, and Future Housing" (e.g., income, educational level, health, race, culture, public policy), identify *which* factors identified in Samuel's story likely influenced how he arrived at his current housing situation. Be sure to also explain *how* and *why* these factors affected his trajectory to his current housing.

3. Using the paper/markers provided, *draw* a visual representation of how you see the previously noted factors influencing Samuel's trajectory/pathway into his *current* housing situation.

Step 2: Looking Forward: Where is he headed?

4. Using the information identified earlier, consider what Samuel's housing situation will be in the future (e.g., as he ages). *What* type of housing will it be? *Why*?

5. Using the paper/markers provided, *draw* a visual representation of what you anticipate Samuel's *future* housing situation will look like. Be sure to include the trajectory/pathway you anticipate he will follow, as well as the factors (and their specific influences) that you expect will lead to his future housing situation.

Step 3: Class Discussion:

6. Be prepared to describe/explain your group's findings for Step 1 and Step 2, using the visual representations you have prepared:

   a. What do you see as the factors that led Samuel to his current housing situation? Why?

   b. What do you see as the factors that will lead to Samuel's future housing situation? Why?

   c. What roles do public policies play in determining Samuel's past, current, and future housing situations?

d. What challenges did your group experience in interpreting Samuel's life course?

e. How did you resolve these challenges?

f. What role did your own social location have on how you interpreted Samuel's past and future?

GROUP 2

Instructions: Using the materials provided, read the vignette and consider, discuss, and then record your group's responses to the questions that follow.

Samuel is a 56-year-old science teacher who both lives and works in Robbinsdale, MN. He and Lisa have been married for 7 years—not long after they met at a support group for widowed spouses. After Lisa's son, now 23, moved away for college, Samuel and Lisa moved into a split-level condo so that there would be room for Samuel's father to come live with them some day. Samuel's father, who spent much of WWII as an officer in Fort Dix, NJ, is a quiet but fiercely independent man who has other ideas. His father's current memory lapses, however, have Samuel concerned that his father probably shouldn't live on his own much longer.

Step 1: Looking Back: How did he get there?

1. Based on his life story and the information in the "Housing Policies and Race Relations" historical chart, identify *which* policies/historical events likely influenced how Samuel arrived at his current housing situation. Be sure to also explain *how* and *why* these policies affected his trajectory to his current housing.

2. Based on his life story and the variables listed in "Factors That Impact Past, Current, and Future Housing" (e.g., income, educational level, health, race, culture, public policy), identify *which* factors identified in Samuel's story likely influenced how he arrived at his current housing situation. Be sure to also explain *how* and *why* these factors affected his trajectory to his current housing.

3. Using the paper/markers provided, *draw* a visual representation of how you see the previously noted factors influencing Samuel's trajectory/pathway into his *current* housing situation.

Step 2: Looking Forward: Where is he headed?

4. Using the information identified earlier, consider what Samuel's housing situation will be in the future (e.g., as he ages). *What* type of housing will it be? *Why*?

5. Using the paper/markers provided, *draw* a visual representation of what you anticipate Samuel's *future* housing situation will look like. Be sure to include the trajectory/pathway you anticipate he will follow, as well as the factors (and their specific influences) that you expect will lead to his future housing situation.

Step 3: Class Discussion:

6. Be prepared to describe/explain your group's findings for Step 1 and Step 2, using the visual representations you have prepared:

a. What do you see as the factors that led Samuel to his current housing situation? Why?

b. What do you see as the factors that will lead to Samuel's future housing situation? Why?

c. What roles do public policies play in determining Samuel's past, current, and future housing situations?

d. What challenges did your group experience in interpreting Samuel's life course?

e. How did you resolve these challenges?

f. What role did your own social location have on how you interpreted Samuel's past and future?

GROUP 3

Instructions: Using the materials provided, read the vignette and consider, discuss, and then record your group's responses to the questions that follow.

Samuel is a 56-year-old science teacher who both lives and works in Robbinsdale, MN. He and Lisa have been married for 7 years—not long after they met at a support group for widowed spouses. After Lisa's son, now 23, moved away for college, Samuel and Lisa moved into a split-level condo so that there would be room for Samuel's father to come live with them. Samuel's father, who spent much of WWII in an internment camp in Idaho, is a quiet but fiercely independent man who has other ideas. His father's current memory lapses, however, have Samuel concerned that his father probably shouldn't live on his own much longer.

Step 1: Looking Back: How did he get there?

1. Based on his life story and the information in the "Housing Policies and Race Relations" historical chart, identify *which* policies/historical events likely influenced how Samuel arrived at his current housing situation. Be sure to also explain *how* and *why* these policies affected his trajectory to his current housing.

2. Based on his life story and the variables listed in "Factors That Impact Past, Current, and Future Housing" (e.g., income, educational level, health, race, culture, public policy), identify *which* factors identified in Samuel's story likely influenced how he arrived at his current housing situation. Be sure to also explain *how* and *why* these factors affected his trajectory to his current housing.

3. Using the paper/markers provided, *draw* a visual representation of how you see the previously noted factors influencing Samuel's trajectory/pathway into his *current* housing situation.

Step 2: Looking Forward: Where is he headed?

4. Using the information identified earlier, consider what Samuel's housing situation will be in the future (e.g., as he ages). *What* type of housing will it be? *Why*?

5. Using the paper/markers provided, *draw* a visual representation of what you anticipate Samuel's *future* housing situation will look like. Be sure to include the trajectory/pathway you anticipate he will follow, as well as the factors (and their specific influences) that you expect will lead to his future housing situation.

Step 3: Class Discussion:

6. Be prepared to describe/explain your group's findings for Step 1 and Step 2, using the visual representations you have prepared:

   a. What do you see as the factors that led Samuel to his current housing situation? Why?

   b. What do you see as the factors that will lead to Samuel's future housing situation? Why?

   c. What roles do public policies play in determining Samuel's past, current, and future housing situations?

d. What challenges did your group experience in interpreting Samuel's life course?

e. How did you resolve these challenges?

f. What role did your own social location have on how you interpreted Samuel's past and future?

GROUP 4

Instructions: Using the materials provided, read the vignette and consider, discuss, and then record your group's responses to the questions that follow.

Samuel is a 56-year-old science teacher who both lives and works in Robbinsdale, MN. He and Lisa have been married for 7 years—not long after they met at a support group for widowed spouses. After Lisa's son, now 23, moved away for college, Samuel and Lisa moved into a split-level condo so that there would be room for Samuel's father to come live with them. Samuel's father, who immigrated from Cuba as a worker in 1946, is a quiet but fiercely independent man who has other ideas. His father's current memory lapses, however, have Samuel concerned that his father probably shouldn't live on his own much longer.

Step 1: Looking Back: How did he get there?

1. Based on his life story and the information in the "Housing Policies and Race Relations" historical chart, identify *which* policies/historical events likely influenced how Samuel arrived at his current housing situation. Be sure to also explain *how* and *why* these policies affected his trajectory to his current housing.

2. Based on his life story and the variables listed in "Factors That Impact Past, Current, and Future Housing" (e.g., income, educational level, health, race, culture, public policy), identify *which* factors identified in Samuel's story likely influenced how he arrived at his current housing situation. Be sure to also explain *how* and *why* these factors affected his trajectory to his current housing.

3. Using the paper/markers provided, *draw* a visual representation of how you see the previously noted factors influencing Samuel's trajectory/pathway into his *current* housing situation.

Step 2: Looking Forward: Where is he headed?

4. Using the information identified earlier, consider what Samuel's housing situation will be in the future (e.g., as he ages). *What* type of housing will it be? *Why*?

5. Using the paper/markers provided, *draw* a visual representation of what you anticipate Samuel's *future* housing situation will look like. Be sure to include the trajectory/pathway you anticipate he will follow, as well as the factors (and their specific influences) that you expect will lead to his future housing situation.

Step 3: Class Discussion:

6. Be prepared to describe/explain your group's findings for Step 1 and Step 2, using the visual representations you have prepared:

a. What do you see as the factors that led Samuel to his current housing situation? Why?

b. What do you see as the factors that will lead to Samuel's future housing situation? Why?

c. What roles do public policies play in determining Samuel's past, current, and future housing situations?

d. What challenges did your group experience in interpreting Samuel's life course?

e. How did you resolve these challenges?

f. What role did your own social location have on how you interpreted Samuel's past and future?

APPENDIX 6.5F: HOUSING POLICIES AND RACE RELATIONS: A CONTEXT FOR LIFE-COURSE ANALYSIS

Housing for Older Adults in the U.S.	Race Relations in the U.S.
Mid 1700s: • **1776–1800:** Relied on personal resources, children, or poorhouses	• **1661–1865:** De jure slavery • **1790:** Naturalization Law
Mid 1800s: • Reforms for *"deserving poor"* but poorhouse still main option if poor • Emergence of mental facilities/institutions; non-profit "old age" homes; and proprietary boarding houses and private "homes" for non-indigent elders • Early planned "retirement communities" *1833: Sailor's Snug Harbor "Old worn out seaman"*	• **1830:** Indian Removal Act • **1846–1848:** Mexican–American War • **1850:** Compromise of 1850 • **1857:** Dred Scott Case • **1861–1865:** Civil War
Late 1800s – Early 1900s: • Early planned "retirement communities" *1889: William Enston Home* • Emergence of professional home care	• **1865–1877:** Reconstruction 13th, 14th, 15th amendments • Literacy tests, poll taxes, lynching • **1882:** Chinese Exclusion Act • **1887:** Dawes Act (allotment and assimilation) • **1896:** *Plessy v. Ferguson* • **1898:** Spanish–American War • **1890s – 1950s, 60s:** Jim Crow laws (restrictive ordinances or covenants that denied housing to racial and ethnic minorities) • Influx of immigrants—Slums, Eugenics movement

(continued)

(continued)

Housing for Older Adults in the U.S.	Race Relations in the U.S.
1900–1929: • More voluntary and non-profit old-age homes built (often on farms) • Urbanization: Less room for elders to live with family in cities (tenements) • Spread of tuberculosis ("consumption") leads to development of public institutions for chronic care • **1908:** Presidential Housing Commission (under Roosevelt) appointed to look into problem of slums in United States • **1914:** Arizona outlaws almshouses (poorhouses), provides pensions for old and disabled (declared unconstitutional in 1916) • **1918:** (Post WWI) Congress authorized loan program for housing construction for shipyard and defense workers	• **1902:** Extension of the Chinese Exclusion Act • **1908:** "Gentlemen's Agreement" (restriction of Japanese immigration to United States) • **1914–1918:** WWI • **1924:** Immigration Act (limits immigration through a national origin quota and prohibits immigration from Asian nations to United States)
The Depression: 1930–1941 • **1932:** Emergency Relief & Construction Act • **1934:** Feds move to eliminate care for old people in "public institutions" (poor houses) for cheaper alternatives (stay at home) • **1934:** National Housing Act creating the Federal Housing Administration (FHA) • **1935:** Social Security Act • **1937:** Federal Public Housing Program established • Fewer old women co-residing with their children • Decline in home care popularity	• **1930s:** Deportation of Mexicans and Mexican Americans • **1932–1972:** Tuskegee Syphilis Experiments • **1933–1942:** New Deal (original Social Security program) excluded farm workers and domestics (most of whom were people of color) • **1934:** National Housing Act (endorsed the practice of redlining) • **1934–1962:** Federal government underwrote 120 billion dollars in new housing; less than 2% went to people of color • **1937:** Housing Act (public housing, created greater racial segregation because majority of poor population at the time were minorities)

(continued)

(continued)

Housing for Older Adults in the U.S.	Race Relations in the U.S.
World War II: 1941–1945	• **1941:** Tuskegee Airmen (Army Air Corps) forms • **1941:** Executive Order 8802 (Fair Employment Practices Committee) • **1942:** Executive Order 9066 (authorized military areas in United States) • **1942 – 1946:** Internment of Japanese Americans • **1942 – 1964:** Bracero Program • **1944:** GI Bill (African American access limited, furthering segregation practices)
Baby Boom: 1946–1964 • **1946:** Hospital Survey and Construction (Hill-Burton) Act (financing for new hospital construction; led to conversion of older hospitals to nursing homes) • **1949:** Housing Act of 1949; beginning of modern era in federal housing programs • **1950–1956:** Amendments to Social Security Act led to increase in Feds paying for nursing home (NH) care • **1952:** NH Fire Hillsboro, MO	• **1949:** Housing Act of 1949—Public housing (Concentration of people of color in one place. Blacks exposed to largely public housing in central city.); urban renewal (90% of all housing destroyed by urban renewal not replaced. Two-thirds of those displaced were Black or Latino) • For most families of color who stayed in urban neighborhoods, the housing market open to them in the 1950s and 1960s was a rental market. (Rentals didn't gain equity) • **1950s:** "Operation Wetback" (deportation of Mexicans and Mexican Americans) • **1950–1953:** Korean War • **1952:** Voluntary Relocation Program *(later became 1962 Employment Assistance Program)* • **1952:** McCarren–Walter Act

(continued)

(continued)

Housing for Older Adults in the U.S.	Race Relations in the U.S.
• **1953:** State regulation of nursing homes/state. surveys of nursing homes emerged	• **1953:** Termination Act
• **1954:** 1st national survey of nursing homes	• **1954:** *Brown v. Board of Education*
• **1954:** Hill–Burton Act amended to include. development of skilled nursing facilities (SNF). Increase in for-profit SNF construction	• Civil Rights Movement, social movements by various groups of color
• **1957:** NH Fire Warrenton, MO	
• **1959:** Housing Act of 1959; provided public housing specifically for older persons; creation of: **Section 202** (loan program to build senior housing); **Section 231** (FHA Mortgage Insurance for Rental Senior Housing projects); Section 232 (loans to build SNF, ALF, B&C); Section 502 (rural housing loans)	• **1959–1975:** Vietnam War
• **1959:** Problems of the Aged and Aging Senate Subcommittee established over concerns regarding quality of NH care	
• **1960:** Kerr–Mills bill Old Age Assistance (OAA) amended and Medical Assistance for Aged (MAA) established	
• **1962:** Section 515 of Federal Housing Act	
• **1962:** Minimum age for Social Security lowered to 62 for reduced benefits	• **1963:** Equal Pay for Equal Work Act.
Post "Boom": 1964-Present	• **1964:** Civil Rights Act
• **1965:** Medicare and Older American's Act	• **1965:** Immigration and Nationality Act

(continued)

(continued)

Housing for Older Adults in the U.S.	Race Relations in the U.S.
• **1967:** Age Discrimination in Employment Act	• **1968:** Fair Housing Act (racial language was removed from federal housing policy) • "Block-busting": Real estate agents preyed on the fears of White homeowners to sell their homes quickly. (It wasn't Blacks moving in, it was White flight that caused housing values to go down.) • **1971:** Nixon's Fair Housing Policy of 1971—Undermined the Fair Housing Act (further exacerbated housing inequality by not supporting subsidized housing programs to help desegregation)
• **1974:** Section 8 of Federal Housing Act • **1974:** Housing and Community Development Act enacted (provided for low-income housing for the elderly and handicapped) • **1975:** OAA Amendments (grants to Indian tribal organizations for transportation, home care, home renovation/repair)	• **1974:** Equal Credit Opportunity Act of 1974—To supplement Fair Housing Act, protection against discrimination in lending practices • **1975:** The Home Mortgage Disclosure Act of 1975—To supplement Fair Housing Act, to prevent lending discrimination in certain localities • **1975:** Indian Self-Determination Act • **1977:** The Community Reinvestment Act of 1977—Required banks to apply the same anti-discriminatory guidelines to their lending criteria in all circumstances (did not completely stop discriminatory practices)
• **1980:** First Assisted Living Facility (ALF) opened in Portland, OR • **1983:** Social Security amended to gradually increase eligibility age for *full retirement* benefits from 65 to 67 (for persons born 1960 and later)	• **1980:** Refugee Act • **1986:** Immigration Reform and Control Act

(continued)

(continued)

Housing for Older Adults in the U.S.	Race Relations in the U.S.
• **1987:** Nursing Home Reform Act (OBRA; Ombudsman)	• **1988:** Fair Housing Amendments of 1988—Increased enforcement authority given to the federal government (discriminatory acts continue)
• **1990s:** Assisted Living (ALF) "boom"	• **1990:** Immigration Act of 1990
	• **1996:** Illegal Immigration Reform and Immigrant Responsibility Act of 1996
	• **1996:** Personal Responsibility and Work Opportunity Act
	• **2001:** 9/11/2001 terrorist attacks
	• **2001:** "War on Terror" originates
	• **2005:** Hurricane Katrina
• **2008:** First Baby Boomers (age 62) draws Social. Security retirement benefit	• **2008:** Barack Obama elected president of United States
• **2011:** First Baby Boomers turn 65	
	• **2016:** Donald Trump elected president of the United States

CONTENT SOURCES

Atchley, R. C. (1982). Retirement as a social institution. *Annual Review of Sociology, 8,* 263–287.

Atchley, R. C. (1987). *Aging: Continuity and change.* Belmont, CA: Wadsworth.

Blake, K. S., & Simic, A. (2005). *Elderly housing consumption: Historical patterns and projected trends.* Fairfax, VA: ICF Consulting.

Bridges, B., & Choudhury, S. (2009). Examining Social Security benefits as a retirement resource for near-retirees, by race and ethnicity, nativity, and disability status. *Social Security Bulletin, 69* (1), 19–44.

Bureau of Labor Statistics. (2015). Retrieved from http://www.bls.gov/cps

Costa, D. L. (1998). The evolution of retirement. In *The evolution of retirement: An American economic history, 1880–1990* (pp. 6–31). Chicago, IL: University of Chicago Press.

Davies, G. & Derthick, M. (1997). Race and social welfare policy: The Social Security Act of 1935. *Political Science Quarterly, 112*(2), 217–235.

ElderWeb. (2016). History of long term care (ElderWeb). Retrieved from www.elderweb.com/book/export/html/2806

Karasik, R. J., & Kishimoto, K. (2016). Is gerontology ready for anti-racist pedagogy? A survey of educators' practices and perspectives. *Gerontology and Geriatrics Education.* doi:10.1080/02701960.2015.1115984

Kastenberg, E. C., & Chasin, J. (2004). Elderly housing evolution of retirement: An American economic history, 1880–1990

Kishimoto, K. (2016). Anti-racist pedagogy: From faculty's self-reflection to organizing within and beyond the classroom. *Race Ethnicity and Education*. doi: 10.1080/13613324.2016.1248824

Lamb, C. M. (2005). *Housing segregation in suburban America since 1960*. Cambridge, UK: Cambridge University Press.

Lee, S. J., Parrott, K. R., & Ahn, M. (2014). Housing adequacy: A well-being indicator for elderly households in southern U.S. communities. *Family and Consumer Sciences Research Journal, 42*(3), 235–251.

Massey, D. S., & Denton, N. A. (1993). *American apartheid: Segregation and the making of the underclass*. Cambridge, MA: Harvard University Press.

McKernan, S. M., Ratcliffe, C., Steuerle, C. E., & Zhang, S. (2013). *Less than equal: Racial disparities in wealth accumulation*. Washington, DC: Urban Institute.

McNamara, T., & Williamson, J. (2004). Race, gender, and the retirement decisions of people ages 60 to 80: Prospects for age integration in employment. *International Journal of Aging and Human Development, 59*(3), 255–286.

Portacolone, E., & Halpern, J. (2014). "Move or suffer": Is age-segregation the new norm for older Americans living alone? *Journal of Applied Gerontology, 35* (8), 836–856. doi:10.1177/0733464814538118

Pounder, C. H., Adelman, L., Cheng, J., Herbes-Sommers, C., Strain, T. H., Smith, L., & Ragazzi, C. (2003). *Race: The power of an illusion [videorecording]*. San Francisco, CA: California Newsreel.

Ransom, R. L., & Sutch, R. (1986). The labor of older Americans: Retirement of men on and off the job, 1870–1937. *The Journal of Economic History, 46*(01), 1–30.

Seitles, M. (1998). The perpetuation of residential racial segregation in America: Historical discrimination, modern forms of exclusion, and inclusionary remedies. *Journal of Land Use & Environmental Law, 14*(1), 89–124.

Stoloff, J. A. (2004). *A brief history of public housing*. Paper presented at the annual meeting of the American Sociological Association, San Francisco, CA. Retrieved from http://citation.allacademic.com/meta/p_mla_apa_research_citation/1/0/8/8/5/p108852_index.html

Trotman, F. K. (2002). Historical, economic, and political contexts of aging in African America. *Journal of Women & Aging, 14*(3/4), 121–138.

U.S. Census Bureau. (n.d.). Website. Retrieved from http://www.census.gov

U.S. Census Bureau. (2015). ACS demographics and housing estimates from 2015. https://factfinder.census.gov/faces/tableservices/jsf/pages/productview.xhtml?pid=ACS_15_5YR_DP05&src=pt

Willamson, J. B. (1984). Old age relief policy prior to 1900: The trend toward restrictiveness. *American Journal of Economics and Sociology, 43*(3), 369–384.

Workplace Flexibility. (2010). *A timeline of the evolution of retirement in the United States*. Washington, DC: Georgetown University Law Center.

APPENDIX 6.5G: FACTORS THAT IMPACT PAST, CURRENT, AND FUTURE HOUSING

Consider these factors that would impact the past, current, and future housing situation of Samuel. Provide specific descriptions of what some of these factors would be for Samuel.

INDIVIDUAL

- Access to health care
- Education
- Functional status
- Health
- Income
- Internalized racism
- Mobility
- Race
- Social role
- Social support
- Socioeconomic status
- Values and beliefs

PUBLIC POLICY

- Federal Housing Administration Redlining
- Federal/State regulations
- G.I. Bill
- Housing Acts

HOUSING ENVIRONMENT

- Attitudes and values
- Culture
- Family relations
- Policies/Programs
- Race
- Racism

- Safety
- Services (health care to groceries)
- Social climate
- Staff characteristics
- Tenant population
- Transportation
- White flight

REFERENCES

Angel, J. L., & Angel, R. J. (2006). Minority group status and healthful aging: Social structure still matters. *American Journal of Public Health, 96*(7), 1152–1159.

Ferraro, K. F., & Shippee, T. P. (2009). Aging and cumulative inequality: How does inequality get under the skin? *The Gerontologist, 49*(3), 333–343.

Golant, S. M. (2015). *Aging in the right place.* Baltimore, MD: Health Professions Press.

Sheehan, N. W. (1992). *Successful administration of senior housing: Working with elderly residents.* Newbury Park, CA: Sage.

CHAPTER 7

PHYSICAL AGING

Rona J. Karasik and Tina M. Kruger

From current media portrayals, one might expect that aging is simply a series of significant losses and rapid, inevitable decline. Although there are certainly physical changes that occur as we grow older, this stereotyped and negative view of physical aging overlooks important nuances. For example, we do not all start with the same physical condition nor environment, and inequalities accumulate over time leading to very different aging experiences (Ferraro & Shippee, 2009). In fact, contrary to popular belief, there is greater heterogeneity, or *interindividual differences*, among older people than among their younger counterparts (Lowsky, Olshansky, Bhattacharya, & Goldman, 2014). While some people may require assistance (for example, glasses, hearing aids) early on in their lives, others may not encounter such changes until much later, if at all. *Intraindividual changes*, those that take place within a person, can similarly vary with regard to the onset and degree of change experienced. In other words, physical aging is experienced differently by everyone.

Additionally, much of what is generally thought of as *normal aging* (e.g., changes associated with time) is instead actually a function of *pathological aging* (e.g., changes associated with disease or illness). Examples of normal aging include *presbyopia* (characterized by gradual changes in vision leading to difficulty in focusing on close objects or reading small print; National Eye Institute, 2016; Saxon, Etten, & Perkins, 2015) and *presbycusis* (gradual changes in hearing leading to difficulty perceiving higher pitched sounds and/or distinguishing between certain consonant sounds; National Institute of Deafness and Other Communication Disorders [NIDCD], 2016). On the other hand, disease processes, such as *glaucoma* and *macular degeneration*, are examples of pathological changes (Saxon et al., 2015).

Although these conditions are more likely to affect people in their later years rather than when they are younger, their occurrence is not due to time alone. Moreover, such changes are not an inevitable part of aging; many older adults will never experience them (Saxon et al., 2015).

Rowe and Kahn (1987, 1997, 2015) further explored normal aging in terms of *usual aging* (no disease, but high risk) and *successful aging* (low risk of disease/disability, along with high levels of functioning and engagement). While the specific definition of successful aging is an ongoing debate (Martin et al., 2015; Stowe & Cooney, 2015), Rowe and Kahn's work shifted the focus of many away from pathology and toward the need to better understand the paradoxical nature of aging. On the one hand, age is the greatest risk factor for developing health problems and for dying. According to the Administration on Aging (AOA; 2015), "most older persons have at least one chronic condition and many have multiple conditions" (p. 12). On the other hand, the same report also notes that only a little over a third of older adults reported having any type of disability. Thus, people can experience limited or no impact of age-related risks or changes on their functioning and may perceive themselves to be aging successfully, regardless of failing to meet Rowe and Kahn's criteria.

For those older adults who do experience negative physical changes or poor health, interactions with health services providers are more frequent. It is vital that those who will interact with older adults in professional and health settings be well prepared to understand the variability of people's aging experiences. In teaching about physical aging, therefore, it is important to balance providing students with an understanding and empathy for the physical challenges some older adults might face with the important caveat that not all older adults are in poor health, nor do the stereotypical notions of physical aging happen to all, or even most, older adults.

HOUSING EDUCATION ACTIVITIES

The following activities offer the opportunity to provide such balance to students. In Activity 7.1, How It Feels to Be Old, participants experience simulated challenges with vision, hearing, and mobility while they attempt to perform ordinary tasks. Similarly, Activity 7.2, Hands-On Experience With the Americans With Disabilities Act (ADA), uses an obstacle course to raise participants' awareness of how the physical environment can influence one's ability to be independent.

Activity 7.3, Hearing Aids and Pizza, provides participants with hands-on experience, not only with the challenges of hearing impairment, but also with the intricacies of using adaptive technology (e.g., hearing aids). In this activity, students are asked to wear hearing aids in a variety of settings, as well as to perform basic maintenance (e.g., changing and testing the hearing aid batteries) that users are routinely called upon to do.

Finally, Activity 7.4, Thinking Critically About Autonomy and Dependency in Aging, challenges participants to step back from specific aging pathologies to reflect on the connections (and disjoints) between autonomy and independence. Recognizing that we all depend on others in a variety of ways (e.g., making the clothes we wear), this activity highlights the true meaning of autonomy (being able to enact personally meaningful choices) and the ways in which depending on others can facilitate autonomy throughout life.

REFERENCES

Administration on Aging. (2015). *A profile of older Americans: 2015.* Retrieved from https://www.acl.gov/sites/default/files/Aging%20and%20Disability%20 in%20America/2015-Profile.pdf

Ferraro, K. F., & Shippee, T. P. (2009). Aging and cumulative inequality: How does inequality get under the skin? *The Gerontologist, 49*(3), 333–343. doi:10.1093/ geront/gnp034

Lowsky, D. J., Olshansky, S. J., Bhattacharya, J., & Goldman, D. P. (2014). Heterogeneity in healthy aging. *Journals of Gerontology Series A: Biological Sciences and Medical Sciences, 69*(6), 640–649. doi:10.1093/gerona/glt162

Martin, P., Kelly, N., Kahana, B., Kahana, E., Willcox, B. J., Willcox, D. C., & Poon, L. W. (2015). Defining successful aging: A tangible or elusive concept? *The Gerontologist, 55*(1), 14–25.

National Eye Institute. (2016). Facts about presbyopia. Retrieved from https://nei .nih.gov/health/presbyopia

National Institute of Deafness and Other Communication Disorders. (2016). Age-related hearing loss. Retrieved from https://www.nidcd.nih.gov/health/ age-related-hearing-loss

Rowe, J. W., & Kahn, R. L. (1987). Human aging: Usual and successful. *Science, 237*(4811), 143–149.

Rowe, J. W., & Kahn, R. L. (1997). Successful aging. *The Gerontologist, 37*(4), 433–440.

Rowe, J. W., & Kahn, R. L. (2015). Successful aging 2.0: Conceptual expansions for the 21st century. *Journals of Gerontology Series B: Psychological Sciences and Social Sciences, 70*(4), 593–596.

Saxon, S., Etten, M. J., & Perkins, E. (2015). *Physical change & aging: A guide for the helping professions* (6th ed.). New York, NY: Springer Publishing.

Stowe, J. D., & Cooney, T. M. (2015). Examining Rowe and Kahn's concept of successful aging: Importance of taking a life course perspective. *The Gerontologist, 55*(1), 43–50.

ACTIVITY 7.1 HOW IT FEELS TO BE OLD

Hallie E. Baker

ACTIVITY INFORMATION

Type

____X____ In class

_____ Online

_____ Take home

_____ In community

Difficulty

____X____ Introductory

_____ Intermediate

_____ Advanced

OVERVIEW

This activity, based on the work of Pastalan (1979), builds on one from Dr. Baker's first gerontology class in the early 1990s. To this day she still remembers it as one of the inspirations of her love of gerontology.

The goal then and now is to help students who are often in prime physical health understand what the physical changes that occur with aging really mean. With a focus on the changes that occur with normal biological aging, the activity provides a more universal version of the aging experience. Specific changes highlighted include the yellowing of the lenses of the eye, impairments in mobility caused by changes in the feet such as bunions or arthritis, loss of mobility in the hands, and hearing loss. Two abnormal aspects of physical aging are included, specifically hearing loss and the impact of arthritis. Hearing loss was added to emphasize how important it is for the students to take action now and throughout their life course to protect their hearing to maximize their hearing in later life. From 2010 to 2012, 49.7% of individuals 64 or older have a diagnosis of arthritis, making it the most common chronic condition for older adults (Hootman, Helmick, Barbour, Theis, & Boring, 2016). Thus, it is important for students to understand the impact the condition can have on elders.

The activity provides a break from lectures and a chance to interact with peers and faculty. Further, students develop critical thinking and problem-solving skills as they seek to cope with their new "condition." Often students laugh and joke as they complete the activity, but they do come away with the message about the physical changes and which changes they can prevent versus which ones are normal, but not life ending, simply something one learns to work around.

ACTIVITY LEARNING GOALS

Following this activity, students should be able to . . .

- Provide practical applications of in-class discussions about physical aging, specifically normal biological changes.
- Identify and discuss how physical aging might affect everyday life for an elder.

ASSOCIATION FOR GERONTOLOGY IN HIGHER EDUCATION COMPETENCIES

- Relate biological theory and science to understanding senescence, longevity, and variation in aging.
- Develop a gerontological perspective through knowledge and self-reflection.

MINIMUM/MAXIMUM NUMBER OF PARTICIPANTS

- 10 to 50

TIME NEEDED TO IMPLEMENT ACTIVITY

- 20 minutes

SETTING

- A classroom with area to walk about in, either a hallway or large clear area in the classroom

MATERIALS

Required

1. Paper bags to hold each kit (12)
2. Gardening gloves pairs (cheap brown ones)—enough for 12 kits
3. Candy
   a. It is suggested that one use plain M&Ms and Skittles, individually packaged like those given at Halloween, to provide sanitary conditions for the candy prior to the students consuming it.
   b. Be sure to ask about food allergies! If anyone has food allergies, adapt the activity (specifically the candy) as needed. Dr. Baker usually asks about it a couple weeks before doing the activity.
   c. Dr. Baker usually buys extra so everyone in the class can get at least one bag of candy. This practice keeps the peace in the classroom.

4. Orange or yellow translucent plastic, to cover the eyes or look through
5. Bag of soup beans
6. Cotton balls

PROCEDURES

Preparation

Create the kits so they contain: a pair of gardening gloves (cheap brown ones), two cotton balls, yellow or orange plastic, two packets each of M&Ms and Skittles (like given at Halloween) or more if possible, and the activity worksheet.

Introduction

After the lecture(s) on physical aging, introduce the activity and split the class into groups of four to five members.

Activity

1. Instruct students to pick a scribe (someone to do the writing) and someone to come up and get their kit.
   a. Note Dr. Baker usually gives candy to everyone, but makes them come get it during the activity to encourage the individuals with different conditions to have to move about and engage with the environment.
2. Allow 10 to 15 minutes to complete the exercise.
3. As the instructor one will need to move around and speak with each group, engaging them about how their "condition" impacts them. Include what those conditions would impact in their everyday life and plans for their idealized retirement.

Discussion/Reflection

- The worksheet includes reflection, but often the groups will discuss with each other and within the groups beyond the worksheet prompts.
- It is important for the instructor to move about the class prompting discussion within the groups.

Wrap-Up

- Call the groups back together as a class and ask for reactions.
  - Prompt discussion by asking them what they thought. Ask if there were any surprises, how they overcame any challenges, or if they were frustrated by anything.
- Validate and reflect back any themes or comments the students provide.
- Be aware and address any negative or ageist comments that arise during the discussion, using the comments as a chance to discuss coping strategies and concepts such as selection, optimization, and compensation.

- Note if you saw any creative problem solving by individuals or group members.
  - Once Dr. Baker observed the "arthritis" individual teaming up with the visually impaired member. The one with limited hand mobility provided the eyes for the pill sorting task while the individual with eye issues provided the hands to do the task. This was pointed out to the class and connected to coping strategies often used by individuals who are aging to maximize their self-esteem and function.
- Collect the worksheets at the end of the time.

Assessment

- The worksheet is handed in and can provide insight into how the students did.
- Credit can be provided for participation or a grade assigned along with using the feedback to assess the activity's effectiveness.
- Dr. Baker also will add an essay question to the next exam specifically asking the students to identify two or three physical changes that occur with age with an example of how each would impact everyday life.

  - For students present for the activity, the answers reflect the experience and the examples often come from the activity itself. For students who missed that class day, scores tend to be lower with fewer being able to identify the changes and their examples are of a lesser quality or missing altogether.

ADDITIONAL CONSIDERATIONS

- The instructor needs to encourage the students to really try it and get into the exercise. They will have fun with it. Also, if one is able they should bring the extra candy to class and give it out. The students not acting out the roles that require candy will be thankful and not jealous.

REFERENCES

Hootman, J. M., Helmick, C. G., Barbour, K. E., Theis, K. A., & Boring, M. A. (2016). Updated projected prevalence of self-reported doctor-diagnosed arthritis and arthritis-attributable activity limitation among US adults, 2015–2040. *Arthritis and Rheumatology, 68*(7), 1582–1587. doi:10.1002/art.39692

Pastalan, L. (1979). Sensory changes and environmental behavior. In T. O. Byerts, S. C. Howell, & L. A. Pastalan (Eds.), *Environmental context of aging: Life-styles, environmental quality, and living arrangements. (pp. 118–126)* New York, NY: Garland STPM Press.

APPENDIX 7.1: "HOW IT FEELS TO BE OLD" WORKSHEET

Group members:

1. _____
2. _____
3. _____
4. _____
5. _____

TASKS

Group member with "arthritis" (wearing the gloves) separate out six different colored pills and pick them up.

Group member with "bunions" (beans in their shoes) make two laps of the classroom.

Group member with "hearing issue" (cotton balls in ears) sit still and listen to the group work.

Group member with "old eyes" (using the colored plastic) pick out:

1-red skittle, 1-blue M&M, 2-orange "pills," 1-green skittle, and 1-red M&M.

1. For the individual with "arthritis" what is your reaction to your task? What did you have to do to complete the task?
2. For the individual with "old eyes" what is your reaction to your task? What did you have to do to complete the task?
3. For the individual with "bunions" what is your reaction to your task? What did you have to do to complete the task?
4. For the individual with "hearing issues" what is your reaction to your task? What did you have to do to complete the task?
5. How might these conditions impact your day-to-day living?
6. For those who didn't have a condition, what did you see? What's your reaction?
7. Other comments?

ACTIVITY 7.2 HANDS-ON EXPERIENCE WITH THE AMERICANS WITH DISABILITIES ACT (ADA)

Phyllis A. Greenberg

ACTIVITY INFORMATION

Type

__X__	In class
_____	Online
_____	Take home
__X__	In community

Difficulty

__X__	Introductory
__X__	Intermediate
__X__	Advanced

This activity can be modified to suit all levels and for both in class and in community.

OVERVIEW

This activity covers aspects of universal design, the Americans with Disabilities Act (ADA), and accessibility for persons with varying abilities and challenges in public spaces. To make the activity interactive an obstacle course was created in which participants (students, staff, faculty, and community members) attempted to maneuver with a range of simulated disabilities. Wheelchairs and walkers were used to simulate mobility issues, ear plugs were used to simulate hearing loss, and vision goggles were used to simulate types of visual impairments. Participants were asked to read signs, understand and follow simple instructions/directions, travel over carpeting and laminated floors, and maneuver through a "hallway" created by tables and chairs that followed ADA regulations for width.

There are a variety of components that can be used to demonstrate how persons with physical mobility, hearing and vision limitations, and the design of physical spaces can create challenges that persons without these challenges may not be aware of. The "course" is designed for students, staff, faculty, community members, and partners to experience trying to navigate "challenges" that are faced by people with varying abilities on a daily basis.

ACTIVITY LEARNING GOALS

Following this activity, students, community members, and participants should be able to . . .

- Have greater understanding of the ADA.
- Have greater awareness of the limitations of the ADA to ensure that people with physical challenges (i.e., mobility, vision, and hearing) have access to government, social, and recreational spaces.
- Have greater awareness and empathy for those with physical challenges as they, albeit momentarily, struggle with navigating the built environment even in those areas that comply with ADA regulations.

ASSOCIATION FOR GERONTOLOGY IN HIGHER EDUCATION COMPETENCIES

- Relate psychological theories and science to understanding adaptation, stability, and change in aging.
- Adhere to ethical principles to guide work with and on behalf of older persons.
- Engage collaboratively with others to promote integrated approaches to aging.
- Promote older persons' strengths and adaptations to maximize well-being, health, and mental health.
- Promote quality of life and positive social environment for older persons.
- Employ and design programmatic and community development with and on behalf of the aging population.
- Employ and generate policy to equitably address the needs of older persons.

MINIMUM/MAXIMUM NUMBER OF PARTICIPANTS

- 10 to 50

TIME NEEDED TO IMPLEMENT ACTIVITY

- Approximately 45 minutes, depending on the number of wheelchairs, goggles, and so on, and the number of activity guides. Each participant takes about 5 to 10 minutes to complete the course. Participants should also be allowed approximately 20 minutes for set-up time.

SETTING(S)

- Could be in a classroom or open space as long as you can arrange barriers and make use of wheelchairs, walkers, ear plugs, and vision goggles.

MATERIALS

Required

- Wheelchairs, walkers, low vision simulation device (goggles), ear plugs, eye chart, pre–post survey or document for students to read/fill out during the activity, tables and chairs or something to create a hallway/doorway if using an open space. You will need a tape measure or yardstick to be sure you are adhering to ADA specifications.

Optional

- Canes, carpet swatches, or something to make minor change in the flooring elevation.

PROCEDURES

Preparation

Using measurements/requirements from ADA (see Appendix 7.2B), set up a course that requires participants to navigate either while in a wheelchair, using a walker, using vision goggles or ear plugs, or all three. Do not do this near stairs. You need a sufficient number of volunteers (students) to help guide participants through the course. The course can be set-up using tables and chairs if in an open space.

Introduction

Pretest (see Appendix 7.2A) to determine knowledge participants have regarding the ADA or persons with physical challenges and what challenges might be experienced in trying to navigate the built environment. Participants are asked such questions as "Have you heard of the Americans with Disabilities Act?" and "Do you think your community (building, facility) is accessible for people with disabilities?"

Activity

After completing the pretest (see Appendix 7.2A), participants are randomly assigned the use of a wheelchair, walker, or vision simulation goggles and earplugs. They are instructed to complete the obstacle course, which includes reading directions with goggles or having someone verbally give the instructions while the participant is wearing ear plugs. They are asked to read an eyechart and then navigate a course that meets ADA specifications in a wheelchair or using a walker (i.e., 3-foot width). The course has been designed using long tables and chairs to construct a hallway/doorway in open spaces. This provides barriers that participants must navigate through.

Discussion/Reflection

After completing (or attempting to complete) the activity, participants are asked to complete a posttest (see Appendix 7.2A). An activity guide will review the posttest and ask if they were surprised at how difficult or easy it was to complete the activity.

Wrap-Up

The participant is given a handout that provides an overview of the ADA (see Appendix 7.2B) and the issues that persons with physical challenges might have with navigating the built environment.

Assessment

- Analysis of pre/post surveys

ADDITIONAL CONSIDERATIONS

Low vision goggles (www.lowvisionsimulators.com/product/full-set) are recommended over cardboard glasses. They are sustainable and provide a more accurate visual experience and a greater variety of visual limitations. Having students act as activity guides is very important. Having people who have not experienced physical challenges try to complete the obstacle course is very "eye opening" for them. Do not do this near stairs. This would be a great experience for architects and administrators at universities, schools, and government officials so they would have a better idea of how important the built environment is. They may often follow the letter of ADA but not always the intent.

CONTENT SOURCES

U. S. Department of Justice, Civil Rights Division. (n.d.). Information and technical assistance on the Americans With Disabilities Act. Retrieved from https://www.ada.gov/ada_intro.htm

U.S. Department of Labor. Americans With Disabilities Act. Retrieved from https://www.dol.gov/general/topic/disability/ada

APPENDIX 7.2A: PRE- AND POSTTEST QUESTIONS

HANDS-ON EXPERIENCE WITH THE AMERICANS WITH DISABILITIES ACT (ADA): PRETEST SURVEY QUESTIONS

Please circle the answers as they relate to you.

1. How many years have you been at (name of institution)?
   a. Less than 1 year
   b. 1 to 2 years
   c. 3 to 5 years
   d. More than 5 years
   e. N/A
2. Are you a faculty or staff, a student, or a community member?
   a. Faculty or staff
   b. Student
   c. Community member
   d. N/A
3. How much do you know about the ADA?
   a. A lot
   b. A little bit
   c. Never heard
4. Do you think your community is accessible for people with disabilities?
   a. Yes
   b. No
5. Have you ever heard of universal design?
   a. Yes
   b. No
6. Please circle any of the following that you have used.
   Earplugs
   Walker
   Wheelchair
   Crutches
7. Do you know where the emergency/fire alarms are?
   a. Yes
   b. No

HANDS-ON EXPERIENCE WITH THE AMERICANS WITH DISABILITIES ACT (ADA): POSTTEST SURVEY QUESTIONS

Please circle the answers as they relate to you.

1. Please circle any of the following that you had difficulty with.

   Earplugs

   Walker

   Wheelchair

   Goggles

2. Please circle which caused the most difficulty for you and indicate why.

   Earplugs

   Walker

   Wheelchair

   Goggles

   Why? _____

   _____

   _____

3. Now that you have had this experience, do you think your community is accessible for people with disabilities?

   a. Yes

   b. No

4. What recommendations do you have to increase accessibility?

   _____

   _____

   _____

   Thanks for your participation!

APPENDIX 7.2B: ADA HANDOUT

After completing the pretest, course, and posttest participants were given the following.

DID YOU KNOW?

Americans With Disabilities Act (ADA)

- The ADA was enacted in 1990.
- ADA "prohibits discrimination against people with disabilities in . . . "
  - Employment
  - Transportation
  - Public accommodation
  - Communications
  - Government activities
- An individual with a disability is a person who
  - Has a physical or mental impairment that substantially limits one or more major life activities;
  - Has a record of such impairment; or
  - Is regarded as having such an impairment.
- Advocacy resources:
  - American Association of People With Disabilities (AAPD)
  - Disabled American Veterans (DAV)
  - National Association of the Deaf
  - National Coalition on Self-Determination (NCSD)
  - World Institute on Disability (WID)

Public Accommodations and ADA

Public Accommodations must

- Provide goods and services in an integrated setting;
- Furnish auxiliary aids when necessary to ensure effective communication;
- Remove architectural and structural communication barriers in existing facilities where readily achievable;
- Provide equivalent transportation services;
- Maintain accessible features of facilities and equipment; and
- Design and construct new facilities and, when undertaking alterations, alter existing facilities in accordance with the ADA Accessibility Guidelines.

  Examples of areas impacted by accessible design:

- Elevators

- Drinking fountain knee clearance and spout height
- Single user toilet door swing
- Detectable warnings
- Slope and clear floor space
- Maneuvering clearance

Universal design is the design of products and environments to be usable by all people, to the greatest extent possible, without the need for adaptation or specialized design.

For more information, see www.ada.gov/ada_title_III.htm.

ACTIVITY 7.3 HEARING AIDS AND PIZZA

Elaine M. Shuey and Susan Dillmuth-Miller

ACTIVITY INFORMATION

Type

__X__   In class

_____   Online

_____   Take home

_____   In community

Difficulty

__X__   Introductory

_____   Intermediate

_____   Advanced

OVERVIEW

According to the National Institutes of Health, 33% of people age 65 to 74 have some degree of hearing loss. That increases to 50% after age 75. Older adults often get hearing aids but discontinue use due to difficulty acclimating to them. Hearing aid management can be problematic, as modern hearing aids are small and require dexterity and visual acuity to manipulate. Further, professionals who aren't audiologists or speech-language pathologists often are afraid to help with their management. The hearing aid activity was designed for students in a communication and aging class to learn how to manipulate and manage the use and care of hearing aids. They learn why the acclimatization process is difficult by experiencing what it is like to wear a hearing aid in a public place while eating pizza together in the student union. Students come from a variety of majors and hopefully after this activity will understand why older adults have difficulty listening in noise with their hearing aids and feel comfortable changing a battery, manipulating the controls, cleaning, and helping to place the hearing aid in a person's ear.

KEY TERMS

Conductive hearing loss
Hearing aids
Presbycusis
Sensorineural hearing loss

ACTIVITY LEARNING GOALS

Following this activity, students should be able to . . .

- Change the battery on a hearing aid.
- Test the battery on a hearing aid.
- Manipulate the volume control and program buttons on a hearing aid.
- Clean a hearing aid and insert it in a user's ear.
- Describe how users can acclimate to hearing aid use and may still experience difficulties listening in noisy backgrounds.

ASSOCIATION FOR GERONTOLOGY IN HIGHER EDUCATION COMPETENCIES

- Promote older persons' strengths and adaptations to maximize well-being, health, and mental health.
- Promote quality of life and positive social environment for older persons.
- Develop a gerontological perspective through knowledge and self-reflection.
- Relate biological theory and science to understanding senescence, longevity, and variation in aging.

MINIMUM/MAXIMUM NUMBER OF PARTICIPANTS

- 20 to 40

TIME NEEDED TO IMPLEMENT ACTIVITY

- 2 hours

SETTING(S)

- Classroom with chairs; then public place

MATERIALS
Required

- Enough behind-the-ear hearing aids for at least half the class. One battery tester and a battery for each aid. A generic ear piece for each student. Hearing aid brush and wax loop. Materials to cut tubing length if needed.

PROCEDURES
Preparation (2 hours for students new to the topic)

- Explain the basic process of how we hear
  - Parts of the ear
  - How sound is transmitted from the world to the brain

- o Explain conductive versus sensorineural hearing loss (which includes presbycusis)
- Explain presbycusis—the hearing loss that occurs with age
  - o Discuss prevalence data
- Introduce hearing aids
  - o Look at different types with photos and actual aids if possible
  - o Review what a hearing aid does and doesn't do
  - o Discuss impediments to hearing aid use including cost, social resistance, cognitive issues, dexterity issues, declining vision, and lack of assistance with hearing aid use and care

Introduction (1–1.5 hours depending on size of class)

- The audiologist introduces a behind-the-ear hearing aid: parts, testing the battery, inserting the battery, cleaning the hearing aid, volume, and other controls.
- The audiologist checks participants' ears with an otoscope to see if it is safe to wear the aid.
  - o If the class is large, examination of ears may have to be done prior to class.
- Distribute the aids, cut the tubing to fit each individual, place the aid appropriately on the student, and adjust the volume.
  - o Prior to class, the aids are adjusted so that the maximum output is set for a mild hearing loss.
  - o If the class is large, students could work in pairs for this, with one wearing the aid for the first half of the activity and the other wearing it for the second half.

Activity (1.5 hours)

- Go to a noisy public place and engage in conversation; if students are sharing an aid, switch at the midpoint.
- Possible locations/activities:
  - o Share pizza at the dining hall or union.
  - o Students and faculty bring food and eat at an area that will provide background noise.
  - o Attend a sporting event as a class, being certain that it won't be too loud.
  - o Gather at a noisy place and simply converse.

Discussion/Reflection (1 hour)

- Return to the classroom to remove the batteries and clean the aids.
- Discuss problems encountered with the aid or with communication.
- Relate aging issues such as visual and dexterity issues to the use of the aid.

Wrap-Up (1 hour)

- Continue the discussion the following week/class to see what other hearing observations students have made throughout the week.

Assessment

- Test questions about hearing aid facts
  - Types of aids, controls, and parts
  - Lists, multiple choice, and identifying on a diagram
- Open-ended questions about hearing aid use
  - Difficulties with use specifically related to older adults (dexterity, visual, or cognitive issues)
  - Hindrances to usage of aids in general (cost and appearance)
- Journal type report of the experience

ADDITIONAL CONSIDERATIONS

- Students enjoy the activity and feel more confident in helping clients/patients deal with hearing aids.

RECOMMENDED RESOURCES

- Information on the general anatomy of the ear and how sound is transmitted to the brain.
  - www.betterhearing.org/hearingpedia/how-we-hear
  - www.asha.org/public/hearing/How-We-Hear
- Information on hearing loss in general and presbycusis in particular.
  - www.nidcd.nih.gov/health/hearing/Pages/older.aspx
  - www.nidcd.nih.gov/health/hearing-loss-older-adults
- Descriptions of the various types of hearing aids and information on what a hearing aid does to the sound.
  - www.nidcd.nih.gov/health/hearing/pages/hearingaid.aspx
  - www.betterhearing.org/hearingpedia/hearing-aids
  - www.asha.org/public/hearing/Hearing-Aids

ACTIVITY 7.4 THINKING CRITICALLY ABOUT AUTONOMY AND DEPENDENCY IN AGING

Russell J. Woodruff

ACTIVITY INFORMATION

Type

  __X__   In class

  _____   Online

  _____   Take home

  _____   In community

Difficulty

  __X__   Introductory

  _____   Intermediate

  _____   Advanced

OVERVIEW

There is a common tendency to see autonomy as synonymous with independence, implying that dependency means a loss of autonomy. Based on an understanding of autonomy developed by George Agich (1990), this activity challenges the identification of autonomy and independence, and reveals how dependencies can in many cases promote autonomy.

Agich provides a way to understand which dependencies are threats to autonomy and which are not by conceiving of autonomy not in terms of minimal constraints on one's choices ("ideal autonomy"), but in terms of being able to identify with one's choices—what he calls "actual autonomy." For example, a college philosophy professor's self-conception and conception of a personal good life might typically involve teaching and writing philosophical essays. Such a person's sense of who they are—their self-identity—is defined by those choices, and not, for example, with the choice to make one's own clothes. The person chooses to be completely dependent on others to supply their clothing, thus allowing them to attend to other activities with which they more strongly identify. Agich provides the following example to illustrate the difference between the concrete concept of "actual autonomy" and the abstract concept of "ideal autonomy" that he finds prevalent in liberal political philosophy:

> The paradigm case of an actually autonomous person and a liberal nonautonomous person would be a wheelchair-bound individual assisted by others in various activities of daily living. At the same time, this person is devoted to

the cause of Food for Peace (FFP). What this woman can do for FFP is limited, yet she identifies strongly with it. She stuffs envelopes twice a week for the local chapter and rejoices when she sees a television feature on FFP's projects. She has visitors from FFP. Her choices are meaningful in the context of her identifications with FFP. She does not care whether she has her bath at 6:00 am on Thursday or at 2:00 on Friday. Not all choices matter to her, just those that are meaningful in terms of her participatory identification in a larger social context. (p. 15)

The dependencies of the philosophy professor and Agich's FFP member enhance autonomy, allowing each to act in ways that matter to them. In Agich's words, such dependencies "help to maintain a sense of functional integrity in the areas of life that individuals value" (p. 16).

The activity presented here is designed to be a practical exploration of Agich's model of the relations between autonomy and dependency. The first part of this activity—the reading—is best done in advance at home. The follow-up questions should then be answered by students individually, either at home or in the classroom or community setting. The discussion portion is carried out with the whole group, either in class or in the community. The required reading is at an intermediate level, and activity leaders may find it desirable to condense or annotate the reading for some participants. Once the concept of "actual autonomy" is grasped, the activity itself is at an introductory level.

ACTIVITY LEARNING GOALS

Following this activity, students should be able to . . .

- Identify cases in which dependencies can undermine autonomy.
- Identify cases in which dependencies can preserve or promote autonomy.
- Describe the basis for such identifications.
- Apply this model to the lives of older adults.

ASSOCIATION FOR GERONTOLOGY IN HIGHER EDUCATION COMPETENCIES

- Develop comprehensive and meaningful concepts, definitions, and measures for well-being of older adults and their families, grounded in humanities and arts.
- Develop a gerontological perspective through knowledge and self-reflection.
- Promote older persons' strengths and adaptations to maximize well-being, health, and mental health.
- Engage in research to advance knowledge and improve interventions for older persons.

TIME NEEDED TO IMPLEMENT ACTIVITY

- 70 minutes

SETTING(S)

- Classroom or meeting space

MATERIALS

- Agich, "Reassessing Autonomy in Long Term Care"; pen and paper or computer

PROCEDURES

Preparation

- Have students read Agich prior to meeting.

Activity

Have each student write out, either in advance or in class, answers to the following five questions. If the time spent in group will be relatively short, it is best if their answers are prepared in advance at home, as that will allow more time for discussion and reflection.

1. Identify five ways in which you are dependent upon others.
2. Determine which if any of these dependencies hinder your actual autonomy, that is, restrict your ability to act in ways that matter to you.
3. Determine which if any of these dependencies promote your actual autonomy, allowing you to act in ways that matter to you.
4. Consider how growing older might affect these two sets of dependencies. Among dependencies that might hinder your actual autonomy, do you foresee any as becoming more likely to occur as you age? Could any autonomy-hindering dependencies become less likely? What about the dependencies that promote actual autonomy: Are any of these likely to be enhanced or diminished as you age?
5. Consider the older adults in your lives: Do you see dependencies in their lives that hinder their autonomy? Do you see dependencies that preserve or promote their autonomy?

Discussion/Reflection

Instructors have several options for facilitating discussion. Which option is best depends on factors such as the time available, the number of participants, and the participants' comfort level with each other and the instructor. Ideally all participants should share their responses in class with at least one other person. With a small group, especially with those who already know each other, this can be achieved by the instructor simply asking each member to share their answers to the questions with the whole group. With a larger group it may be more effective to have participants share their responses initially with a subgroup, such as by means of the "pair, square, share" technique: have students pair up to discuss their answers, then form groups of four, then have each group report to the larger class.

Whichever format is chosen, the following guidelines can aid discussion:

1. Instructors should ask the students to listen carefully to their peers' responses, and to identify any similarities, differences, and patterns that emerge.

2. Given that Question 4 specifically addresses the relationships between aging, autonomy, and dependency, particular attention should be paid to the answers to it. Instructors may choose to solicit answers to the first three questions and discuss those first, before moving on to focus on Question 4.

3. If the group has participants of different ages, it is worthwhile to attend to the ways that their answers might differ. For example, typical undergraduates often note that dependencies upon their parents will likely decrease while differing on whether those decreases will likely hinder or enhance autonomy. Older participants will likely have different perspectives, and the contrasts can be illuminating.

4. When older adults are participants, or when participants have thought carefully about the extent to which dependencies enhance or restrict the autonomy of the elders that they know (Question 5), an opening is created for a further discussion of the ways in which individuals or institutions can work to ensure that the dependencies in elders' lives are as far as possible autonomy-enhancing, or at least not autonomy-restricting.

Wrap-Up

Reiterate the main point about dependency as not necessarily being the enemy of autonomy; and summarize any other conclusions derived from the group's work, as well as any areas for further exploration.

Assessment

Students will have achieved the learning goals when they can examine the life situations of specific individuals and clearly distinguish any dependencies of those individuals that undermine their actual autonomy from any dependencies that preserve or enhance it. Achievement can be assessed by examining the responses students wrote for this activity, or, better yet, by reviewing a follow-up assignment in which students are required to apply this framework to one or more new cases, for example, conducting semi-structured interviews of elders to elicit how those elders' dependencies affect their actual autonomy.

ADDITIONAL CONSIDERATIONS

Another good article for students to read in this context is Lustbader's "Thoughts on the Meaning of Frailty" (1999). Her hypothetical description of being cared for in a long-term care facility captures from a first-person perspective a number of the points Agich makes about the possibility of autonomy in the face of dependency: "being known," being "difficult," and having "a conversation rather than a feeding" are ways in which the self is asserted, thus creating the possibility that one can identify with the actions that others do on one's behalf.

Woodruff (2016) frames the issue of the relation between dependency and autonomy in terms of the maintenance of dignity, which he understands as the capacity for creating meaningfulness in one's life. He argues that the capacities for making meaning are generally distinct from, and not as easily compromised as, the capacities involved in the activities of daily life (ADLs), such as bathing and cooking. Thus, ADL dependencies do not necessarily undermine what matters most to people.

REFERENCES

Agich, G. (1990). Reassessing autonomy in long-term care. *Hastings Center Report, 20*(6), 12–17.

Lustbader, W. (1999). Thoughts on the meaning of frailty. *Generations, 23*(4), 21–24.

Woodruff, R. (2016). Aging and the maintenance of dignity. In G. Scarre (Ed.), *The Palgrave handbook of the philosophy of aging* (pp. 225–246). London, UK: Palgrave Macmillan.

CHAPTER 8

PUBLIC POLICY AND AGING

Phyllis A. Greenberg

Public policy is an essential component to quality of life for older adults and provides funding and guidelines for the agencies and staff that provide services. Oftentimes, students may find this topic to be dry and not pertaining to their lives. This can be a challenge for those who teach in gerontology. Social Security, Medicare/Medicaid, and the Older Americans Act (OAA) often seem distant and remote—"that is just for old people" and "those programs won't even exist when I am old." How do you make it come alive, interesting, accessible, and relevant? Or is it "urban myth" that students do not want to learn and are disconnected from public policy in general and age-based policy in particular? A review of literature showed that there were no current studies on this topic, but those of us who teach and write about policy know this is no myth.

First, here is a "primer" on age-based policy. A link to sites where you can find additional information is included for each of the primary age-based policies—Social Security, Medicare/Medicaid, and the OAA.

SOCIAL SECURITY

Enacted in 1935 under President Franklin D. Roosevelt, during the height of the Depression, this was the first large-scale social insurance program in the United States. At its inception, it was a retirement system for people 65+. Over the years several programs have been added, and, for the Baby Boomers, the age of eligibility has changed. The oldest of the Baby Boom Generation (1946–1964) are the first cohort that will not be able to collect full benefits at age 65 under Social Security, but will need to wait until they turn 66.

Resources

- National Academy of Social Insurance—www.nasi.org/learn/socialsecurity/overview
- Social Security Administration—www.ssa.gov/history/briefhistory3.html
- Social Security Administration video history—www.ssa.gov/history/video
- Glossary of Social Security Terms—www.ssa.gov/agency/glossary

MEDICARE/MEDICAID

In 1965, President Lyndon Johnson initially sought to provide health insurance to older adults (Medicare for people age 65+) and persons with low incomes (Medicaid). Over the years both programs have changed to expand the numbers of persons covered. The two also differ in funding sources. **Medicare** is funded by the federal government and through taxes. **Medicaid** is also funded through the federal government, but individual states are required to provide matching funds to receive any federal monies.

Originally, Medicare consisted of two parts: Part A, Hospital Insurance; and Part B, Medical Insurance. Two more parts have been added: Part C, Medicare Advantage; and Part D, Prescription Drug Coverage. Medicare (A and B) *does not* provide coverage for dental care/dentures, hearing aids, and glasses. Under Part C one contracts with a private insurance company, pays higher premiums, and can receive comprehensive coverage.

Medicaid eligibility is based on need. Medicaid has a much broader scope of coverage than Medicare (A and B) and is the primary source of payment for long-term-care (nursing home) services. People can be on both Medicaid and Medicare. Eligibility for Medicaid varies from state to state and is usually based on income and medical needs.

Resources

- www.medicare.gov
- www.cms.gov

OLDER AMERICANS ACT

This program was enacted in 1965 under President Lyndon Johnson. It was the first federal level program that was age-based policy (age 60+). The funding for the OAA is federal and based on a formula that includes general population, population of older adults, cost of living, and incomes. Such services as Meals on Wheels, senior centers, employment, transportation, congregate nutrition, and education are at the core of the OAA.

Resource

- www.cms.gov

POLICY AND POLITICS EDUCATION ACTIVITIES

The following three sections provide information and activities you can use for students to develop a better understanding of public policy and aging. Activity 8.1, Examining Organizations That Benefit Older Adults in the Local Community, provides a venue for students, community, and educators to "explore the local network of organizations that exist for older adults." Students will have the opportunity to research a single organization and identify strengths, gaps, and limitations of services to support older adults.

In Activity 8.2, Letter to a Legislator: Civic Engagement for Gerontology Students, students have the opportunity to "write a persuasive letter to a legislator to support or oppose a proposed aging related social policy." Students learn about the policy process and how it fosters greater civic engagement.

Activity 8.3, What Will Your Future Look Like? Financing Retirement Exercise, provides a means for students to understand how "events in the economy, political spheres, and personal health status can influence their retirement income." Students are given budgets and are then exposed to different scenarios that may impact their financial security. They become aware of personal choices and outside influences.

RECOMMENDED RESOURCES

National Council on Aging. (2016). Older Americans Act. Retrieved from https://www.ncoa.org/public-policy-action/older-americans-act

U.S. Centers for Medicare & Medicaid Services. (2016). The different parts of Medicare in 2017. Retrieved from https://medicare.com/about-medicare/changes-2017-different-parts-medicare

U.S. Centers for Medicare & Medicaid Services. (n.d.). Overview. Retrieved from https://www.medicaid.gov/medicaid/index.html

U.S. Centers for Medicare & Medicaid Services. (2017). Medicare 2017 costs at a glance. Retrieved from https://www.medicare.gov/your-medicare-costs/costs-at-a-glance/costs-at-glance.html

U.S. Social Security Administration. (n.d.). Glossary of terms. Retrieved from https://www.ssa.gov/glossary

U.S. Social Security Administration. (n.d.). A hope of many years (video). Retrieved from https://www.ssa.gov/history/video

U.S. Social Security Administration. (2017). Basic facts. Retrieved from https://www.ssa.gov/news/press/factsheets/basicfact-alt.pdf

ACTIVITY 8.1 EXAMINING ORGANIZATIONS THAT BENEFIT OLDER ADULTS IN THE LOCAL COMMUNITY

Heather R. Rodriguez

ACTIVITY INFORMATION

Type

__X__	In class
__X__	Online
__X__	Take home
__X__	In community

Difficulty

__X__	Introductory
__X__	Intermediate
_____	Advanced

OVERVIEW

This activity helps students explore the local network of organizations that exist for older adults. Each student selects a single organization to research and report on. This activity helps students identify any strengths, gaps, or limitations of services and organizations that currently exist to support older adults. The lecture preceding this activity focuses on social groups, formal organizations, social isolation, activity theory, and benefits gained from being socially engaged.

KEY TERMS

Activity theory
Community
Formal organization
Group
Primary group
Voluntary association

ACTIVITY LEARNING GOALS

Following this activity, students should be able to . . .

- Evaluate the various kinds of organizations currently present in their local community.

- Understand the role organizations can play in the overall well-being of older adults.
- Examine various ways in which older adults can be engaged in society or in social groups.
- Describe the overall benefits older adults can gain from being involved in different organizations.
- Explain the difference between the various kinds of organizations that benefit older adults.

ASSOCIATION FOR GERONTOLOGY IN HIGHER EDUCATION COMPETENCIES

- Promote engagement of older people in the arts and humanities.
- Acknowledge and promote unique contributions older adults can make to the social environment.
- Interpret the gerontological frameworks in relationship to aspects and problems of aging adults, their families, and their environment and communities.
- Recognize older adults' potential for wisdom, creativity, life satisfaction, resilience, generativity, vital involvement, and meaningful engagement.

MINIMUM/MAXIMUM NUMBER OF PARTICIPANTS

- The minimum number of recommended students needed is one. The maximum number of recommended students is 50. Students can be paired into small groups of two to four and present together if there are more than 25 students in the class or if time is limited.

TIME NEEDED TO IMPLEMENT ACTIVITY

- Students need time to locate and research an appropriate organization, gather information on their selected organization, and create a presentation. The student then presents this information to the class. Presentations can be 10 to 15 minutes long.

SETTING

- The room should be equipped with chairs, tables, Internet access, an overhead projector, a computer, sound, and the ability to play a video. Lights will likely need to be dimmed during the presentation.

MATERIALS
Required

- Formal presentation and brief report/paper with summary of organization and website (if available) for each organization. Textbook or notes that contain discussion on either social groups, organizations, social isolation, activity theory, and/or role loss.

Optional

- The student may gather and bring to class informational or promotional handouts from the organization.

PROCEDURES

Preparation

Prior to the assignment the instructor lectures on topics related to groups, social organizations, role loss, activity theory, social isolation, and other relevant information. The instructor discusses different kinds of organizations that are beneficial to older adults. Hillier and Barrow (2015) discuss the importance of social networks and being part of social organizations. Friendship and companionship among older adults helps decrease feelings of social isolation. Harris (2007) defines the various kinds of formal organizations in society with a focus on primary groups and volunteer associations. The definitions and examples provided by these authors clarify to the student what is meant by an organization.

Introduction

This activity helps students explore the local network of organizations that exist for older adults. It also helps students identify any strengths, gaps, or limitations of services and organizations that currently exist to support older adults.

Activity

1. The instructor lectures on organizations and discusses various kinds of organizations that can benefit older adults.
2. Students are instructed to find a local organization that is beneficial to older adults. The purpose of this activity is to help students examine local and currently existing organizations. This helps place course material in a more tangible and local perspective.
3. Once the student locates an organization, the student gathers information on the organization including but not necessarily limited to the function of the organization, location, hours, ways in which the organization serves older adults, benefits of being part of the organization, and any upcoming events. It is helpful if the organization has a website that the student can exhibit during the presentation, and helpful if the student is able to collect brochures, pamphlets, or other informational materials from the organization. These items are then shared with the class during the student's presentation.
4. After the student has gathered all necessary information, the student writes a three-page report discussing the points from number 3 in the list. The report summarizes the information found and applies course material to the structure of the organization.

5. A few weeks before the student's presentation, the instructor passes around a sign-up sheet and students sign up for a day to present their organization to the class. It works well to have five to six students present per class period, or fewer, pending class time allotted.

6. On their presentation day, the student comes prepared with a formal presentation, their paper, and any relevant information. The presentation lasts 10 to 15 minutes.

Discussion/Reflection

After all presentations for the day are completed, students are asked to reflect on the following questions which can be posted on an overhead or passed out on pieces of paper:

1. What kinds of organizations do you think are still needed for older adults, if any?
2. Were you surprised by the plethora or lack of social organizations available for older adults?
3. Do you believe organizations assist older adults in a beneficial manner?

Wrap-Up

The instructor addresses the importance of being aware of different organizations in the area and reiterates the importance of engaging older adults in social activities. The discussion ends with a quick brainstorming of organizations that were not found or did not exist, but that perhaps should exist (i.e., anti-bullying campaigns for older adults, protecting older adults from online predators, and rehabilitation for older adults coming out of the prison system).

Follow-Up

Optional: After class, the instructor creates a typed list of each organization that students presented on and includes corresponding web links. This is then posted online for students to access, or it is passed out in class the following class period.

Assessment

Using the Association of American Colleges and Universities (AACU, 2016) value rubrics, student presentations could be assessed in the following areas:

1. Identifies a creative, focused, and manageable topic that addresses potentially significant yet previously less explored aspects of the topic, as opposed to simply giving a general presentation on defining organizations.
2. A variety of types of supporting materials (explanations, examples, illustrations, statistics, analogies, quotations from relevant authorities) make appropriate reference to information or analysis that significantly supports the presentation or establishes the presenter's credibility/authority on the topic, as opposed to making no links to course material and no links to the older adult population.
3. Meaningfully synthesizes connections among experiences outside of the formal classroom (including life experiences and academic experiences such as internships and travel abroad) to deepen understanding of fields of study and to broaden own points of view, as opposed to stereotyping older adults or demeaning older adult populations.

ADDITIONAL CONSIDERATIONS

It is useful to show students examples of different types of organizations. Some students may not realize that there are community organizations in the area that benefit older adults. Part of the exercise is to encourage students to search for organizations, locally, that benefit older adults. This can be done by visiting different community buildings, walking around town, conducting a basic Google search, observing advertisements on billboards or local newspapers, and so forth.

REFERENCES

Association of American Colleges & Universities. (2016). Value rubrics. Retrieved from http://www.aacu.org/value-rubrics

Harris, D. K. (2007). *The sociology of aging* (3rd ed.). New York, NY: Rowman & Littlefield.

Hillier, S. M., & Barrow, G. M. (2015). *Aging, the individual, and society* (10th ed.). Stamford, CT: Cengage.

ACTIVITY 8.2 LETTER TO A LEGISLATOR: CIVIC ENGAGEMENT FOR GERONTOLOGY STUDENTS

April Temple

ACTIVITY INFORMATION

Type

__X__	In class
_____	Online
__X__	Take home
_____	In community

Difficulty

_____	Introductory
__X__	Intermediate
_____	Advanced

OVERVIEW

According to the political economy of aging perspective (Estes, 2001), political, economic, and sociocultural factors contribute to the experience of old age and aging as well as to social policy and the distribution of resources to older adults. Consequently, it's important to understand the changing landscape of the politics on aging throughout U.S. history and its potential impact on the lives of older adults. From the 1930s until the late 1970s, social programs and policies such as the Social Security Act (1935), Medicare and Medicaid (1965), and the OAA and the Aging Network (1965) were facilitated by "compassionate ageism," or the notion that older adults were needy and deserving of government support (Binstock, 2010). Despite the successes of these programs, by the late 1970s, neoliberalism ideology emerged emphasizing individual responsibility, a free-market economy, and reductions in government spending and regulation. Thus, the political discourse in the 1980s and 1990s characterized older adults as prosperous and powerful "greedy geezers" who are an increasing burden to society at the expense of younger generations, leading to debates on intergenerational equity (Binstock, 2010). More recently, attention has been focused on policies that address entitlement reform in Social Security, Medicare, and Medicaid to reduce the growing federal deficit (Binstock, 2010). A major challenge for the future of social policies on aging will be how to avoid intergenerational conflict while protecting old-age policies and programs.

The purpose of this activity is for students to learn to write a persuasive letter to a legislator to support or oppose a proposed aging-related social policy. Students use critical thinking skills to synthesize research on a public issue affecting older adults and to analyze the implications of the proposed policy. This activity also improves students' written communication skills by learning to write professional correspondence. Furthermore, it fosters civic engagement as it teaches students the policy-making process and the importance of social activism. This activity works particularly well in upper-level undergraduate or graduate courses with an emphasis on social gerontology.

KEY TERM

Civic engagement

ACTIVITY LEARNING GOALS

Following this activity, students should be able to . . .

- Synthesize and discuss research on a public issue affecting older adults.
- Analyze and articulate a position on a proposed social/aging policy.
- Develop a letter to a legislator on a proposed aging policy as a form of civic engagement.

ASSOCIATION FOR GERONTOLOGY IN HIGHER EDUCATION COMPETENCIES

- Relate social theories and science of aging to understanding heterogeneity, inequality, and context of aging.
- Distinguish factors related to aging outcomes, both intrinsic and contextual, through critical thinking and empirical research.
- Develop a gerontological perspective through knowledge and self-reflection.
- Engage, through effective communication, older persons, their families, and the community, in personal and public issues in aging.
- Employ and generate policy to equitably address the needs of older persons.

MINIMUM/MAXIMUM NUMBER OF PARTICIPANTS

- As a short writing assignment, this take-home activity works well in all class sizes.

TIME NEEDED TO IMPLEMENT ACTIVITY

- For this take-home activity, students research a Congressional Bill and complete the writing assignment outside of class time. It may take approximately 1 to 2 hours of class time to provide a contextual background of the policy-making process and aging social policies as well as to explain the guidelines for the activity (see Appendices 8.2A & 8.2B). Upon completion of the activity, the instructor may also wish to use a class meeting to facilitate a discussion of students' findings of current, proposed policies affecting the older adult population. It is suggested to give the students at least a few weeks to complete the assignment, preferably toward the end of the semester when most of the course content has been covered.

SETTING(S)

- Students complete the assignment on their own time outside of class. The initial introduction of the activity and final reflection occur within class meeting(s).

MATERIALS

Required

- Students are responsible for finding and selecting a Congressional Bill for this assignment. The instructor may wish to limit bills to a specific time period, such as within the past year. An online database of Congressional Bills is available from the U.S. Government Publishing Office: www.gpo.gov/fdsys/search/home.action

PROCEDURES

Preparation

To prepare for this activity, instructors will need to become familiar with the online database of Congressional Bills to be able to assist students with the search process, if necessary. The instructor should also review the relevant content sources listed in Appendix 8.2A to gain a general understanding of the policy-making process and aging social policies. Lastly, the instructor will need to review and potentially adapt the assignment guidelines included in Appendix 8.2B.

Introduction

It is suggested to take approximately 1 to 2 hours to introduce the activity to students. The introduction should include a brief contextual background of the policy-making process as well as an overview of social policies and aging (see content sources listed in Appendix 8.2A). It is recommended that students are already familiar with the major aging policies and programs either covered in the current course or in previous course(s). The instructor should also discuss and review the objectives of the activity and the guidelines and evaluation criteria of the written assignment (see Appendix 8.2B).

Activity

For this activity, students are first instructed to find a current Congressional Bill affecting older adults using the online database via the U.S. Government Publishing Office found at www.gpo.gov/fdsys/search/home.action. In the search box in the center of this webpage, click "Advanced Search." In the drop-down menu for date, select "date is after" and enter [insert specific dates].

Next, under "Available Collections" add "Congressional Bills" only to the selected collections to be searched. Finally, enter any relevant search term related to aging or older adults in the "for" box (e.g., Alzheimer's disease, Medicare, nursing homes, caregiving, hospice). A list of search results will appear and selected bills can be downloaded as a PDF file.

After selecting a bill, students need to read through and understand the basics of the bill including its purpose, statement of the problem, and proposed legislative action. Instructors may need to provide some guidance on the interpretation of a bill if requested by a student(s) who needs additional assistance.

Each student will write a one-page letter to petition a legislator to support or oppose the selected bill. The letter should discuss and synthesize research from class lectures, course readings, and/or outside research on the problem or issue the policy is attempting to address. It should also include a brief analysis of how the proposed policy will or will not address the problem.

Sample instructions for students, including a sample letter format, are included in Appendix 8.2B.

Discussion/Reflection

Upon submission of the activity, the instructor may wish to use a class meeting to facilitate a discussion and evaluation of the aging policies identified in select bills. This discussion could take the form of a larger class discussion or students could be put into smaller groups. Discussion questions could include the following:

- What are the salient proposed policies identified by the class?
- For each proposed policy, how does it address a significant problem/issue faced by older adults? What are the implications of the bill, if passed?
- How could a particular proposed policy be strengthened?
- How would the proposed policy contribute to the intergenerational equity debate?
- Do you foresee intergenerational conflict emerging in policies in the future as we become an aging society?

Wrap-Up

In addition to the discussion/reflection described earlier, the instructor can wrap-up the activity by describing the next steps needed to send the letter, such as how to check the status of a bill. The instructor could also wrap up the activity within the context of the importance of civic engagement and advocacy. See Appendix 8.2A for suggested content sources.

Follow-Up

By reading individual student letters, the instructor will be able to grasp whether students have a solid understanding of the proposed aging policy and the problem or issue it attempts to address. Individual follow-up with students can be conducted by providing feedback on their papers. If certain misinformation is consistent across several letters, the instructor has the opportunity to provide clarification to the whole class.

Assessment

The topics of individual letters will vary depending upon the bill selected and the aging-related issue/problem it attempts to address. A sample grading rubric can be adapted from the Association of American Colleges and Universities, (2009) *Civic Engagement VALUE Rubric* and *Written Communication VALUE Rubric*.

REFERENCES

American Psychological Association. (2016). Civic engagement. Retrieved from http://www.apa.org/education/undergrad/civic-engagement.aspx

Association of American Colleges and Universities. (2009). Civic engagement VALUE rubric. Retrieved from https://www.aacu.org/value/rubrics

Association of American Colleges and Universities. (2009). Written communication VALUE rubric. Retrieved from https://www.aacu.org/value/rubrics

Binstock, R. H. (2010). From compassionate ageism to intergenerational conflict? *Gerontologist, 50*(5), 574–585. doi:10.1093/geront/gnq056

Estes, C. L. (2001). *Social policy and aging: A critical perspective*. Thousand Oaks, CA: Sage.

APPENDIX 8.2A: CONTENT SOURCES

For access to Congressional Bills, please see:

- U.S. Government Printing Office. (2016). Federal digital system. Retrieved from www.gpo.gov/fdsys/search/home.action

For a detailed review of the legislative process, please see:

- Sullivan, J. V. (2007). *How our laws are made*. Washington, DC: United States House of Representatives. Retrieved from www.congress.gov/resources/display/content/How+Our+Laws+Are+Made+-+Learn+About+the+Legislative+Process

For more information on social policies and aging, please see:

- Estes, C. L. (2001). *Social policy and aging: A critical perspective*. Thousand Oaks, CA: Sage.

- Shulz, J. H., & Binstock, R. H. (2008). *Aging nation: The economics and politics of growing old in America*. Baltimore, MD: Johns Hopkins University Press.

For an overview of civic engagement in higher education, please see:

- Reich, J. N. (2014). *Civic engagement, civic development, and higher education*. Washington, DC: Bringing Theory to Practice. Retrieved from http://archive.aacu.org/bringing_theory/documents/4civicseries_cecd_final_r.pdf

APPENDIX 8.2B: LETTER TO A LEGISLATOR: ASSIGNMENT SHEET

LETTER TO A LEGISLATOR: CIVIC ENGAGEMENT FOR GERONTOLOGY STUDENTS

Sample Guidelines for Students

For this assignment, first find a current Congressional Bill relating to older adults you wish to petition your legislator to support or oppose. Bills in Congress can be found at www.gpo.gov/fdsys/search/home.action. In the search box in the center of this webpage, click "Advanced Search." In the drop-down menu for date, select "date is after" and enter [specify dates]. Next, under "Available Collections" add "Congressional Bills" only to the selected collections to be searched. Finally, enter any relevant search term related to aging or older adults in the "for" box (e.g., Alzheimer's disease, Medicare, nursing homes, caregiving, hospice,). A list of search results will appear, and selected bills can be downloaded as a PDF file to review.

Once you have selected a bill, please read through the basics of the bill, including its purpose, statement of the problem, and proposed legislative action. These bills can be lengthy and challenging to comprehend; however, you should understand enough about the problem/issue and proposed policy to articulate an intelligible argument in your letter.

The final outcome of this assignment is a short, one-page letter that petitions your legislator to support or oppose your selected bill on a proposed aging policy. The letter *must* include the following requirements:

- If you have selected a House bill (H. R. XX), you will be writing to your district's representative in the U.S. Congress. If you have selected a Senate bill (S. XX), you will write to your state's senator in the U.S. Congress. You will need to identify your representative or senator (see www.house.gov/representatives/find or www.senate.gov/senators/contact).

- Your letter should clearly state whether you want your legislator to support or oppose your selected bill. Include the official bill number, title, and a brief summary of the bill.

- The letter should discuss and synthesize research from class lectures, course readings, and/or outside research on the problem or issue the policy is attempting to address. It should also include a brief analysis of how the proposed policy will or will not address the problem.

- Please limit your letter to one single-spaced page. These letters are quicker to read, and busy legislators will appreciate your brevity.

- Since this assignment will be considered as a formal letter to a legislator, it is expected to look professional and to be free of spelling or grammatical errors.

A sample letter format is included on the following page.

LETTER TO A LEGISLATOR: CIVIC ENGAGEMENT FOR GERONTOLOGY STUDENTS

Sample Letter Format

[Date]

The Honorable [full name of representative or senator]
Street Address
City, State, and Zip
Dear Senator or Representative [last name],

The first paragraph is the introduction to your letter. In this paragraph, you need to introduce yourself and clearly state whether you would like your elected official to support or oppose a specific bill (include the official bill number and its full title or short title). You also need to include a one- or two-sentence summary of the bill or portion of the bill you wish to discuss.

The main body of your letter follows. This is where you explain why your elected official should support your point of view. This is achieved by discussing the current problem/issue and the need for this piece of legislation or why it should be opposed. You must include *objective information* such as facts, figures, or findings from outside research to support your statements. (*Do not* simply recite the background already included in the bill!) This information must be cited in the text of your letter and included as a full reference(s) in a footer or on a separate page. You may also share a relevant personal story, but only if you have also presented several facts to support your position. The last sentence(s) of this section should relate back to the bill by specifically stating what the proposed legislation would do to address the problem/issue you identified.

To conclude, clearly restate what you would like your legislator to do—to support or oppose the bill. You may also politely request a response.

Respectfully/Sincerely/Best regards,
[Your Name]
[Your Mailing Address]*
[Your City, State, Zip]*

*Your contact information should correspond to the correct senator or representative.

ACTIVITY 8.3 WHAT WILL YOUR FUTURE LOOK LIKE? FINANCING RETIREMENT EXERCISE

Hallie E. Baker and Pamela Pitman Brown

ACTIVITY INFORMATION

Type

__X__ In class

_____ Online

_____ Take home

_____ In community

Difficulty

__X__ Introductory

_____ Intermediate

_____ Advanced

OVERVIEW

One challenge of teaching financing in retirement is making the topic real and relevant to students. Often simply relating to students what the average monthly Social Security benefit is ($1,298.57 in May 2017) does not capture students' attention or imagination (Social Security, 2017). Thus, using a Harvard Business School's investment game as a model, the author created a similar game to engage students in discussing the topic and to make students realize how choices made earlier in life impact their later life. The bonus of using the game is that it allows students to see how decisions can impact their later life without them experiencing the consequences of poor decisions that could occur in real-life settings and promotes critical thinking (Evans, Lombardo, Belgeri, & Fontane, 2005; Schmall, Grabinski, & Bowman, 2008).

Specifically, the activity uses the metaphor of the "three-legged stool" often used in gerontology textbooks (Social Security Administration, 1996). The legs consist of Social Security, pensions, and private savings, each of which is impacted by choices made by the individual over the course of one's life and by macro forces including the government and/or the private sector. The game promotes critical thinking of how different events in the economy, political spheres, and personal health status can influence retirement income by giving students budgets and then exposing them to different scenarios that change one or more of the income sources from the "legs" over time.

Feedback from students who have participated in the game in the past have included comments such as "(I have) a better understanding of the importance of really saving for my retirement as early as possible, like NOW!" Overall, students note an increased level of personal responsibility needed in order to provide an adequate retirement income and financial security in later life. Besides being fun, the game can make students really reflect upon how the choices they make now can impact their later life.

ACTIVITY LEARNING GOALS

Following this activity, students should be able to . . .

- Identify and discuss practical applications of financing in retirement, including the three-legged stool of retirement income.
- Identify and discuss of how different events in the economy, political spheres, and personal health status can influence their retirement income.

ASSOCIATION FOR GERONTOLOGY IN HIGHER EDUCATION COMPETENCIES

- Relate social theories and science of aging to understanding heterogeneity, inequality, and context of aging.
- Promote quality of life and positive social environment for older persons.
- Address the roles of older persons as workers and consumers in business and finance.

MINIMUM/MAXIMUM NUMBER OF PARTICIPANTS

- 15 to 50

TIME NEEDED TO IMPLEMENT ACTIVITY

- 20 minutes

SETTING

- Classroom with chairs

MATERIALS
Required

- One set of dice
- Retirement financial scenarios cards (Appendix 8.3C) printed out or cut to size (*Note:* Print them back to back so the number is all the student will see.)

- Retirement financial change scenarios cards (Appendix 8.3D) printed out or cut to size (*Note:* Print them back to back so the number is all the student will see.)

PROCEDURES

Preparation

The students will need to have had background materials on Social Security, financing retirement, and the three-legged stool of retirement model of financing retirement (see Appendix 8.3A). Once that background is present, they are ready for the "game."

Introduction

- First provide the background on the "Three-Legged Stool of Retirement Income." One could use the PowerPoint provided to introduce the concept and what each "leg" represents in terms of income stream.
- Introduce this as a scenario to see how well the students can do in retirement and to test their budgeting skills. Challenge them to try and maintain their idealized retirement lifestyle on the budget they will be given.
- Remind the students that they could live 20 or more years on their savings. Will that be enough?

Activity

1. Split the class into groups of three to four students per group and hand out the worksheet (Appendix 8.3B).
2. Have one member of each group come to you to get their initial retirement financial scenario (Appendix 8.3C) by rolling one of the dice and then picking the card that matches the number that turns up. Each group's representative will then return to the group to answer the first prompts on the worksheet. Once all the groups have their initial scenario, put away those cards and pull out the change cards.
   a. Challenge the students to really think about what that budget means for their ideal retirement and to really think about the prompts on the worksheet.
3. Over the next 10 to 15 minutes the groups will send up a member three more times to roll one of the dice to get a change card (Appendix 8.3D); each time they will have to go back and deal with what the change means for their retirement.
   a. As the instructor, you will need to move around and speak with each group, engaging them about how their income has changed or not. Include what those changes mean for day-to-day life as well as long-term plans.

Discussion/Reflection

- The worksheet will ask the students to reflect upon the whole experience.
- By giving points for the game, you can encourage students to fully participate.
- However, when the groups are done, the whole class will reflect as well.

Wrap-Up

- Once all the groups are done, pull the class back together.
- Ask each group to discuss their situation, how it changed over the draws, and what surprised them.
- Ask the group as a whole what other reactions they had.
- Validate and reflect back any themes or comments the students provide.
- Collect the worksheets at the end of the time.

Follow-Up

- Often the next class is a great time to discuss Social Security reform as the students have had time to really process the experience and will come back with even more questions and will challenge many of the proposed reforms for Social Security.

Assessment

- The worksheet is handed in and can provide insight into how the students did.
- Credit can be provided for participation or a grade assigned along with using the feedback to assess the activity's effectiveness.

ADDITIONAL CONSIDERATIONS

- The activity can be a lot of fun as their fates go up and down. . . . Just make sure they don't blame one individual for any bad draws. Often you will hear joking and teasing about "bad" luck.

SOURCE ACTIVITY IS BASED ON/MODIFIED FROM:

- The idea to roll dice for the group's fate comes from a Harvard Business School investment game that teaches about the ups and downs of the market. However, the content of this activity is original.

REFERENCES

Evans, S., Lombardo, M., Belgeri, M., & Fontane, P. (2005). The Geriatric Medication Game in pharmacy education. *Journal of Pharmaceutical Education, 69*(3), 304–310.

Schmall, V., Grabinski, C. J., & Bowman, S. (2008). Use of games as a learner-centered strategy in gerontology, geriatrics, and aging-related courses. *Gerontology & Geriatrics Education, 29*(3), 225–233. doi:10.1080/07399330802359443

Social Security Administration. (1996). Research notes & special studies by the historian's office. Research note #1: Origins of the three-legged stool metaphor for Social Security. Retrieved from http://www.ssa.gov/history/stool.html

Social Security Administration. (2017). Monthly statistical snapshot, June 2017. Retrieved from https://www.ssa.gov/policy/docs/quickfacts/stat_snapshot

CONTENT SOURCES

More information is available about this activity in this article:

Baker, H., & Brown, P. (2015). Teaching retirement financial literacy in an undergraduate gerontology classroom: Broadening the concept of the tripod or three-legged stool of retirement income utilizing active learning. *Gerontology & Geriatrics Education, 36*(4), 416–424. Published online: May 7, 2015.

APPENDIX 8.3A: SOURCES OF INCOME IN RETIREMENT: BACKGROUND INFORMATION

SOURCES OF INCOME IN RETIREMENT

- Asset income
  - Unevenly distributed, larger disparities intensified by race/gender
- Pensions
  - 1974 Employment Retirement Income Security Act (ERISA) strengthened private pension systems
- Earnings
  - Currently form about 28% of older adults' income

THREE-LEGGED STOOL OF RETIREMENT INCOME

- Legs:
  - Personal savings/investments
  - Private pension plans
  - Social Security

Private Savings: Leg 1

- 58% of older adults claimed some asset in 2001 including:
  - Savings and checking accounts
  - Financial investments (stocks, bonds)
  - Other investments such as bank deposits (CDs), art, or rare collections
    - Don't rely upon rare collectables though; just look at Beanie Babies, for example
- Tend to be younger older adults who actually get income from these sources
  - Could be they outlived their savings?
- Many elders do not have this as much as policy folks would like

Private Pension Plans: Leg 2

- These are needed for maintaining preretirement income.
- Around one-half of all retirees today have a pension either from their own or a spouse's past employer.
- Pensions peaked in the 1980s with 46% of employees being in a private pension plan.
  - Therefore, not as universal as the original conceptualization of retirement plans.

- Reform of pension plans led to the ability of workers to take part of their pension with them when they leave the company.
  - Key especially in today's work because of the high amount of job turnover; in the past, adults often thought of only working in one job for life.
  - Now workers can expect 5+ jobs in their lives.
  - How many jobs have you had already? How about your parents?
- In general, there are more options for pension programs for workers than ever before.
  - This means you need to be savvy now or pay in the future.

Social Security: Leg 3

- Social Security was not meant to be the entire source of income for elders.
  - Instead, it was conceptualized as only one of the "legs" of a stool.
  - Within Social Security is Supplemental Security Income.
  - It was only a safety net to keep elders out of poverty, a last resort in the original planning of the program.
  - However, for many it is their only retirement, especially those in lower socioeconomic statuses.

APPENDIX 8.3B: WORKSHEET FOR STUDENTS

FINANCING RETIREMENT

Group members:

1. _____

2. _____

3. _____

4. _____

5. _____

You are planning your retirement. For this exercise your group will have a budget determined by luck. Each group will draw a starting income level. Then at three different times, you will draw another slip that will tell you what will affect your retirement next. At the end, you will reflect on the experience.

1. What was your starting monthly budget?
2. How do you think this income level will affect your retirement?
3. What happened with the first draw? What is your monthly budget now? How will this impact your retirement?
4. What happened with the second draw? What is your monthly budget now? How will this impact your retirement?
5. What happened with the third draw? What is your monthly budget now? How will this impact your retirement?
6. How does your retirement look now compared to at the beginning of the exercise?
7. What is your reaction to this exercise?

APPENDIX 8.3C: INITIAL SCENARIO CARDS

INITIAL SCENARIO CARD SET 1

Your monthly retirement income is made up of: Social Security: $1,200.00 Private pension: $500.00 Savings: $300.00 Total: $2,000.00 Total monthly expenses (not optional) = $1,200	Your monthly retirement income is made up of: Social Security: $1,200.00 Private pension: $500.00 Savings: $300.00 Total: $2,000.00 Total monthly expenses (not optional) = $1,200
Your monthly retirement income is made up of: Social Security: $1,200.00 Private pension: $500.00 Savings: $300.00 Total: $2,000.00 Total monthly expenses (not optional) = $1,200	Your monthly retirement income is made up of: Social Security: $1,200.00 Private pension: $500.00 Savings: $300.00 Total: $2,000.00 Total monthly expenses (not optional) = $1,200
Your monthly retirement income is made up of: Social Security: $1,200.00 Private pension: $500.00 Savings: $300.00 Total: $2,000.00 Total monthly expenses (not optional) = $1,200	Your monthly retirement income is made up of: Social Security: $1,200.00 Private pension: $500.00 Savings: $300.00 Total: $2,000.00 Total monthly expenses (not optional) = $1,200
Your monthly retirement income is made up of: Social Security: $1,200.00 Private pension: $500.00 Savings: $300.00 Total: $2,000.00 Total monthly expenses (not optional) = $1,200	Your monthly retirement income is made up of: Social Security: $1,200.00 Private pension: $500.00 Savings: $300.00 Total: $2,000.00 Total monthly expenses (not optional) = $1,200

INITIAL SCENARIO CARD SET 2

Your monthly retirement income is made up of: Social Security: $1,000.00 Private pension: $200.00 <u>Savings: $100.00</u> Total: $1,300.00 Your monthly expenses (not optional) = $1,200	Your monthly retirement income is made up of: Social Security: $1,000.00 Private pension: $200.00 <u>Savings: $100.00</u> Total: $1,300.00 Your monthly expenses (not optional) = $1,200
Your monthly retirement income is made up of: Social Security: $1,000.00 Private pension: $200.00 <u>Savings: $100.00</u> Total: $1,300.00 Your monthly expenses (not optional) = $1,200	Your monthly retirement income is made up of: Social Security: $1,000.00 Private pension: $200.00 <u>Savings: $100.00</u> Total: $1,300.00 Your monthly expenses (not optional) = $1,200
Your monthly retirement income is made up of: Social Security: $1,000.00 Private pension: $200.00 <u>Savings: $100.00</u> Total: $1,300.00 Your monthly expenses (not optional) = $1,200	Your monthly retirement income is made up of: Social Security: $1,000.00 Private pension: $200.00 <u>Savings: $100.00</u> Total: $1,300.00 Your monthly expenses (not optional) = $1,200
Your monthly retirement income is made up of: Social Security: $1,000.00 Private pension: $200.00 <u>Savings: $100.00</u> Total: $1,300.00 Your monthly expenses (not optional) = $1,200	Your monthly retirement income is made up of: Social Security: $1,000.00 Private pension: $200.00 <u>Savings: $100.00</u> Total: $1,300.00 Your monthly expenses (not optional) = $1,200

INITIAL SCENARIO CARD SET 3

Your monthly retirement income is made up of: Social Security: $800.00 Private pension: $200.00 <u>Savings: $0.00</u> Total: $1,000.00 Your monthly expenses (not optional) = $900	Your monthly retirement income is made up of: Social Security: $800.00 Private pension: $200.00 <u>Savings: $0.00</u> Total: $1,000.00 Your monthly expenses (not optional) = $900
Your monthly retirement income is made up of: Social Security: $800.00 Private pension: $200.00 <u>Savings: $0.00</u> Total: $1,000.00 Your monthly expenses (not optional) = $900	Your monthly retirement income is made up of: Social Security: $800.00 Private pension: $200.00 <u>Savings: $0.00</u> Total: $1,000.00 Your monthly expenses (not optional) = $900
Your monthly retirement income is made up of: Social Security: $800.00 Private pension: $200.00 <u>Savings: $0.00</u> Total: $1,000.00 Your monthly expenses (not optional) = $900	Your monthly retirement income is made up of: Social Security: $800.00 Private pension: $200.00 <u>Savings: $0.00</u> Total: $1,000.00 Your monthly expenses (not optional) = $900
Your monthly retirement income is made up of: Social Security: $800.00 Private pension: $200.00 <u>Savings: $0.00</u> Total: $1,000.00 Your monthly expenses (not optional) = $900	Your monthly retirement income is made up of: Social Security: $800.00 Private pension: $200.00 <u>Savings: $0.00</u> Total: $1,000.00 Your monthly expenses (not optional) = $900

INITIAL SCENARIO CARD SET 4

Your monthly retirement income is made up of: Social Security: $800.00 Private pension: $100.00 <u>Savings: $0.00</u> Total: $900.00 Your monthly expenses (not optional) = $850	Your monthly retirement income is made up of: Social Security: $800.00 Private pension: $100.00 <u>Savings: $0.00</u> Total: $900.00 Your monthly expenses (not optional) = $850
Your monthly retirement income is made up of: Social Security: $800.00 Private pension: $100.00 <u>Savings: $0.00</u> Total: $900.00 Your monthly expenses (not optional) = $850	Your monthly retirement income is made up of: Social Security: $800.00 Private pension: $100.00 <u>Savings: $0.00</u> Total: $900.00 Your monthly expenses (not optional) = $850
Your monthly retirement income is made up of: Social Security: $800.00 Private pension: $100.00 <u>Savings: $0.00</u> Total: $900.00 Your monthly expenses (not optional) = $850	Your monthly retirement income is made up of: Social Security: $800.00 Private pension: $100.00 <u>Savings: $0.00</u> Total: $900.00 Your monthly expenses (not optional) = $850
Your monthly retirement income is made up of: Social Security: $800.00 Private pension: $100.00 <u>Savings: $0.00</u> Total: $900.00 Your monthly expenses (not optional) = $850	Your monthly retirement income is made up of: Social Security: $800.00 Private pension: $100.00 <u>Savings: $0.00</u> Total: $900.00 Your monthly expenses (not optional) = $850

INITIAL SCENARIO CARD SET 5

Your monthly retirement income is made up of: Social Security: $1,200 Private pension: $200 Savings: $100 Total: $1,500 Your monthly expenses (not optional) = $1,200	Your monthly retirement income is made up of: Social Security: $1,200 Private pension: $200 Savings: $100 Total: $1,500 Your monthly expenses (not optional) = $1,200
Your monthly retirement income is made up of: Social Security: $1,200 Private pension: $200 Savings: $100 Total: $1,500 Your monthly expenses (not optional) = $1,200	Your monthly retirement income is made up of: Social Security: $1,200 Private pension: $200 Savings: $100 Total: $1,500 Your monthly expenses (not optional) = $1,200
Your monthly retirement income is made up of: Social Security: $1,200 Private pension: $200 Savings: $100 Total: $1,500 Your monthly expenses (not optional) = $1,200	Your monthly retirement income is made up of: Social Security: $1,200 Private pension: $200 Savings: $100 Total: $1,500 Your monthly expenses (not optional) = $1,200
Your monthly retirement income is made up of: Social Security: $1,200 Private pension: $200 Savings: $100 Total: $1,500 Your monthly expenses (not optional) = $1,200	Your monthly retirement income is made up of: Social Security: $1,200 Private pension: $200 Savings: $100 Total: $1,500 Your monthly expenses (not optional) = $1,200

INITIAL SCENARIO CARD SET 6

Your monthly retirement income is made up of: Social Security: $1,000.00 Private pension: $200.00 Savings: $0.00 Total: $1,200.00 Your monthly expenses (not optional) = $1,200	Your monthly retirement income is made up of: Social Security: $1,000.00 Private pension: $200.00 Savings: $0.00 Total: $1,200.00 Your monthly expenses (not optional) = $1,200
Your monthly retirement income is made up of: Social Security: $1,000.00 Private pension: $200.00 Savings: $0.00 Total: $1,200.00 Your monthly expenses (not optional) = $1,200	Your monthly retirement income is made up of: Social Security: $1,000.00 Private pension: $200.00 Savings: $0.00 Total: $1,200.00 Your monthly expenses (not optional) = $1,200
Your monthly retirement income is made up of: Social Security: $1,000.00 Private pension: $200.00 Savings: $0.00 Total: $1,200.00 Your monthly expenses (not optional) = $1,200	Your monthly retirement income is made up of: Social Security: $1,000.00 Private pension: $200.00 Savings: $0.00 Total: $1,200.00 Your monthly expenses (not optional) = $1,200
Your monthly retirement income is made up of: Social Security: $1,000.00 Private pension: $200.00 Savings: $0.00 Total: $1,200.00 Your monthly expenses (not optional) = $1,200	Your monthly retirement income is made up of: Social Security: $1,000.00 Private pension: $200.00 Savings: $0.00 Total: $1,200.00 Your monthly expenses (not optional) = $1,200

APPENDIX 8.3D: CHANGE SCENARIO CARDS

CHANGE SCENARIO CARD SET 1

A recession has hit the country, as a result, your income from savings and private pensions have decreased by half (1/2).	A recession has hit the country, as a result, your income from savings and private pensions have decreased by half (1/2).
A recession has hit the country, as a result, your income from savings and private pensions have decreased by half (1/2).	A recession has hit the country, as a result, your income from savings and private pensions have decreased by half (1/2).
A recession has hit the country, as a result, your income from savings and private pensions have decreased by half (1/2).	A recession has hit the country, as a result, your income from savings and private pensions have decreased by half (1/2).
A recession has hit the country, as a result, your income from savings and private pensions have decreased by half (1/2).	A recession has hit the country, as a result, your income from savings and private pensions have decreased by half (1/2).

CHANGE SCENARIO CARD SET 2

Congress has passed a cost of living increase in Social Security. This means you can add 10% to your Social Security payments.	Congress has passed a cost of living increase in Social Security. This means you can add 10% to your Social Security payments.
Congress has passed a cost of living increase in Social Security. This means you can add 10% to your Social Security payments.	Congress has passed a cost of living increase in Social Security. This means you can add 10% to your Social Security payments.
Congress has passed a cost of living increase in Social Security. This means you can add 10% to your Social Security payments.	Congress has passed a cost of living increase in Social Security. This means you can add 10% to your Social Security payments.
Congress has passed a cost of living increase in Social Security. This means you can add 10% to your Social Security payments.	Congress has passed a cost of living increase in Social Security. This means you can add 10% to your Social Security payments.

CHANGE SCENARIO CARD SET 3

Inflation has hit the country hard. Your monthly expenses have increased by $100 if you make equal to or less than $1000 and $200 if your monthly income is more than $1000.	Inflation has hit the country hard. Your monthly expenses have increased by $100 if you make equal to or less than $1000 and $200 if your monthly income is more than $1000.
Inflation has hit the country hard. Your monthly expenses have increased by $100 if you make equal to or less than $1000 and $200 if your monthly income is more than $1000.	Inflation has hit the country hard. Your monthly expenses have increased by $100 if you make equal to or less than $1000 and $200 if your monthly income is more than $1000.
Inflation has hit the country hard. Your monthly expenses have increased by $100 if you make equal to or less than $1000 and $200 if your monthly income is more than $1000.	Inflation has hit the country hard. Your monthly expenses have increased by $100 if you make equal to or less than $1000 and $200 if your monthly income is more than $1000.
Inflation has hit the country hard. Your monthly expenses have increased by $100 if you make equal to or less than $1000 and $200 if your monthly income is more than $1000.	Inflation has hit the country hard. Your monthly expenses have increased by $100 if you make equal to or less than $1000 and $200 if your monthly income is more than $1000.

CHANGE SCENARIO CARD SET 4

The economy is booming. Your savings income has increased as a result. Thanks to smart investments you can double your income from savings.	The economy is booming. Your savings income has increased as a result. Thanks to smart investments you can double your income from savings.
The economy is booming. Your savings income has increased as a result. Thanks to smart investments you can double your income from savings.	The economy is booming. Your savings income has increased as a result. Thanks to smart investments you can double your income from savings.
The economy is booming. Your savings income has increased as a result. Thanks to smart investments you can double your income from savings.	The economy is booming. Your savings income has increased as a result. Thanks to smart investments you can double your income from savings.
The economy is booming. Your savings income has increased as a result. Thanks to smart investments you can double your income from savings.	The economy is booming. Your savings income has increased as a result. Thanks to smart investments you can double your income from savings.

CHANGE SCENARIO CARD SET 5

No change in your income has occurred this time.	No change in your income has occurred this time.
No change in your income has occurred this time.	No change in your income has occurred this time.
No change in your income has occurred this time.	No change in your income has occurred this time.
No change in your income has occurred this time.	No change in your income has occurred this time.

CHANGE SCENARIO CARD SET 6

Poor health has hit you and your spouse hard. You now require assistance to maintain your home and health. This adds $300.00 to your monthly expenses. If your income is under $1000 you may qualify for assistance with the cost.	Poor health has hit you and your spouse hard. You now require assistance to maintain your home and health. This adds $300.00 to your monthly expenses. If your income is under $1000 you may qualify for assistance with the cost.
Poor health has hit you and your spouse hard. You now require assistance to maintain your home and health. This adds $300.00 to your monthly expenses. If your income is under $1000 you may qualify for assistance with the cost.	Poor health has hit you and your spouse hard. You now require assistance to maintain your home and health. This adds $300.00 to your monthly expenses. If your income is under $1000 you may qualify for assistance with the cost.
Poor health has hit you and your spouse hard. You now require assistance to maintain your home and health. This adds $300.00 to your monthly expenses. If your income is under $1000 you may qualify for assistance with the cost.	Poor health has hit you and your spouse hard. You now require assistance to maintain your home and health. This adds $300.00 to your monthly expenses. If your income is under $1000 you may qualify for assistance with the cost.
Poor health has hit you and your spouse hard. You now require assistance to maintain your home and health. This adds $300.00 to your monthly expenses. If your income is under $1000 you may qualify for assistance with the cost.	Poor health has hit you and your spouse hard. You now require assistance to maintain your home and health. This adds $300.00 to your monthly expenses. If your income is under $1000 you may qualify for assistance with the cost.

CHAPTER 9

POSITIVE INTERACTIONS WITH OLDER ADULTS

Mary C. Ehlman

Activities promoting positive interactions between young adults and older adults are often embedded in gerontology courses. These assignments have the potential to inspire undergraduate students to consider careers in gerontology-related fields, connect the generations, improve student attitudes about aging, and promote transformational learning.

Utilizing assignments focused on positive interactions with older adults in higher education is especially important as the United States' population ages. One in five individuals is expected to be aged 65 or older by the year 2030. Between 2015 and 2060, the percentage of the population that is 65 and older is expected to grow from 15% to 24% (Colby & Ortman, 2015). The population aged 85 and over, known as the oldest-old population, is expected to grow exponentially from 5.9 million in 2012 to 8.9 million in 2030 to 18 million in 2050. The oldest-old population is expected to account for 4.5% of the total population in 2050, up from 2.5% in 2030 (Ortman, Velkoff, & Hogan, 2014). As the population ages, demand for professionals working with older adults and having knowledge of the aging process also increases (Eshbaugh, Gross, Hillebrand, Davie, & Henninger, 2013) in both clinical and nonclinical gerontology-related fields. Recruiting students into gerontology and gerontology-related fields can be a challenge for educators in a youth-centric society, but connecting the generations through positive interactions opens the door for students to explore the multi-faceted field of gerontology.

Robert Butler describes **ageism** as "prejudice by one age group toward another age group" (Butler, 1969, p. 243). Negative attitudes about aging and negative attitudes about older adults can influence a person's ageist feelings (Cummings, Kropf, & DeWeaver, 2000) and contribute to the common anxiety and fear about aging in our society (Barrett & Toothman, 2016; Cummings et al., 2000). It is not uncommon for young adults to have these negative attitudes. As such, educators should examine ways to shift these attitudes. Incorporating activities promoting positive interactions between young adults and older adults in higher education can positively shift students' attitudes toward aging and students' attitudes toward older adults (Anderson-Hanley, 1999; Ehlman, Ligon, Moriello, Welleford, & Schuster, 2011; Ligon, Ehlman, Moriello, & Welleford, 2009; Moriello, Ligon, & Ehlman, 2016; Penick, Fallshore, & Spencer, 2014; Snyder, 2005).

At the heart of teaching, educators look to inspire learners. This may be the primary reason educators in the field of gerontology include activities promoting positive interactions between young adults and older adults. These experiential learning activities have the potential for transformational learning, which is more than acquiring facts or learning new skills. In transformational learning learners are struck by a new concept or a new way of thinking through an *experience* and then follow-through to make a life change (Cranton, 1994). **Transformational learning** is defined as "the process of using a prior interpretation to construe a new or a revised interpretation of the meaning of one's experience in order to guide future action" (Mezirow, 1996, p. 162). Transformational learning is sparked by a **disorienting dilemma** which is described as an experience testing one's own beliefs (Taylor, 1998). When educators design experiential learning opportunities, such as those that involve positive interactions with older adults, they are creating opportunities for a student to experience a disorienting dilemma. Equally important to the disorienting dilemma in the transformational learning process is the need for *reflection*. Reflecting on the process challenges students to examine how the experience aligns or does not align with one's previous ideas and thus allows for attitude and belief changes (Kolb, 1984; Mezirow, 1996). When educators create and implement activities promoting positive interactions with elders, they are creating a space where students may experience a disorientating dilemma. Upon reflection, this experience may result in transformational learning.

EDUCATION EXERCISES FOR INTERACTING WITH OLDER ADULTS

The following sections outline details for four activities promoting positive interactions with older adults. Activity 9.1, Intergenerational Speed Greeting Activity, is based on the idea of "speed dating" and gives younger and older adults an opportunity to come together and answer questions around shared experiences. Students engaging in Activity 9.2, Life History Interview Project, conduct multiple life history interviews with an older adult living in a nursing home or in assisted living and then compare these interviews with an older adult relative. Activity 9.3, Service Learning Fair (SLF) in Gerontology, introduces students to the range and scope of gerontology-related agencies and services. Additionally, this activity exposes students to future internship and employment possibilities. Activity 9.4, Site Visits as a Requirement for an Introductory Gerontology Course: Social and Demographic Implications of Aging, allows students to visit and tour an organization within the aging network. Students learn about the roles and qualification needed to work within the aging network and observe the interactions between staff members and older adults at the site.

REFERENCES

Anderson-Hanley, C. (1999). Experiential activities for reaching psychology of aging. *Educational Gerontology, 29,* 449–456.

Barrett, A. E., & Toothman, E. L. (2016). Explaining age differences in women's emotional well-being: The role of subjective experiences of aging. *Journal of Women & Aging, 28*(4), 285–296. doi:10.1080/08952841.2015.1017426

Butler, R. N. (1969). Age-ism: Another form of bigotry. *The Gerontologist, 9*(4), 243.

Colby, S. L., & Ortman, J. L. (2015). *Projections of the size and composition of the U.S. population,* Current Population Reports, P25–1143. Washington, DC: U.S. Census Bureau.

Cranton, P. (1994). *Understanding and promoting transformative learning: A guide for educators of adults.* San Francisco, CA: Jossey-Bass.

Cummings, S. M., Kropf, N. P., & DeWeaver, K. L. (2000). Knowledge of and attitudes among non-elders: Gender and race differences. *Journal of Women & Aging, 12*(1), 77–91. doi:10.1300/J074v12n01_06

Ehlman, M. C., Ligon, M. B., Moriello, G., Welleford, E. A., & Schuster, K. (2011). Oral history in the classroom: A comparison of traditional and on-line gerontology classes. *Educational Gerontology, 37*(9), 772–790. doi:10.1080/03601271003780917

Eshbaugh, E., Gross, P. E., Hillebrand, K., Davie, J., & Henninger, W. R. (2013). Promoting careers in gerontology to students: What are undergraduates seeking in a career? *Gerontology & Geriatrics Education, 34*(2), 150–160. doi:10.1080/0270 1960.2012.679373

Kolb, D. A. (1984). *Experiential learning: Experience as the source of learning and development.* New York, NY: Prentice Hall.

Mezirow, J. (1996). Contemporary paradigms of learning. *Adult Education Quarterly, 46*(3), 158–172. doi:10.1177/074171369604600303

Moriello, G., Ligon, M., & Ehlman, M. C. (2016). Don't [have to] talk to strangers? Findings from an intergenerational oral history project. *The International Journal of Reminiscence and Life Review, 12*(1), 40–53.

Ortman, J. M., Velkoff, V. A., & Hogan, H. (2014). *An aging nation: The older population in the United States,* Current Population Reports, P25–1140. Washington, DC: U.S. Census Bureau.

Penick, J. M., Fallshore, M., & Spencer, A. M. (2014). Using intergenerational service learning to promote positive perceptions about older adults and community service in college students. *Journal of Intergenerational Relationships, 12*(1), 25–39. doi: 10.1080/15350770.2014.870456

Snyder, J. (2005). The influence of instruction on college students' attitudes toward older adults. *Gerontology & Geriatrics Education, 26*(2), 69–79.

Taylor, E. W. (1998). *The theory and practice of transformational learning: A critical review.* Columbus: The Ohio State University. Retrieved from ERIC database. (ED423422).

ACTIVITY 9.1 INTERGENERATIONAL SPEED GREETING

Carrie Andreoletti and Joann M. Montepare

ACTIVITY INFORMATION

Type

   X   In class

_____   Online

_____   Take home

   X   In community

Difficulty

   X   Introductory

_____   Intermediate

_____   Advanced

OVERVIEW

Negative stereotypes about aging and older adults are pervasive in our youth-oriented culture (North & Fiske, 2012). Some older adults may also hold negative stereotypes about young people (Matheson, Collins, & Kuehne, 2000). One reason why these views continue to exist is because younger and older adults often have limited contact with each other. Indeed, many college students may not have the opportunity to engage in conversations with older adults outside of their own families, and older adults (particularly those who have moved from their homes) have limited opportunities for interacting with young people. Given the increasing age diversity of our society, it is important to promote intergenerational communication and understanding.

This "speed greeting" activity, based on the popular idea of "speed dating," aims to give younger and older adults the opportunity to come together as equal partners and to develop common ground for improved intergenerational communication and understanding. Toward this end, icebreaker questions are designed to direct the discussion around common, shared experiences as opposed to age differences. While differences in experience will certainly emerge during the conversations, they will more likely reflect individual than age differences.

The speed greeting activity is geared toward interactions with college-age or graduate level students, and may be conducted in a variety of settings such as at a college/university, senior/community center, or assisted living facility as appropriate. For example, this activity could be done at the onset of a college class, a community program, or other exchange between younger and older adults. It could also work as a stand-alone program where younger adults engage with older adults in care settings, senior centers, or service-learning programs.

ACTIVITY LEARNING GOALS

Following this activity, students should be able to . . .

- Initiate conversations with older adults with greater confidence.
- Demonstrate the ability to overcome communication barriers.
- Recognize the diversity of older adults.
- Identify commonalities across the generations.

ASSOCIATION FOR GERONTOLOGY IN HIGHER EDUCATION COMPETENCIES

- Attitudes and perspectives—Develop a gerontological perspective through knowledge and self-reflection.
- Social health—Promote quality of life and positive social environment for older persons.
- Education—Encourage older persons to engage in life-long learning opportunities.

MINIMUM/MAXIMUM NUMBER OF PARTICIPANTS

- The number of participants can vary from as few as 15 to a larger group of 45.

TIME NEEDED TO IMPLEMENT ACTIVITY

- The total time needed for the activity is approximately 45 to 60 minutes, which does not include time to set-up the room.

SETTING(S)

- College/university, senior/community center, or assisted living facility.
- The ideal set-up is a large room with chairs set in small circles, or round tables and chairs.

MATERIALS

Required

- Multiple sets of icebreaker questions for each group
- Paper or index cards and paper bags or envelopes

PROCEDURES

Preparation

Prior to the session, the instructor should prepare multiple sets of interest and experience questions (see Appendix 9.1 for sample questions; questions may be edited as desired), and each question should be printed separately on paper or index cards. The number of questions to use will depend on the number of participants and groups. Each group will get different sets of questions during the activity. Each group should also have a small paper bag or large envelope to put the questions in, so participants can randomly pull one out at a time.

Activity

Younger and older adults should first be organized into small groups of approximately the same size, with a maximum of five to seven people per group (e.g., four to five young adults and one to two older adults). Next, the instructor introduces the activity by explaining the procedure and saying that the goal is for the participants to begin to get to know one another. Participants should be encouraged to use the questions as a starting point, but should be allowed to deviate as long as the conversation is stimulating and everyone is participating. Then, the instructor gives each group the first set of questions. Group members are instructed to pull out one question at a time, and told that they will have 10 to 15 minutes to answer the first set of questions (groups may or may not get to all questions). After 10 to 15 minutes, the young adults in each group are asked to rotate to the next table and the instructor collects the old questions and gives each group the next set of questions. This procedure is followed two more times until time is up and all four sets of questions have been discussed in the different intergenerational groups. For larger groups of participants, it would be helpful for the instructor to train a student to assist with distributing the materials as groups rotate.

One advantage of this rotation method is that participants will have the opportunity to interact with a variety of younger and older adults. In addition, participants enjoy the fun-loving nature of actively conversing that the "speed greeting" rotation instills.

Discussion/Reflection

Following completion of the speed greeting activity, the instructor can open the floor for a group discussion, asking participants to share the most interesting or surprising things they learned about one another.

Follow-Up

If this activity is conducted as part of a college class, the instructor may wish to follow up with students to explore what they learned from the experience and how their observations relate to issues being examined in the class. Instructors may also assign reflection papers on specific topics such as intergenerational communication and have a class discussion once students have had the opportunity to reflect on their experience.

Assessment

This activity is aimed to challenge the stereotypes that young and older adults may have about one another by promoting intergenerational interaction. To assess its impact, the instructor may assign reflection papers and/or follow the activity with a class discussion about age stereotypes to see whether students report any changes in their views of older adults. Possible reflection questions are: How did the experience meet with your expectations? Was it different than you expected? What is something that surprised you about the experience? Did this activity influence your views on aging and older adults?

If a more systematic assessment of changes in age perceptions is desired, the instructor may wish to give participants a pre- and postsurvey with measures that tap beliefs about younger and older adults (e.g., Fraboni, Saltstone, & Hughes, 1990; Polizzi, 2003).

ADDITIONAL CONSIDERATIONS

This activity could be adapted to a variety of settings and situations. Although typically done in a small group format, it could also be used more like speed dating where the activity is done in dyads. Dyads or groups could be given longer than 10 minutes and groups could rotate fewer times depending on how much time is allocated. Questions can be revised as needed.

REFERENCES

Fraboni, M., Saltstone, R., & Hughes, S. (1990). The Fraboni scale of ageism (FSA): An attempt at a more precise measure of ageism. *Canadian Journal on Aging, 9,* 56–66. doi:10.1017/S0714980800016093

Matheson, D. H., Collins, C. L., & Kuehne, V. S. (2000). Older adults' multiple stereotypes of young adults. *The International Journal of Aging & Human Development, 51*(4), 245–257. doi:10.2190/LL3H-VKE8-QAT1-7M9M

North, M. S., & Fiske, S. T. (2012). An inconvenienced youth? Ageism and its potential intergenerational roots. *Psychological Bulletin, 138*(5), 982–997. doi:10.1037/a0027843

Polizzi, K. G. (2003). Assessing attitudes toward the elderly: Polizzi's refined version of the Aging Semantic Differential. *Educational Gerontology, 29*(3), 197–216. doi:10.1080/713844306

CONTENT RESOURCES

The following resources provide additional information for instructors using reflection for assessment.

Karasik, R. J. (2013). Reflecting on reflection: Capitalizing on the learning in intergenerational service-learning. *Gerontology & Geriatrics Education, 34,* 78–98.

Marchel, C. A. (2004). Evaluating reflection and sociocultural awareness in service learning classes. *Teaching of Psychology, 31*(2), 120–123.

The following resource provides detail on the development of an intergenerational service-learning program that used similar activities.

Andreoletti, C., & Howard, J. L. (2016). Bridging the generation gap: Intergenerational service-learning benefits young and old. *Gerontology & Geriatrics Education,* 1–15. doi:10.1080/02701960.2016.1152266

APPENDIX 9.1: ACTIVITY INSTRUCTION SHEET

Activity Instruction Sheet

Speed Greeting Exercise

Time needed = 45 to 60 minutes

Instructions: Organize students and older adults into eight groups of five to seven people (four to five students and one to two older adults). Divide the following questions into four groups (five questions each). Each group begins with the same set of five questions. Place questions in a bag and have a group member pull out one question at a time. Groups will have 10 minutes to answer the first set of questions (groups may or may not get to all questions). After 10 minutes, have students rotate to the next group and all groups get the next set of five questions. Follow this procedure two more times until 40 minutes are up and all four sets of questions have been distributed. You can end the session with a group discussion asking participants to share the most interesting or surprising things they learned about one another.

- What is the greatest invention that has come along in your lifetime so far?
- If you could go anywhere on a trip right now, where would you go?
- What was one of the best gifts you have ever received?
- Is there something you have always wanted to do that you have never done?
- What do you know about your ancestors?
- What was your first job?
- What was your worst job?
- Where were you born?
- What did you hate to eat as a child?
- What is your favorite movie?
- Are you a "morning" or "evening" person?
- What was your first pet?
- What is your favorite dessert?
- What was your favorite toy as a child?
- What is your favorite holiday?
- What is your favorite sport?
- What is your favorite leisure activity?
- What is your favorite kind of music?
- Do you play an instrument?
- What was your worst date?

ACTIVITY 9.2 LIFE HISTORY INTERVIEW PROJECT

Monika Ardelt

ACTIVITY INFORMATION

Type

___X___   Take home

_____   In class

___X___   In community

Difficulty

_____   Introductory

_____   Intermediate

___X___   Advanced

OVERVIEW

The five principles of the life course perspective propose that (a) human development and aging are lifelong processes, (b) people shape their own life course through the choices they make within the opportunities and constraints of history and social circumstances, (c) the life course of individuals is influenced by the historical times and places they live in, (d) people live in a network of interdependent relationships that is affected by socio-historical events and shape their life course, and (e) the impact of life transitions, such as marriage and childbearing, and social events, such as a war or an economic depression, on the life course depends on the timing and the ages of the individuals when these events happen (Elder, 1994, 1995). The life history interview project provides an opportunity for students to identify the applications of these principles in the life course of the participants. It illustrates in a very concrete way how factors related to historical times, childhood family environment, socioeconomic status, culture, race, and/or gender influenced the participants' life course.

Students should also be able to recognize how cumulative advantage and cumulative disadvantage of socioeconomic status, race, and/or gender affects the life course of individuals. The theory of cumulative advantage and cumulative disadvantage states that diversity and inequality regarding socioeconomic resources and health increases among age peers as they move through the life course (Dannefer, 2003). By comparing nursing home or assisted living residents with their relatively healthy older relatives, students might see some of the forces at work that led to greater inequality across the life course.

ACTIVITY LEARNING GOALS

Following this activity, students should be able to . . .

- Compare the life of the nursing home/assisted living facility resident with the life of their older relative.
- Use the life course perspective on aging to analyze how factors related to historical times, childhood family environment, socioeconomic status, culture, race, and/or gender impact the participants' life course.
- Analyze whether the theory of cumulative advantage and disadvantage is applicable to the participants' life course.
- Examine the participants' current life to see whether it best fits the activity, continuity, or disengagement theory of aging.
- Better understand what life in a nursing home/assisted living facility entails.

ASSOCIATION FOR GERONTOLOGY IN HIGHER EDUCATION COMPETENCIES

- Utilize gerontological frameworks to examine human development and aging.
- Relate psychological theories and science to understanding adaptation, stability, and change in aging.
- Relate social theories and science of aging to understanding heterogeneity, inequality, and context of aging.
- Distinguish factors related to aging outcomes, both intrinsic and contextual, through critical thinking and empirical research.

MINIMUM/MAXIMUM NUMBER OF PARTICIPANTS

- No minimum/maximum: 130

TIME NEEDED TO IMPLEMENT ACTIVITY

- 8 weeks

SETTING(S)

- Nursing home or assisted living facility

MATERIALS
Required

- Computer to write down interview notes and analyze the notes

PROCEDURES

Preparation

Before the semester starts, institutional review board (IRB) approval for the interview project is obtained, and the written informed consent form for the resident and the oral informed consent form for the students' older relative are included in the course packet. Sample informed consent forms are presented in Appendix 9.2A.

To secure permission to conduct the interview project, phone calls are made and/or emails are sent to the activity directors and/or volunteer coordinators of the local nursing homes and assisted living facilities. An example email is included in Appendix 9.2B.

Introduction

At the beginning of the semester, students are informed that they will conduct and analyze 30-minute qualitative interviews with *two* older adults, age 55 or above, every week for a total of 8 weeks over the course of the semester. Preferably, students should interview one of their older relatives and one nursing home or assisted living facility resident. If they do not have an older relative who is 55 or above and willing to participate, they are allowed to interview any other older adult in this age group that they know or a second nursing home or assisted living facility resident. If any participant is unable to continue with the interview project midway, students are allowed to conduct the remaining interviews with another participant from the same group (i.e., either a nursing home/assisted living resident or an older relative). Students are told to ask for permission to conduct the interview project from their older relatives or friends/acquaintances within the first 2 weeks of the semester, using the oral informed consent form.

As soon as it can be arranged, students are paired with a resident at one of the nursing homes/assisted living facilities that agreed to participate in the project. Students receive volunteer training in class and at the site for conducting the interviews.

Activity

Students visit and interview "their" resident each week for at least 30 minutes about their past and present life, starting with a life history review that inquires about the resident's past life in a chronological order (see Appendix 9.2C). The life history review chart, which is included in the course packet (see Appendix 9.2D), might help students to conduct those interviews, but they are not required to use this chart. Possible interview topics include childhood and family of origin, adolescence and dating, marriage or partnership history across the life course, relationship with children across the life course, work life (including child rearing and volunteering), personal/psychosocial/spiritual development across the life course, and current situation.

Students conduct the same kind of interviews with one of their older relatives for comparison purposes. Students are allowed to conduct the interviews with their relative by phone but are required to do all interviews with the resident face-to-face. Students are taught in class that the "trick" to good interviewing is to learn how to listen. Knowing how to truly listen is a valuable skill that can benefit both one's professional and private life. Mindful listening also appears to be a skill that is exceedingly rare in our society. Although individuals are constantly connected to others electronically, at the same time it seems to become more difficult to pay complete attention to each other due to multiple sources of distraction. For this project, students are instructed not to take notes during the interview but to pay 100% attention to the conversation instead. Yet, immediately after each interview, they are told to write down what the respondent said in as much detail as possible and then compare and analyze the interviews of their two respondents. Students are asked to use the life course perspective on aging to analyze how factors related to historical times, childhood family environment, socioeconomic status, culture, race, and/or gender impacted their respondents' life course. They are also asked to examine whether their respondents' current life best fits the activity, continuity, or disengagement theory of aging.

Discussion/Reflection

We periodically discuss the interview project and its challenges in class and connect the class lessons to the concrete lives of the interview participants. This makes the information more relevant and memorable to the students.

Wrap-Up

At the end of the semester, students are asked about their interview project experiences and what they think they have learned from the project.

Assessment

Students write at least 500 words of interview notes per interview session. In addition, they analyze each set of interview notes and compare the resident interview with the interview of their relative. Students write at least 250 words of analysis, containing their ideas, hypotheses, assumptions, impressions, and so on. In total, students write at least 1,250 words per week for 8 weeks for the interview project. Students receive full credit if they write at least 500 words of interview notes per interview and at least 250 words of analysis notes per interview set.

Students also have the option to write an 8- to 10-page term paper, based on a particular topic derived from the interview notes. Students are asked to utilize their interview notes and previous analyses to write about this topic in detail, comparing the interviews with the nursing home/assisted living facility resident and their older relative and incorporating theoretical and empirical issues that were discussed in class or that they read in the literature. The term paper is graded based on the criteria listed in Appendix 9.2E.

ADDITIONAL CONSIDERATIONS

When doing this activity with graduate students, they have to interview the nursing home/assisted living facility resident for 1 hour rather than 30 minutes. Graduate students write at least 1,000 words of interview notes per interview session and at least 300 words of analysis, containing their ideas, hypotheses, assumptions, impressions, and so on. In total, graduate students write at least 2,300 words per week for 8 weeks for the interview project. Students receive full credit if they write at least 1,000 words of interview notes per interview and at least 300 words of analysis notes per interview set.

For graduate students, the final paper is required rather than optional. In addition, graduate students also give an oral presentation of their findings.

For their final paper, graduate students compare the life course of four older adults (age 55 or older): one nursing home or assisted living facility resident, one of their older relatives, friends, or acquaintances (e.g., a grandparent or great-grandparent), and two contemporary persons of their choice based on their biography or autobiography. They also have the option to replace both of the autobiographical accounts with another set of "live" interviews and then compare the lives of three older adults. However, in this case, they have to write at least 3,300 words per week. A detailed description of the life history project for graduate students is given in Appendix 9.2F.

It is recommended that a list of nursing homes/assisted living facilities that have agreed to accept student volunteers should be provided for this activity.

REFERENCES

Dannefer, D. (2003). Cumulative advantage/disadvantage and the life course: Cross-fertilizing age and social science theory. *Journals of Gerontology Series B: Psychological Sciences and Social Sciences, 58B*(6), P327–P337. doi:10.1093/geronb/58.6.S327

Elder, G. H., Jr. (1994). Time, human agency, and social change: Perspectives on the life course. *Social Psychology Quarterly, 57*(1), 4–15.

Elder, G. H., Jr. (1995). The life course paradigm: Social change and individual development. In P. Moen, G. H. Elder, Jr., & K. Lüscher (Eds.), *Examining lives in context: Perspectives on the ecology of human development* (pp. 101–139). Washington, DC: American Psychological Association.

APPENDIX 9.2A: EXAMPLE INFORMED CONSENT FORMS

Monika Ardelt

INFORMED CONSENT FORM

You are invited to participate in a class project "Sociology of Aging and the Life Course" led by Professor Monika Ardelt, Department of Sociology, at the University of Florida. The purpose of this project is to help students understand the process of aging from a life course perspective, learn about the problems older people face in their daily lives, and discover the strengths that older people possess.

If you decide to participate in this study, a student will visit you weekly during the semester for at least 30 minutes and talk to you about issues related to your past and present life. Topics may range from your childhood (e.g., how you grew up), to your adult years (e.g., family and adult roles) and your present situation (e.g., what you enjoy and what you like to do). If the student wishes and you consent, interviews may be tape-recorded.

Any information obtained in connection with this study that can be identified with you will be kept confidential to the extent provided by law. To protect your identity all names in the student's notes will be replaced by aliases, and all audio tapes, if they were used, will be erased after the end of the project.

There are no anticipated risks to your participation in this study, and there will be no compensation or other direct benefits to you as a participant. Your participation in the study is completely voluntary, you do not have to answer any question you do not wish to answer, and you are free to withdraw consent and discontinue participation at any time without penalty.

Your signature on this form where noted indicates that you have decided to participate in this study and that you have read and understood the information in this consent form. You also give me permission to report your responses anonymously in a final research paper for my professor that might result from this study. Your decision as to whether or not to participate will not have any bearing on your care nor will it prejudice your relations with the Department of Sociology and Criminology & Law or the University of Florida.

If you have any additional questions, please contact Dr. Ardelt at 352-294-7166 or ardelt@ufl.edu. Questions and concerns about the research participants' rights can be directed to the University of Florida Institutional Review Board office, PO Box 112250, University of Florida, Gainesville, FL 32611-2250.

Thank you very much!

I have read the procedure described. I voluntarily agree to participate in the procedure, and I have received a copy of this description.

Participant's signature _____ Date _____

Investigator's signature _____ Date _____

ORAL INFORMED CONSENT SCRIPT FOR TELELPHONE INTERVIEWS

You are invited to participate in a class project "Sociology of Aging and the Life Course" led by professor Monika Ardelt, Department of Sociology, at the University of Florida. The purpose of this project is to help students understand the process of aging from a life course perspective, learn about the problems older people face in their daily lives, and discover the strengths that older people possess.

If you decide to participate in this study, I will call you weekly during the semester for at least 30 minutes and talk to you about issues related to your past and present life. Topics may range from your childhood (e.g., how you grew up), to your adult years (e.g., family and adult roles) and your present situation (e.g., what you enjoy and what you like to do). If you consent, interviews may be tape-recorded.

Any information obtained in connection with this study that can be identified with you will be kept confidential to the extent provided by law. To protect your identity all names in my interview notes will be replaced by aliases, and all audio tapes, if they were used, will be erased after the end of the project.

There are no anticipated risks to your participation in this study, and there will be no compensation or other direct benefits to you as a participant. Your participation in the study is completely voluntary, you do not have to answer any question you do not wish to answer, and you are free to withdraw consent and discontinue participation at any time without penalty.

If you agree to participate in this study you also give me permission to report your responses anonymously in a final research paper for my professor that might result from this study. Your decision as to whether or not to participate will not prejudice your relations with the Department of Sociology and Criminology & Law or the University of Florida.

If you have any additional questions, please contact Dr. Ardelt at 352-294-7166 or ardelt@ufl.edu. Questions and concerns about the research participants' rights can be directed to the University of Florida Institutional Review Board office, PO Box 112250, University of Florida, Gainesville, FL 32611-2250.

Do you have any questions about the study?

Are you willing to participate in the study?

Thank you very much!

APPENDIX 9.2B: DESCRIPTION OF INTERVIEW PROJECT TO NURSING HOMES AND ASSISTED LIVING FACILITIES

Description of Interview Project to Nursing Homes and Assisted Living Facilities

Subject: Interviewing of residents for Sociology of Aging and the Life Course

Dear . . .,

I am an associate professor in Sociology in the Department of Sociology and Criminology & Law at the University of Florida. In the fall semester, I will teach an undergraduate class on Sociology of Aging and the Life Course. As part of the class, I am asking my students to visit one older nursing home or assisted living resident each week for at least 30 minutes and at least 8 weeks to interview them about issues related to their past and present life. (Students will be told that they do not need to interview the respondent for 30 minutes but may take part of the time to make small talk or tell the respondent about their own life.) Students will start with a life history review, that is, they will ask the resident about their past life in a chronological order starting with their childhood. After completing the life history review, they can then ask about issues that were neglected or that they may want to explore in further detail. Students are also asked to conduct the same kind of interviews with one of their older relatives for comparison purposes. The purpose of this project is to help students understand the process of aging from a life course perspective, learn about the problems older people face in their daily lives, and discover the strengths that older people possess.

I am writing to ask whether some of my students would be permitted to conduct the interview project at. . . . The class has about 50 students. I am also asking other facilities in <city> if they would like to participate, so that the students do not overwhelm one particular facility. The project received approval from the IRB at the University of Florida and informed consent from the residents will be obtained before the interviews begin.

I would be very grateful if you were willing to participate in this project. The students would start to contact you at the [beginning of the semester], and I would like to ask you to pair each student with one resident. I have done the interview project for many years and found that students really come to appreciate their interviews and interactions with the residents. It is this experience that they will remember about the class long after the theoretical class lessons are forgotten.

Many thanks,
Monika Ardelt

APPENDIX 9.2C: ACTIVITY INFORMATION FOR STUDENTS

INTERVIEW PROJECT

Your task will be to interview an older nursing home or assisted living facility resident each week for a total of 8 weeks and compare the interviews with interviews conducted with one of your older relatives (e.g., one grandparent or great-grandparent).

At the beginning of the semester, you will be paired with a nursing home or assisted living facility resident at one of the nursing homes/assisted living facilities that have agreed to participate in this project. After receiving volunteer training, which is provided at each facility and also in class, you will visit the resident each week for at least 30 minutes and interview them about issues related to their past and present life. (You do not need to interview the respondent for 30 minutes but may take part of the time to make small talk or tell the respondent about your own life.) You will start with a life history review, that is, you will ask the resident about their past life in a chronological order starting with their childhood. Possible interview topics include childhood and family of origin, adolescence and dating, marriage or partnership history across the life course, relationship with children across the life course, work life (including child rearing and volunteering), personal/psychosocial/ spiritual development across the life course, and current situation. The life history review chart will help you to conduct those interviews which may take several sessions (take your time). After completing the life history review, you can then ask about issues that were neglected or that you may want to explore in further detail.

You will conduct the same kind of interviews with one of your older relatives for comparison purposes. Therefore, you should choose a relative that is of the same gender and approximately of the same age as your nursing home interviewee if possible. You may conduct the interviews with your relative by phone if necessary but all interviews with the resident are to be conducted face-to-face.

If you like, you may tape-record the interviews but this is not required or even recommended. However, *immediately after each interview you need to write down what happened during the interview and what the respondent said* **in as much detail as possible.** The following are guidelines for writing interview notes.

1. Start all interview notes on a new page. The heading should identify the respondent, the interview number, and the date (e.g., "First Interview with Grandma on September 14 between 2:00 and 2:30 p.m."). Make sure that all participants remain anonymous. If you want to use names give respondents pseudonyms.

2. Write down the location of the interview for each interview (regardless of number of visits).

3. Describe the environment of the respondent even if you do the interviews by phone (does not need to be repeated if the environment does not change in subsequent visits).

4. Describe the respondent in detail, that is, age, gender, race, physical appearance (only for the first visit).

5. Describe what the respondent is doing when you arrive. Give a physical description of the participant—clothes, and so on.
6. Give your impression of the participant—(mental alertness, physical demeanor, etc.).
7. Describe any events that seem noteworthy during the interview in chronological order (e.g., visits from other persons, medication dispensed, frequent stops due to fatigue).
8. Report the interview in chronological order and in as much detail as possible.
9. Include any information that you think would be noteworthy.

You should write **AT LEAST 500 words of interview notes per interview session.** In addition, you should analyze each set of notes and compare the resident interview with the interview of your relative. Use the life course perspective on aging to analyze how factors related to historical times, childhood family environment, socioeconomic status, culture, race, and/or gender impact your respondents' life course and later examine your respondents' current life to see whether it best fits the activity, continuity, or disengagement theory of aging. Start each analysis on a new page. The heading should identify the analysis and the interview number (e.g., "Analysis of First Set of Interview Notes"). You should write **AT LEAST 250 words of analysis,** containing your ideas, hypotheses, assumptions, impressions, and so on. This means that the analysis cannot be simply a summary of the interview notes.

To summarize, you will write AT LEAST 1,250 words per week for 8 weeks for your interview project.

Your first set of interview and analysis notes are due as hard copies during the first weeks of the semester together with the informed consent form that was signed by the nursing home/assisted living respondent. I will review the notes and the analysis and return them to you with my comments. All remaining sets of interview and analysis notes should be submitted via e-Learning. I expect to receive one set of interview and analysis notes per week, but the last opportunity to submit sets of interview and analysis notes will be 1 week before classes end. This date is also your last chance to submit the signed volunteer confirmation form. If I do not receive this form, you will not get any credit for the interview project. Please contact me if you have questions or experience any difficulties with the interview project.

APPENDIX 9.2D: LIFE HISTORY REVIEW CHART

Year	Age	Residence	Mo	Fa	Sib	Sp	So	Da	Oth	Marital Events	Births	Crises	Deaths	Quality of Life	Activities

Mo, Mother; Fa, Father; Sib, Sibling(s); Sp, Spouse; So, Son; Da, Daughter; Oth, Other.

APPENDIX 9.2E: OPTIONAL TERM PAPER

Term Paper (Optional)

For your individual or group term paper, choose a particular topic and use your interview notes and your previous analyses to write about this topic in detail. Your paper should contain a comparison of the interviews with the nursing home/assisted living facility resident(s) and your older relative(s) and incorporate theoretical and empirical issues that were discussed in class or that you read in the literature. You may write this paper as an individual paper, or two to four students can write this paper together as a group term paper. If students work together on this paper, the paper will be based on a comparison of ALL the residents and older relatives that they have interviewed.

The final term paper should be 8 to 10 pages long for an individual paper and 15 to 25 pages long for a group term paper (it can be longer if necessary). The paper is due 1 week before classes end, during regular class time together with the signed volunteer confirmation form (feel free to hand in this form earlier).

I will grade the term paper according to the following criteria:

Form

- Is the paper typed and double-spaced? (Exception: Lengthy quotes should be single-spaced and indented on both sides.)
- Is there a title page that includes the title, your name, and the course title?
- Is the paper organized in a logical way (i.e., introduction, method, results, and conclusion)?
- Were headings and subheadings used?
- Does the paper have 1-in. margins on the left, top, and bottom of the page and a 1.5-in. margin on the right side of the page?
- Is the font size either 11 or 12?
- Except for the title page, are all pages numbered?
- Does the paper contain any grammar and spelling errors?

Content

1. Introduction
   - Describe your research topic.
   - What gap in knowledge does your paper address?
   - Explain how your paper is related to previous theoretical or empirical work in this area (i.e., do a relatively brief literature review using academic journal articles and books—NOT web pages).
   - Present your research question(s).
   - Give an overview of your paper.
2. Method
   - Describe exactly what you did to get your "data," that is, your interview notes.
   - Describe the settings (i.e., the nursing home and your relative's home) and the people you interviewed in detail.

3. Results
   - Describe your findings in detail. Give evidence from your interview notes to illustrate your points. Be explicit! Quote from your interview notes.
   - Were you surprised by any of your findings? If yes, why? What did you discover that was different from your initial assumptions and preconceptions? Which findings confirmed your initial assumptions and preconceptions?

4. Conclusion
   - Present a short summary of your major findings and insights in relation to your research question(s).
   - How do those findings relate to past research? Do they confirm or contradict prior research?
   - Make suggestions for further research based on your findings and, if appropriate, recommendations for social policy and practice.

5. References
   - List all the articles and/or books that are cited in the paper, using APA reference style. You need to have **a minimum of five academic references per group member**. Web pages do not count!

If you encounter any problems pertaining to this interview project (e.g., choosing a topic, writing the notes, analyzing the notes, or writing the term paper) come and talk to me.

APPENDIX 9.2F: DESCRIPTION OF LIFE HISTORY PROJECT FOR GRADUATE STUDENTS

LIFE HISTORY PROJECT

For your term paper, you will compare the life course of four older adults (age 55 or older): one nursing home or assisted living facility resident, one of your older relatives, friends, or acquaintances (e.g., a grandparent or great-grandparent), and two contemporary persons of your choice based on their biography or auto-biography (e.g., *Having Our Say: The Delany Sisters' First 100 Years*). If you do not know any older adults personally, you can interview two nursing home/assisted living residents. Moreover, you also have the option to replace both of the auto-biographical accounts with another set of "live" interviews and then compare the lives of three older adults.

More specifically, your task will be to interview one (or two) older nursing home or assisted living facility resident(s) each week for a total of 8 weeks and compare the interviews with interviews conducted with one (or two) of your older relatives, friends, or acquaintances (e.g., a grandparent or great-grandparent), and two biographies or autobiographies of your choice. At the beginning of the semester, you will be paired with one (or two) nursing home or assisted living facil-ity resident(s) at one of the nursing homes/assisted living facilities that have agreed to participate in this project. After receiving volunteer training, which is provided at each facility and also in class, you will visit the resident each week for at least 1 hour to ask them about their life. (You do not need to interview the respondent for 1 hour but may take part of the time to make small talk or tell the respondent about your own life.) You will start with a life history review, that is, you will ask the resident about their past life in chronological order, starting with their child-hood. Possible interview topics include childhood and family of origin, adolescence and dating, marriage or partnership history across the life course, relationship with children across the life course, work life (including child rearing and volunteering), personal/psychosocial/spiritual development across the life course, and current situation. The life history review chart will help you to conduct those interviews, which may take several sessions (take your time). After completing the life history review, you can then ask about issues that were neglected or that you may want to explore in further detail.

You will conduct the same kind of interviews with one of your older relatives for comparison purposes. Therefore, you might want to choose a relative that is of the same gender and approximately of the same age as your nursing home/assisted living interviewee if possible. You may conduct the interviews with your relative by phone if necessary, but all interviews with the resident are to be con-ducted face-to-face.

You may tape-record the interviews, but it is not required that you transcribe the interviews verbatim. However, immediately after each interview you need to write down what happened during the interview and what the respondent said **IN AS MUCH DETAIL AS POSSIBLE.** The following are guidelines for writing interview notes.

1. Start all interview notes on a new page. The heading should identify the respondent, the interview number, and the date (e.g., "First Interview with Grandma on September 14 between 2:00 and 3:00 p.m."). Make sure that all participants remain anonymous. If you want to use names give respondents pseudonyms.

2. Write down the location of the interview for each interview (regardless of number of visits).

3. Describe the environment of the respondent even if you do the interviews by phone (does not need to be repeated if the environment does not change in subsequent visits).

4. Describe the respondent in detail, that is, age, gender, race, physical appearance (only for the first visit).

5. Describe what the respondent is doing when you arrive. Give a physical description of the participant—clothes, and so on.

6. Give your impression of the participant—(mental alertness, physical demeanor, etc.).

7. Describe any events that seem noteworthy during the interview in chronological order (e.g., visits from other persons, medication dispensed, frequent stops due to fatigue).

8. Report the interview in chronological order and in as much detail as possible.

9. Include any information that you think would be noteworthy.

You should write **AT LEAST 1,000 words of interview notes per interview session.** In addition, you should analyze each set of notes and compare the resident interview with the interview of your relative. Use the life course perspective on aging to analyze how factors related to historical times, childhood family environment, socioeconomic status, culture, race, and/or gender impact your respondents' life course and whether the theory of cumulative advantage and cumulative disadvantage can be applied. Start each analysis on a new page. The heading should identify the analysis and the interview number (e.g., "Analysis of First Set of Interview Notes"). You should write **AT LEAST 300 words of analysis,** containing your ideas, hypotheses, assumptions, impressions, and so on. This means that the analysis cannot be simply a summary of the interview notes.

To summarize, you will write at least 2,300 words per week for 8 weeks for your life history project or at least 3,300 words if you interview three older adults.

Your first set of interview and analysis notes are due as hard copies during the first weeks of the semester together with the informed consent form that was signed by the nursing home/assisted living respondent. I will review the notes and the analysis and return them to you with my comments. All remaining sets of interview and analysis notes should be submitted via e-Learning. I expect to receive one set of interview and analysis notes per week, but the last opportunity to submit sets of interview and analysis notes is 1 week before classes end. Please contact me if you have questions or experience any difficulties with the life history project.

For your term paper, choose a particular topic and compare the interviews with your two respondents and the two (auto)biographies to write about this topic in detail. Your paper should be between 15 and 25 pages long and incorporate some of the topics that were discussed in class. You should examine at least eight different academic references (academic books or journal articles—not websites), which should be included in the paper. The paper is due 1 week before classes end.

Oral presentations of the research findings will take place on the last day of class.

I will grade the term paper according to the following criteria:

Form

- Is the paper typed and double-spaced? (Exception: Lengthy quotes should be single-spaced and indented on both sides.)
- Is there a title page that includes the title, your name, and the course title?
- Is the paper organized in a logical way (i.e., introduction, method, results, and conclusion)?
- Were headings and subheadings used?
- Does the paper have 1-in. margins on the left, top, and bottom of the page and a 1.5-in. margin on the right side of the page?
- Is the font size either 11 or 12?
- Except for the title page, are all pages numbered?
- Does the paper contain any grammar and spelling errors?

Content

1. Introduction
   - Describe your research topic.
   - What gap in knowledge does your paper address?
   - Explain how your paper is related to previous theoretical or empirical work in this area (i.e., do a relatively brief literature review using academic journal articles and books).
   - Give an overview of your paper.

2. Method
   - Describe exactly what you did to get your "data," that is, your interview notes and the biographies.
   - Describe the settings (i.e., the nursing home and your relative's home), the people you interviewed, and the background of your biography subjects in detail.

3. Results
   - Describe your findings in detail. Give evidence from your interview notes and biographies to illustrate your points. Be explicit! Quote from your interview notes and biographies.

4. Conclusion
   - Present a short summary of your major findings and insights.
   - How do those findings relate to past research? Do they confirm or contradict prior research?
   - Make suggestions for further research based on your findings and, if appropriate, recommendations for social policy and practice.

5. References
   ○ List all the articles and/or books that are cited in the paper, using APA reference style. You should have a minimum of eight *academic* references. Web pages do not count!

If you encounter any problems pertaining to this life history project (e.g., choosing a topic, writing the notes, analyzing the notes, or writing the term paper) come and talk to me.

ACTIVITY 9.3 SERVICE-LEARNING FAIR (SLF) IN GERONTOLOGY

Maria Claver, Casey Goeller, and Elena Ionescu

ACTIVITY INFORMATION

Type

_____ Take home

__X__ In class

__X__ In community

Difficulty

_____ Introductory

__X__ Intermediate

_____ Advanced

OVERVIEW

The SLF in Gerontology is a tool to introduce gerontology students to the range and scope of agencies and services considered the "network of aging." Although the Service Learning (SL) educational approach is not new to the gerontology field (e.g., Gorelik, Damron-Rodriguez, Funderburk, & Solomon, 2000; Hanks & Icenogle, 2001; Vandsberger & Wakefield, 2005), the SLF may be an underutilized best practice that is both a component of the service learning experience and a stand-alone tool for introducing students to career and volunteer options within the field. As part of the greater service-learning experience, SLF is an important opportunity for community partners to meet with students and brainstorm about the upcoming semester-long collaboration. Allowing students the choice of agency based on a particular population of interest, location, and/or hours of operation promotes buy-in and flexibility. A pre-service-learning reflection assignment further promotes student buy-in to the experience, fosters a baseline for growth as the service-learning experience progresses, and establishes the practice of reflection, a hallmark of service-learning (Anstee, Harris, Pruitt, & Sugar, 2008; Hatcher, Bringle, & Muthiah, 2004), before the service-learning hours begin. The SLF brings together community partners, students, and faculty and serves the added purpose of connecting the university with representatives of services and programs aimed at older adults for other types of partnerships such as guest lectures, community engagement, and research. Establishing connections with community agencies and an assessment of the appropriateness of the agency for service learning (vs. internship placements) is an ongoing process and achieved through alumni relationships, invitations to agencies to provide guest lectures in classes, and attendance at conferences and health/aging fairs. Continued efforts in connecting with community agencies is important for maintaining quality service learning experiences. This can be achieved through site visits and email communication throughout the semester, but a gathering to include several agencies once per semester (i.e., the SLF) serves to build more of a "community," including fostering inter-agency relationships.

ACTIVITY LEARNING GOALS

Following this activity, students should be able to . . .

- Describe the services provided by agencies represented at the SLF in Gerontology.
- Identify the needs of older adults and their families that might be met by programs in the community.
- Discuss differences and commonalities between agencies in the "aging network" regarding populations served, funding sources, and organization.
- Reflect on expectations for personal and professional learning opportunities through service learning at a particular agency.

ASSOCIATION FOR GERONTOLOGY IN HIGHER EDUCATION COMPETENCIES

Participation in the SLF in Gerontology will prepare students to:

- Appreciate the diversity of the older population based on age, functioning, gender, culture, language, religion, immigration status, sexual orientation, and/or other variables.
- Assess and reflect on one's work in order to continuously learn and improve outcomes for older persons.
- Advocate for and develop effective programs to promote the well-being of older persons.
- Council individuals to utilize available services that promote well-being and quality of life.
- Inform the public of the spectrum of aging services that provide older persons with preventive, treatment, supportive programs.

MINIMUM/MAXIMUM NUMBER OF PARTICIPANTS

- 1 to 80+

TIME NEEDED TO IMPLEMENT ACTIVITY

- 2 hours

SETTING(S)

- Classroom or conference room with open space

MATERIALS
Required

- Table and two chairs per agency

Optional

- Request that agencies bring handouts
- Chairs for students
- Name badges
- Refreshments

PROCEDURES

Preparation

- Set a date for the SLF and decide where SLF will take place (school campus or community).
- Invite the collaborating community partners to the SLF. The community partners are profit and nonprofit organizations serving the older adults within the proximity of the educational institution campus.
- If possible, arrange parking for community partners.
- Prepare students for the SLF by sharing a list of the participating agencies and encourage students to do some research about the agencies before the SLF.
- Set up the classroom/conference room in a way that tables are around the edges of the room and there is open space in the middle of the room for student movement.
- Print out the class roster.

Introduction

- At the beginning of the SLF, ask each student to sign in, using the class roster.
- Each agency representative is asked to introduce oneself, provide a description of populations served by the agency, and describe the services provided by the agency they represent.
- In addition, the agency representative provides students with a brief description of the types of activities they would be doing at that site during their SL hours.

Activity

- After introductions, allow students to circulate around the room and interact with agency representatives.
- After students have made their decision, they can sign up for the site.
- Each student's decision is tracked by an agency representative and instructor on a computerized system such as SLPro or simply on a spreadsheet (Word table or Excel).

Discussion/Reflection

- Before attending the SLF, students need to research the agencies presented at the event.

- After the SLF, students must complete a Service Learning Expectations Paper, noting all of the project's outcomes (e.g., things they expect to see, do, hear, feel, and even smell!).

Follow-Up

- Student reports the SL experiences in the form of SL journal reflections, which are submitted weekly to the instructor—the SL journal reflection correlates the field experience with class material and is tied back to the pre-SL Expectations Paper.

Assessment

- The SLF is assessed based on the student's attendance, student's registration with the preferred presented agency, and SL Expectations Paper.
- Grading rubric: see Appendix 9.3.

Example of SLF assessment (30 points)

1. SLF participation points are given based on the student's signature on the provided class roster (5 points).
2. SL Expectations Paper—includes student's registration with the preferred presented agency (25 points).

The SL Expectations Paper is two to three well-developed paragraphs students must submit within a week after they attend the SLF. In the SL Expectations Paper students include the name of the SL placement and what they will expect to do, see, hear, and even smell during the SL hours at the agency. The points can be distributed as following:

a. A student reports what they expect to do at the chosen agency (5 points).
b. A student reflects on how they expect to feel in regard to the SL experience (5 points).
c. A student identifies the importance of SL into the student's professional growth by recognizing the application of gerontological concepts presented in class throughout the expected experiences at the chosen agency (15 points).

ADDITIONAL CONSIDERATIONS

If your campus has a Center for Community Engagement (this office may have a different name at different campuses), ask for their support for the SLF in the way of funding, attendance to introduce the center to students and community partners, and so on.

REFERENCES

Anstee, J. L. K., Harris, S. G., Pruitt, K. D., & Sugar, J. A. (2008). Service-learning projects in an undergraduate gerontology course: A six-stage model and application. *Educational Gerontology, 34*(7), 595–609.

Gorelik, Y., Damron-Rodriguez, J., Funderburk, B., & Solomon, D. H. (2000). Undergraduate interest in aging: Is it affected by contact with older adults? *Educational Gerontology, 26*(7), 623–638.

Hanks, R. S., & Icenogle, M. (2001). Preparing for an age-diverse workforce: Intergenerational service-learning in social gerontology and business curricula. *Educational Gerontology, 27*(1), 49–70.

Hatcher, J. A., Bringle, R. G., & Muthiah, R. (2004). Designing effective reflection: What matters to service-learning? *Michigan Journal of Community Service Learning, 11*(1), 38–46.

Vandsberger, E., & Wakefield, M. (2005). Service learning with rural older adults: Effects on students' career perspectives in gerontology. *Journal of Intergenerational Relationships, 3*(4), 83–97.

CONTENT SOURCE

National Service Learning Clearinghouse: www.servicelearning.org

APPENDIX 9.3: SL EXPECTATIONS PAPER GRADING RUBRIC

Section	Points	Comments
What you expect to do	5	In-depth response with details about activities you expect to do during the SL project. (Example: I expect to help older adults learn how to utilize technological gadgets such as Apple devices—iPod, iPad, Mac system); Android calendar; or wii, simply for playing a bowling game.)
How you expect to feel	5	Focus on how you expect to feel, rather than what you'll do. (Example: I expect to be amazed to see how an 84-year-old person can learn something such as new technology systems. Such experience can blow away the stereotypes my generation holds with regard to older adults.)
Importance of SL project in correlation to your major and gerontological presented class material	15	Refer to course material in this section by citing two class material sources. (Example: Given the fact that I am a nursing student, I am looking forward to deepening my understanding of dementia. At [site] I observed that seniors with different levels of dementia are taken care of. I will keep an open mind while spending time at this agency and try to enhance my observational skills in order to understand how the integrative BioPsychoSocial model presented in our lecture adds bonus years to the current generation of older adults. In addition, I am curious to understand how positive aging is dramatically influenced by social support.)
TOTAL	25	
Overall grammar/ writing	5	PLEASE take pride in your work and spell check!

ACTIVITY 9.4 SITE VISITS AS A REQUIREMENT FOR AN INTRODUCTORY GERONTOLOGY COURSE: SOCIAL AND DEMOGRAPHIC IMPLICATIONS OF AGING

Nina M. Silverstein

ACTIVITY INFORMATION

Type

_____	Take home
_____	In class
__X__	In community

Difficulty

__X__	Introductory
_____	Intermediate
_____	Advanced

OVERVIEW

Site visits offer an opportunity for students to envision their career options and to understand in what facet of the aging network of programs and services they might imagine their future selves as professionals. This is one of the first networking opportunities for new learners and a beginning orientation to the professional role. The site visit brings life to the in-class readings and discussions.

KEY TERMS

Aging network
Site visit

ACTIVITY LEARNING GOALS

Following this activity, students should be able to . . .

- Understand firsthand one or more of the continuum of services and programs that comprise the aging network and careers in aging.
- Describe one or more of the professionals' roles and qualifications needed to work within the aging network of programs and services.
- Observe firsthand the interactions that staff members have with older adults served by the agency or organization.

- Consider environmental features related to accessibility that add to agency or organizational space serving older adults.

ASSOCIATION FOR GERONTOLOGY IN HIGHER EDUCATION COMPETENCIES

- Develop a gerontological perspective through knowledge and self-reflection.
- Adhere to ethical principles to guide work with and on behalf of older persons.
- Promote quality of life and positive social environment for older persons.
- Employ and design programmatic and community development with and on behalf of the aging population.

MINIMUM/MAXIMUM NUMBER OF PARTICIPANTS

- 1 to 20

TIME NEEDED TO IMPLEMENT ACTIVITY

- 90 minutes

SETTING(S)

- At agency or organizational setting

PROCEDURES

Preparation

- Schedule with agency at least a month before the academic term.
- Include on syllabus that the site visit(s) are required and are outside of class time. Two site visits are required. Sites are chosen that are accessible by public transit or carpools are coordinated, if necessary.

Introduction

- Students are notified in writing in the syllabus and the expectations are reviewed the first day of class.
- The following language is included on the syllabus:

Time needed outside of class
List day of the week, time, and location for each of the scheduled group site visits.

Independent site visit(s):
If the student is unable to attend with a group then instructions are provided for the student to arrange an independent site visit to an agency or organization

(must be approved in advance by the faculty member). The expectations for the individual site visits for students unable to join the group visits on (date) and (date) are (see the description under Activity):

Note: Instructions for independent site visits may also be used when this course is taught online and students are not local to campus.

Activity

The site visits are group site visits arranged by the faculty member. The site visit includes the director and key program staff who provide brief presentations followed by Q/A. The staff describe the agency or organization and share their career paths and current responsibilities, as well as opportunities and challenges faced. The students then are escorted on a tour of the agency or organization.

Appendix 9.4 provides instructions for an independent site visit if a student is unable to participate in the group or the course is offered online.

Discussion/Reflection

- Class time is spent in the session following the site visit for student discussion and reflection and new insights into professional life. Students who do independent site visits are also provided time to share their experiences with the class.

Follow-Up

- In addition to thank you notes (as part of mentoring new professionals to get in the habit of acknowledging others), we also take photographs of students and staff (not older adults without consent) and those photos are helpful to the agency and to the university and program in demonstrating applied learning and community engagement.

Assessment

- As this is a required activity, students who do not participate in the group site visit or who do not arrange for an independent site visit will see that reflected in their final grade—however, students usually welcome this activity and opportunity to expand their network of professional colleagues. The student is responsible for attending the site visit, participating in the discussion with agency staff members, and sharing reflections on new insights on professional life during the subsequent class session.

- Rubric: Has clearly participated in professionally focused activity and begins to reflect or describe how this activity may contribute to one's career path.

ADDITIONAL CONSIDERATIONS

- Students have been gerontology certificate students or majors; and as this course meets the General Education Diversity–U.S. requirement for the campus, it has attracted students from other majors.

- This is a win-win for all involved—the faculty member, the students, and the agency or organizational staff members. Site visits help to keep faculty members current about agencies and organizations in their state; for the students, this activity orients them to careers in aging and specific roles and responsibilities of people who work in the field; for the agency or organization, it reinforces the reputation of gerontology programs, strengthens community partnerships, and introduces students as resources to the aging network through future field placements and internships.

APPENDIX 9.4: INSTRUCTIONS FOR AN INDEPENDENT SITE VISIT

For use if students are unable to participate in the class activity, or are participating online.

1. Arrange to visit an agency or organization that serves older adults by asking for an informational interview. Examples of such agencies or organizations that may be found in communities nationwide include: State Unit on Aging, Area Agency on Aging, Council on Aging/Senior Center, Independent Housing or Assisted Living, Continuing Care Retirement Community (CCRC), or Village model; or organization that serves older adults such as AARP, the Alzheimer's Association, or a faith-based organization whose mission includes older adults.

2. Call ahead and ask for an appointment with the director or program manager— do not just "drop in."

3. Dress professionally—no jeans.

4. Spend no more than 1 hour in an informational interview—learning about the services and programs offered, organizational structure and funding mechanism, and career opportunities/qualifications of staff.

5. Tour the area.

6. Prepare a brief write-up of knowledge gained, your impressions, and observations about your new understanding of professional life (no more than two pages). Be prepared to present in class.

CHAPTER 10

RESEARCH PROJECTS AND PAPERS

Pamela Pitman Brown

Mention the words "research methods" in a classroom and you are likely to hear groaning from a majority of the students. Research is a key component in every discipline and is often considered the most difficult to teach and the most boring to learn. Students frequently ask the greater question, "Why do I need to study research if I am going to be a _____?" Constructing a convincing case for the "why" takes more than one course or one lecture.

Many undergraduate and graduate courses in research methods are across two semesters, which include a course on statistics and then a course on research methods, with a melding of the two during the second course. Universities are encouraging undergraduates to complete a research project with a professor in order to show their abilities prior to joining the workforce or attending graduate school.

WHAT IS RESEARCH?

Simply stated, research is a process of continuous exploration and discovery through systematic steps in order to increase knowledge or to discover new information on a particular topic or question.

Salkind (2017) presents a concise explanation of the characteristics of research, more specifically high-quality research.

High-quality research:

- Is based on the work of others
- Can be replicated
- Is generalizable to other settings
- Is based on some logical rationale and tied to theory
- Is doable
- Generates new questions or is cyclical in nature
- Is incremental
- Is an apolitical activity that should be undertaken for the betterment of society (p. 2)

FORMS OF RESEARCH

There are four main forms of research: *basic* or *pure research*, *applied research*, *evaluation research*, and *action research*.

- **Basic research** is driven by curiosity and is used to increase our knowledge. Typically, it is descriptive in nature and often is used to explain/understand a phenomenon.
- **Applied research** is used to provide information in order to improve the human condition or improve society. It is prescriptive in nature and attempts to offer solutions to practical or real-world problems.
- **Evaluation research** is used to examine the solution to the problem via looking at the processes and outcomes associated with the proposed solution. Evaluation research may be summative, which attempts to evaluate the proposed solution/program. It may be formative, which attempts to improve upon the intervention/solution.
- **Action research** is usually conducted from within an organization or a community, with the research focusing on collecting and analyzing internal data or studying themselves.

METHODOLOGY: QUANTITATIVE/QUALITATIVE

Within methodology there are two main approaches: *qualitative* and *quantitative*.
Qualitative methods are used mainly when the goal of the project is to describe, understand, or examine an issue or a phenomenon.
Research designs that use qualitative methodology include:

- Case studies
- Historical studies/analysis
- Narratives
- Grounded theory
- Phenomenology
- Ethnography

Quantitative methods are used mainly when examining variables and relationships between variables, with the goals of the research project being analysis of testing relationship and examination of cause/effect relationship; they include the ability to present the relationship via statistical analysis.

Research designs that use *quantitative methodology* include:

- Correlational
- Causal comparative
- Experimental
- Quasi-experimental

RESEARCH EDUCATION ACTIVITIES

For those of us who teach research methodology, active learning is time-consuming in construction, presentation, and grading and is sometimes limited by time constraints. Each of the following activities relies on the students' high level of participation outside of delineated class time. Each activity is usable with undergraduates and graduates alike with little to no modification. Each activity is appropriate for a face-to-face or online course.

In Activity 10.1, An Examination of Scholarly Research on Older Adults From the Past 5 Years, students utilize their newly acquired knowledge of research methods to locate current research on older adults. Each student produces a presentation to the class, relating the article to class material learned, such as theory, research designs, and findings. Additionally, the students should be able to discuss/explain the various components of the study, relating to qualitative/quantitative analysis, tools used, methodology, and conclusions. Construction of a class handout by the presenter informs the class of the article's citation, key terms/definitions, article summary, critical thinking questions, and how the article overlaps with class material.

Activity 10.2, Final for Biology of Human Aging Course, incorporates acquired knowledge on biological aspects of aging and links an individual to each biological aging process. The student interviews an aging individual, a caregiver, and a health care professional to gain a holistic perspective of biological processes, which includes normative aging and diseased aging. The activity also prepares students for future research in construction of questions and linking the interviews to class materials. Students are able to place a personal context to each of the biological processes after participation, which expands the students' abilities to connect on a personal level to those whom they later treat or see within clinical experience.

REFERENCE

Salkind, N. (2017). *Exploring research* (9th ed.). Boston, MA: Pearson.

ACTIVITY 10.1 DIVERSITY OF THE AGING EXPERIENCE: AN EXAMINATION OF SCHOLARLY RESEARCH ON OLDER ADULTS FROM THE PAST 5 YEARS

Heather R. Rodriguez

ACTIVITY INFORMATION

Type

___X___ In class (Students present their article in class.)

_____ Online

___X___ Take home (Students spend time at home searching for an article and creating their presentation.)

_____ In community

Difficulty

___X___ Introductory. This activity would work well in any introductory course or in any course when students are coming from different disciplines.

___X___ Intermediate. This activity would work well in any upper level course when students are familiar with research methods or have a foundation in a particular field.

_____ Advanced

OVERVIEW

This activity focuses on helping students learn about the various research methods used in scholarly, peer-reviewed articles about older adults. This activity also focuses on helping students learn about current research findings on older adults. The instructor addresses various research methods (oral histories, longitudinal, cohort studies, etc.) used to study older adults. Students are then asked to find and present on a current scholarly, peer-reviewed article about older adults. The topic of choice is up to the student but students are encouraged to find studies that address unique or overlooked topics. This activity enhances classroom discussion and learning by providing current and up-to-date information on new topics related to older adults. Once the student identifies an appropriate article of interest, the instructor reviews and approves the article. The student then begins working on a 15- to 20-minute presentation with all data coming from the selected and approved article. The presentation covers each section of the research article including the introduction, relevant theories used in the study, research design, findings, conclusion, and concludes with a discussion of how the article overlaps with class material. By the end of the presentation, students are better informed about current day topics impacting older adults.

ACTIVITY LEARNING GOALS

Following this activity, students should be able to . . .

- Comprehend and analyze current topics related to the diversity of the aging experience.
- Report current trends, behaviors, or statistics related to older adults.
- Understand current research methods and theories used to understand older adults.
- Explain various components of a research study and how research studies contribute to our understanding of the aging process.
- Discuss overlap between current research and class material.

ASSOCIATION FOR GERONTOLOGY IN HIGHER EDUCATION COMPETENCIES

- Utilize gerontological frameworks to examine human development and aging.
- Relate social theories and science of aging to understanding heterogeneity, inequality, and context of aging.
- Develop a gerontological perspective through knowledge and self-reflection.
- Promote older adults' strengths and adaptations to maximize well-being, health, and mental health.
- Engage in research to advance knowledge and improve interventions for older adults.
- Use critical thinking to evaluate information and its source (popular media and research publications).
- Recognize the strengths and limitations of reliance on either qualitative or quantitative questions, tools, methods, and conclusions.

MINIMUM/MAXIMUM NUMBER OF PARTICIPANTS

- The minimum number of recommended students is one. The maximum number of recommended students is 100. Students can be paired into small groups of two to four and present together if there are more than 25 students in the class or if time is limited.

TIME NEEDED TO IMPLEMENT ACTIVITY

- Students need adequate time to search and find an appropriate research article, present it to the instructor for approval, and prepare a presentation. A minimum of 3 to 4 weeks advanced notice works best.

SETTING

- The room should be equipped with chairs, tables, Internet access, an overhead projector, a computer, sound, and the ability to play a video. Lights will likely need to be dimmed during the presentation.

MATERIALS
Required
- The student should come prepared with a formal presentation that can be shown on an overhead and a typed, one-page summary handout for classmates to follow along with. The handout should contain correct citation of the research article, a summary of the article, key terms and definitions, ways in which the article overlaps with class material, and three critical thinking questions related to the research article. The student is instructed ahead of time to make copies of the handout and to bring enough copies to class so that each student receives a copy of the handout. The student submits three items to the instructor: a copy of the handout, a copy of the presentation, and the research article being presented.

Optional
- The student may want to pass around a hard copy of the research article that they are presenting. The student may also consider making relevant web links available to classmates.

PROCEDURES
Preparation
This activity helps with keeping course material engaging and applicable to the current student population. Students are asked to find a recent, scholarly research article or report from the past 5 years. The article needs to be about older adults and/or the aging process and can be on a topic of the student's choosing. After the article is approved by the instructor, the student then gives a formal presentation on the article and topic of choice. The presentation should be 15 to 20 minutes in length and can include no more than 5 minutes of video.

Introduction
Students present a peer-reviewed, scholarly research article published within the past 5 years. It is best to have no more than seven presentations in one day; five per day works best. Presentations can be shortened to 10 to 15 minutes if needed. On the day of the presentation, students use the classroom computer to bring up their presentations. Students present their presentation. The instructor monitors time and gives 5-minute and 2-minute warnings to the presenter.

Activity
1. Instructor lectures on research methods used to study the aging process and older adults.
2. Students read relevant texts, chapters, and notes related to research methods used to study the aging process and older adults.
3. Instructor shows students how to locate peer-reviewed, scholarly articles and shows students what a peer-reviewed, scholarly article looks like.
4. Instructor assigns presentation and asks students to find a peer-reviewed, scholarly article (from within the past 5 years) that the student wants to present to the class. Instructor provides a due date when the article of choice is due.

5. Student submits a hard copy of the found article to the instructor for approval.

6. The instructor confirms that the article submitted is a peer-reviewed, scholarly article from within the past 5 years and is related to older adults and/or the aging process. The instructor also confirms that each student submitted a different article and that there are no overlaps in submissions.

7. If the article meets the requirements, the instructor makes note of the article title and authors, and hands the article back to the student with approval. If the article does not meet the requirements, the instructor informs the student how the article does not meet the minimum requirements and gives the student three more days to find a different article.

8. The instructor passes around a sign-up sheet well in advance of the presentation day(s). Students sign up for a day to present. Students note their presentation day.

9. Students are provided specific instructions on what to include in their presentations. Each presentation should cover the main sections of the research article chosen, with a focus on the research methods used. It is suggested that students use PowerPoint and have a range of 10 to 15 slides total. The presentation should conclude with a discussion of how the information in the article overlaps with course material. The presentation ends with the presenter posing three critical thinking questions to the class. The critical thinking questions should go beyond simply asking for definitions of key terms.

10. Approximately 2 to 5 minutes of discussion time is allotted per presentation. To help avoid monopolization of class discussion, it works best to request that students in the audience only remark once, to allow time for others to contribute to class discussion, and to allow time for others to have enough time to present.

11. The student presenter submits all materials to the instructor.

12. Optional: Students in the audience may be given assessment sheets to "grade" each presentation. A scale of 1 to 5 can be used, with 1 being poor and 5 being excellent. Presenters could be assessed by their peers on professionalism (for example, no stereotyping of older adults), discussion of overlap with class material, and presentation of appropriate sections of the research article. The instructor would create this assessment and make enough copies for each student and for each presentation. These assessments are anonymous and are returned to the instructor after completion. Assessments help the instructor develop an understanding of what students gained from the presentation, how students perceived the effectiveness of the presenter, and the quality of information presented.

Discussion/Reflection

Students pose three critical thinking questions to the class at the end of the presentation. The three critical thinking questions should also be printed on the handout and should relate to the information in the article that the student presented.

Wrap-Up

Students in the audience have 2 to 5 minutes to respond to the three critical thinking questions posed by the presenter. Optional: After discussion, students in the audience complete assessment of the presenter and presentation.

Assessment

The instructor assesses which students achieved the learning goals of the activity by assessing:

a. The student presentation and materials submitted to the instructor by the student.

b. How well the student's presentation and handout addressed current day issues.

c. The student's report of key findings from the article.

d. The student's discussion of research methods used for the study.

e. The student's ability to apply course material to the article.

This assessment can be completed using an already established grading rubric from the instructor. In accordance with AACU Value Rubrics (Rhodes, 2009), students can also be evaluated on critical thinking and whether the "issue/problem to be considered critically is stated clearly and described comprehensively, delivering all relevant information necessary for full understanding" versus lacking clarification and information. Second, students can be assessed on information literacy and if the student "effectively defines the scope of the research question or thesis. Effectively determines key concepts. Types of information (sources) selected directly relate to concepts or answer research question" versus has difficulty defining the research study. Last, students can be assessed on inquiry and analysis and whether the student, "Identifies a creative, focused, and manageable topic that addresses potentially significant yet previously less explored aspects of the topic" versus chooses a topic that is too general and not manageable.

ADDITIONAL CONSIDERATIONS

Adapting for Class Size

This activity can be conducted with any small or large group of students, traditional and nontraditional students, and students of various majors or professions. However, if the class size is larger than 25 students, it is best to have students work in groups of two or three.

Suggested Lecture Points

- Research methods
- Longitudinal study designs
- Cohort studies
- Cross-sectional study designs

REFERENCE

Rhodes, T. (2009). *Assessing outcomes and improving achievement: Tips and tools for using the rubrics.* Washington, DC: Association of American Colleges and Universities.

ACTIVITY 10.2 FINAL FOR BIOLOGY OF HUMAN AGING COURSE

Jacquelyn Browne

ACTIVITY INFORMATION

Type

_____ In class

_____ Online

_____ Take home

__X__ In community

Difficulty

_____ Introductory

__X__ Intermediate

_____ Advanced

OVERVIEW

Developed as a final project for biology of aging this course, this assignment is designed to reinforce a humanistic approach to learning about the biology of human aging. By humanistic, the aim is for students to develop sensitivity to and critical thinking about the experiences of those older adults who are living the biological processes presented in the course textbook (Saxon, Ettens, & Perkins, 2015). While the clinical information about the biology of human aging requires familiarity with what constitutes normal aging and what constitutes disease, it is equally important to be aware of and curious about the older individual human being who is experiencing aging, as well as those who are caregivers and health care professionals providing care and treatment. A biological process also includes psychological and social aspects that impact both the process and meaning of what it is like to grow old. To that end, this assignment includes the opportunity to interview an aging individual, a caregiver, and a health care professional in order to expand students' perspectives. Gaining a more holistic perspective is key to this course and this assignment.

For each biological process studied, students are asked not only to learn the biology appropriate for their future work, but also to focus on the experience of an individual who is experiencing that process. This happens each week in discussion posts and readings. The final paper is meant to dive into the experience of an older individual, caregiver, or health professional to gain multiple perspectives on the lived experience of growing older.

Students will practice using open-ended questions. For example: What is your experience with (diabetes, macular degeneration, congestive heart failure, hearing loss, and so on)?

Final project and paper (25% of grade): The final project and paper reflect use of narratives and life stories as a method for learning about the humanistic perspective within the biological experience of aging. The final paper will be a 10-page double-spaced paper (including title page and reference page, appendix is separate) based on interviews with two of the following: (a) an older individual experiencing an acute or chronic illness, (b) a caregiver of that individual, and (c) a health care professional involved directly or indirectly in the care of that individual. The paper shall consist of a biological description of the normal aging process and disease, summary of interviews and interview themes, and conclusions about the experience and meaning of a particular illness or condition for those interviewed.

ACTIVITY LEARNING GOALS

Following this activity, students should be able to . . .

- Demonstrate knowledge of the biology of a particular aging process linked to a person living that process.
- Gain a broader perspective on the meaning of aging and/or illness/disability in the life of an aging individual, caregiver, and/or health care professional.
- Demonstrate an increased ability to be an open, curious, good listener.
- Evaluate awareness of personal attitudes about aging/illness from the interview experience.
- Demonstrate greater understanding of the benefits of a holistic perspective.

ASSOCIATION FOR GERONTOLOGY IN HIGHER EDUCATION COMPETENCIES

- Relate biological theory and science to understanding senescence, longevity, and variation in aging.
- Develop comprehensive and meaningful concepts, definitions and measures for well-being of older adults and their families, grounded in Humanities and Arts.

MINIMUM/MAXIMUM NUMBER OF PARTICIPANTS

- As many as are in a class

TIME NEEDED TO IMPLEMENT ACTIVITY

- 5 to 6 hours

SETTING(S)

- Distance learning program: Students interview in the field and share their experiences through presentations and discussion online. The final paper is sent to instructor for feedback and grading.

PROCEDURES

- Students will share the assignment with prospective interviewees and the reason the interviewee is being asked.

- Students will select interviewees to whom they have access and who agree to be interviewed.

- Interviewees will not be named. All identifying information about any individual interviewed must be removed during the writing process.

- For the interviewee experiencing an acute or chronic illness, the student will obtain the individual's *explanation* of their condition and the experience of living with this condition.

- For a caregiver, the student will obtain the caregiver's understanding of the older adult's condition, understanding of the older adult's personality, explanation of the caregiver's role, and description of how the caregiver experiences giving care.

- For the health care professional, the student will obtain a description of the health care professional's work and role with the older adult, their view of aging, their view of the older adult's condition and prognosis, and the professional's experience treating the older adult.

- An appendix will include a discussion guide that will detail the questions asked by the student to include the assignment questions plus any additional questions asked during the interview.

Assessment

Rubrics are used for direct assessment of elements that distinguish an excellent, adequate, or poorly executed assignment. An excellent paper will have an introduction that includes a discussion of ideas and information from the course that clearly link to a humanistic perspective and a well-written description of the disease in question against the backdrop of normal aging. The body of the paper will include a detailed summary of the interviews followed by a presentation and discussion of main themes. The conclusion will provide insight into perceptions of illness or disease in aging and how perceptions may influence the experience of aging based on the interview experience. An appendix with the students' questions will be included. An adequate paper will include the same or most of the elements just described, but they will be presented with less detail and insight. A poor paper will be missing significant elements and/or the discussions will be superficial. Spelling, grammar, and syntax are additional elements factored into grading the final paper.

ADDITIONAL CONSIDERATIONS

This activity is suitable for students who are diverse in backgrounds and ages but have completed undergraduate work and are striving to progress in the field of gerontology, generally within health care, senior living, or some other aspect of senior services.

REFERENCE

Saxon, S. V., Etten, M. J., & Perkins, E. A. (Eds.). (2015). *Physical change & aging: A guide for the helping professionals*. New York, NY: Springer Publishing.

CHAPTER 11

SPIRITUALITY

Kelly Niles-Yokum

The Little Fish

*"Excuse me," said an ocean fish. "You are older than I so can you tell me
where to find this thing they call the Ocean?"*

"The Ocean," said the older fish, "is the thing you are in now."

*"Oh, this? But this is water. What I'm seeking is the Ocean,"
said the disappointed fish as he swam away to search elsewhere.
(de Mello, 1982)*

In the story of *The Little Fish* (1982), de Mello reminds us that in our searching we
sometimes miss what is right in front of us, and that as we age, we may find ways
to transcend that which we are seeking and finally connect our own selves with
something greater that has been in us and around us all along. Discussions about
later life and spirituality are generally framed around the search for something.
We may not be sure what that something is, but it is in our later lives that we may
come to realize that, in fact, what we have been searching for is here, it is you, it
is in your last step, your next step. What we do know is that spirituality is not
static. Our ideas about spirituality and our connection to others, the universe,
and the world around us vary over time, and, because spirituality is tied to the
search for meaning, it becomes an interesting platform for gerontologists and
their work with older adults.

CONCEPTUALIZING SPIRITUALITY

Spirituality has been conceptualized in a variety of ways. Hooyman and Kiyak (2011, p. 521) provide the following summary of definitions over time:

- A human quest for meaning, sense of purpose, and more principles in relation to one's deepest convictions and experiences about the nature of reality
- A relationship with that which is sacred in life and transcends the ordinary limits of the body, ego, linear space, and time
- Wisdom in which the individual tries to achieve balance in life
- Self-transcendence, or crossing a boundary beyond the self, being supported by some power greater than oneself
- Achievement of meaning and purpose for one's continued existence
- Sense of the wholeness of life and connectedness to the universe, nature, and a higher power
- Awe or unconditional joy
- Giving and receiving support through affiliation with others
- Intuitive nonverbal understanding of how to cope with life's circumstances

Moody and Carroll, in their book *The Five Stages of the Soul* (1997), put forth that the experience of spirituality:

- Shifts our center of being away from the external world and toward the inner life of the soul
- Encourages a sense of disengagement from the ordinary problems of daily living
- Increases our commitment to virtuous behavior—kindness, generosity, unselfishness, love
- Raises our normal state of consciousness to a higher "transpersonal" level that awakens new and extraordinary faculties within us
- Creates a desire to give back to the world what we have gained spiritually and to devote ourselves in service to others (p. 34)

Emmons (2009) presents an additional way of thinking about spirituality, and that is as spiritual intelligence, suggesting that there are five components:

- The capacity for transcendence
- The ability to enter into heightened spiritual states of consciousness
- The ability to invest everyday activities, events, and relationships with a sense of the sacred
- The ability to utilize spiritual resources to solve problems in living
- The capacity to engage in virtuous behavior (to show forgiveness, to express gratitude, to be humble, to display compassion; p. 3)

SPIRITUALITY EDUCATION ACTIVITIES

The two activities in this chapter bring both breadth and depth to the issue of spirituality in the context of end-of-life issues and, specifically, a direct assessment that connects students to their own selves and older adults. In Activity 11.1, Spiritual Assessment, Beran brings to the classroom a tool that allows students to reflect on their own spirituality and then compare that to an understanding of the broad concept of spirituality. This particular activity has an exciting dimension that brings in both intergenerational opportunities and connections around generativity, which students will take with them long after the class is finished.

In Activity 11.2, Exploring Cultural Death Practices Through Group Presentations, Claver and Goeller provide an opportunity for students to become more engaged in considering death and dying and later life in a cultural context. The authors have a creative classroom process that brings students together and allows them to explore their own ideas and beliefs, as well as the opportunity to hear the voices of their peers.

REFERENCES

de Mello, A. (1982). *The song of the bird.* New York, NY: Doubleday.

Emmons, R. A. (2009). Is spirituality an intelligence? Motivation, cognition, and the psychology of ultimate concern. *The International Journal for the Psychology of Religion, 10*(1), 3–26.

Hooyman, N. R., & Kiyak, H. A. (2011). *Social gerontology: A multidisciplinary perspective.* Boston, MA: Allyn & Bacon.

Moody, H. R., & Carroll, D. L. (1997). *The five stages of the soul: Charting spiritual passages that shape our lives.* New York, NY: Doubleday.

ACTIVITY 11.1 SPIRITUAL ASSESSMENT

Connie Beran

ACTIVITY INFORMATION

Type

	In class
	Online
X	Take home
X	In community

Difficulty

	Introductory
X	Intermediate (for undergraduate)
X	Advanced (for graduate)

OVERVIEW

Spirituality has been studied for years and the results have shown that people with a faith life fare better in the aging process than those who do not. Students seem to find the idea of discussing spirituality somewhat daunting. The best way to gain knowledge about an activity is to do the activity, so students create their own spiritual assessment tool and then perform the assessment with an older adult.

ACTIVITY LEARNING GOALS

Following this activity, students should be able to . . .

- Research and develop a spiritual assessment tool.
- Administer a spiritual assessment to an older adult.
- Describe the benefits and challenges associated with conducting a spiritual assessment.
- Evaluate and explain how conducting a spiritual assessment impacts older adults.
- Evaluate the effect of conducting a spiritual assessment on the student through self-reflection.

ASSOCIATION FOR GERONTOLOGY IN HIGHER EDUCATION COMPETENCIES

- Utilize gerontological frameworks to examine human development and aging.
- Relate psychological theories and science to understanding adaptation, stability, and change in aging.

- Develop comprehensive and meaningful concepts, definitions, and measures for well-being of older adults and their families, grounded in Humanities and Arts.
- Develop a gerontological perspective through knowledge and self-reflection.
- Promote older persons' strengths and adaptations to maximize well-being, health, and mental health.
- Promote quality of life and positive social environment for older persons.

MINIMUM/MAXIMUM NUMBER OF PARTICIPANTS

- Variable

TIME NEEDED TO IMPLEMENT ACTIVITY

- 8 to 10 hours

SETTING(S)

- On-ground (face-to-face) classroom or online

MATERIALS
Required

- Textbooks, journal articles, means of transportation

PROCEDURES
Preparation

- Complete assigned readings.
- Research other sources of information on spiritual assessment.
- Discuss questions and ideas concerning creation of a spiritual assessment.

Introduction

- Create a draft of a spiritual assessment based on knowledge gained from readings and research.
- Submit a copy of spiritual assessment for review and evaluation by the instructor and/or peers.
- Finalize the spiritual assessment.

Activity

- Locate an older adult (aged 70 or older) willing to participate in the project.
- Determine the appropriate setting in which to conduct the assessment.

- Establish suitable time(s) for conducting the assessment, keeping in mind the stamina of the older adult.
- Administer the spiritual assessment to the older adult.

Discussion/Reflection

- Reflect on the result of assessment and student thoughts.
- Outline the assessment material, process, and student's self-evaluation.

Wrap-Up

- Synthesize and compose a comprehensive paper on the results of assessment and impact on student's feelings about the construction, implementation, and results of the spiritual assessment.

Assessment

- Grading rubric (see Appendix 11.1)

ADDITIONAL CONSIDERATIONS

- Students really seem to value this assignment, as it is often mentioned in the course reviews as having had an impact on them.

Source activity is based on/modified from:
Adapted and modified from spiritual assessment information found in Ellor, J. W. (Ed). (2009). *Methods in Religion, Spirituality and Aging*. New York, NY: Routledge.

CONTENT SOURCES

Anadarajah, G. (2005). Doing a culturally sensitive spiritual assessment: Recognizing spiritual themes and using the HOPE questions. *American Medical Association Journal of Ethics*. Retrieved from http://journalofethics.ama-assn.org/2005/05/cprl1-0505.html

Hefner, L. (2008). Spiritual assessment 1 comparing and discussing two spiritual assessment tools. Retrieved from https://www.researchgate.net/publication/265149289_Spiritual_Assessment_1_Comparing_and_Discussing_Two_Spiritual_Assessment_Tools

Hodge, D. (2004). Why conduct a spiritual assessment? A theoretical foundation for assessment. *Advances in Social Work, 5*(2), 183–196.

Lifeway. (2006). Spiritual growth assessment process. Retrieved from http://www.lifeway.com/lwc/files/lwcF_PDF_DSC_Spiritual_Growth_Assessment.pdf

Puchalski, C. (1999). Spiritual assessment tool—FICA. Retrieved from http://www.hpsm.org/documents/end_of_life_summit_fica_references.pdf

Puchalski, C. (2015). Fast facts and concepts #274 the FICS Spiritual History Tool. Retrieved from https://www.mypcnow.org/blank-voxrz

Puchalski, C. M. (2008). Spiritual issues as an essential element of quality palliative care: A commentary. *The Journal of Clinical Ethics, 19*(2), 160–162.

APPENDIX 11.1: GRADING RUBRIC FOR SPIRITUAL ASSESSMENT

	Mastery (4 pts.)	Proficient (3 pts.)	Developing (2 pts.)	Aspiring (1 pt.)	Not a Clue (0 pts.)
The Spiritual Assessment	Presents mature, well-developed spiritual assessment	Demonstrates a clear focus on context and purpose of assessment	Exhibits a spiritual awareness but is not fully formulated in the assessment	Demonstrates a simplified understanding of spiritual assessment	Does not demonstrate understanding of spiritual assessment development assignment
Understanding a Spiritual Journey as Part of Assessment	Able to fully articulate the spiritual journey; creates an comprehensive, interesting and understandable assignment	Articulates spiritual journey; creates interesting assignment	Utilizes sources to explain spiritual journey without exhibiting personal understanding	Demonstrates an elementary desire to understand the spiritual journey but has difficulty articulating it	Does not exhibit understanding of a spiritual journey
Critical Thinking About Spirituality	Clearly understands and articulates the challenges and opportunities associated with spiritual assessment	Articulates that there are challenges and opportunities associated with spiritual assessment	Underdeveloped ideas regarding the challenges and opportunities involved in a spiritual assessment	Demonstrates understanding of critical thinking as related to assessment in general	Does not use critical thinking in creating assignment

(continued)

(*Continued*)

	Mastery (4 pts.)	Proficient (3 pts.)	Developing (2 pts.)	Aspiring (1 pt.)	Not a Clue (0 pts.)
Resources and Documentation	Provided extensive relevant sources; correctly cited and formatted	Provided adequate number of relevant sources; correctly cited and formatted	Provided few relevant sources; correctly cited and formatted	Provided sources; incorrectly cited and formatted	No sources cited
Language	Skillfully uses language that communicates with readers and is error-free	Uses language that communicates with readers with only minor grammatical errors	Conveys meaning to readers but has grammatical errors can be distracting	Intends to convey meaning to readers but the grammatical errors are distracting	Does not convey consistent meaning to readers because of extensive grammatical errors

ACTIVITY 11.2: EXPLORING CULTURAL DEATH PRACTICES THROUGH GROUP PRESENTATIONS

Maria Claver and Casey Goeller

ACTIVITY INFORMATION

Type

__X__	In class
_____	Online
_____	Take home
_____	In community

Difficulty

_____	Introductory
__X__	Intermediate
_____	Advanced

OVERVIEW

One of the objectives for this activity is to demonstrate a cross-cultural under-standing of death practices. Rather than solely lecturing about the topic or provid-ing reading material, students become much more engaged in the material when they work with a small group and present the information to their classmates in a creative manner. Students are encouraged to think "outside of the box" when deciding how best to present information about the death and dying practices of the cultural group to which they were assigned (e.g., African/African American, Asian/Asian American, Judaism, Amish, Wiccan, Native American, Mexican/Mexican American). In the past, students have incorporated traditional foods and music, performed role-plays, and shown film clips to educate their classmates.

ACTIVITY LEARNING GOALS

Following this activity, students should be able to . . .

- Discuss cross-cultural perspectives of death.
- Describe how an understanding of issues of diversity (i.e., socioeconomic status, gender, ethnic group, sexual orientation) and death, dying, and bereavement can enhance engagement with clients addressing these issues.
- Evaluate one's own performance and the performance of peers in working with a small group to design and deliver a presentation.

ASSOCIATION FOR GERONTOLOGY IN HIGHER EDUCATION COMPETENCIES

- Utilize gerontological frameworks to examine human development and aging.
- Develop comprehensive and meaningful concepts, definitions, and measures for well-being of older adults and their families, grounded in Humanities and Arts.
- Develop a gerontological perspective through knowledge and self-reflection.
- Engage collaboratively with others to promote integrated approaches to aging.

MINIMUM/MAXIMUM NUMBER OF PARTICIPANTS

- Three to five students per group

TIME NEEDED TO IMPLEMENT ACTIVITY

- 3 hours

SETTING

- Classroom with chairs, but enough room in front of the classroom for setup of props, movement of participants, and projector for those that choose to use PowerPoint/Prezi

MATERIALS
Required

- Peer review worksheets
- Projector
- Laptop
- Tables and chairs
- Props supplied by students

PROCEDURES
Preparation

Preparation includes putting students into small groups (or having them split into small groups) and assigning (random or otherwise) them a cultural group. Cultural groups might be formed along ethnic or racial lines (e.g., Mexican/Mexican American, African/African American) or religious lines (e.g., Buddhist, Christian). Some of the most interesting presentations arise from student suggestions (e.g., Amish, Wiccan), so consider opening up the list to student suggestions. It is best to have distinctly different groups to avoid overlap. For example, a group covering Buddhism is likely to have considerable overlap with a group presenting Asian/Asian American death rituals. Set guidelines in advance, including a time limit for the small group presentation (15 minutes works well). It is helpful to remind students that although creativity and role-play are encouraged for the presentations, they should be handled with the utmost respect. Give groups approximately two weeks to prepare for their presentations.

Introduction

Introduction to this activity should happen when small groups are formed and assignments are made to a specific cultural group (you can have a list, such as Mexican/Mexican American, African/African American, Jewish, Buddhist, and so on, but also welcome suggestions from students). Specify the importance of knowing accept that there is a range of ways in which culture may play a role in decisions about end-of-life care and funeral practices.

Activity

The activity includes the small group presentations, which may include visual aids such as YouTube videos, photographs, skits, or other aids such as music, food, and class participation. Before the presentations, distribute peer evaluation worksheets (see Appendix 11.2) and instruct students to take notes during the presentations. Each group should get about 5 minutes to set up, 15 minutes to present, and 5 minutes for question and answer.

Discussion/Reflection

Discussion should occur after each presentation and students should create interactive experiences for the class as part of their presentations to encourage the postpresentation discussion. Instructors might ask students, "How was this group similar to/different from the previous groups? What are some common threads among all of the groups presented? What looks or sounds familiar to how you and your family (or your clients) deal with death and dying? Did you learn something new you might consider incorporating into your own rituals?"

Wrap-Up

Students will complete a peer review form for each group (other than their own), and these comments will be shared with the groups after the class session.

Assessment

Students are assessed on the quality of the oral presentation/preparedness, creativity/use of audio and visual, content, and a Q&A session. They are also given bonus points based on the peer reviews of the presentation.

ADDITIONAL CONSIDERATIONS

It really helps to encourage students to think outside of the box when planning their small group presentations. Follow-up discussion should include a caveat that just because a person identifies with a certain culture doesn't mean that person will adopt the practices demonstrated and discussed during the presentations. It is always best to allow the client to lead the way.

APPENDIX 11.2: PEER REVIEW WORKSHEET

Group No. 1: _____

Name one thing you learned from this group's presentation.

What were the strengths of this group's presentation?

What could this group work on to improve their presentation?

Note: Repeat this peer review sheet format for all groups and leave enough space between questions so that students can write on the worksheet. Do not require students to write their name on the worksheet. After your review, you can return the worksheets to the small groups of students.

GLOSSARY

Absolute Number of Older People in a Population provides a count of how many adults over the age of 65 are living in the country.

Accessory Apartment (also known as "mother-in-law" apartment) is a unit added to or created within a single family dwelling (e.g., *attached*) with provision for independent cooking, living, bathroom facilities, and sleeping occupying no more than 30% of the gross floor area of the principal structure.

Action Research is usually conducted from within an organization or a community, with the research focusing on collecting and analyzing internal data, or studying themselves.

Activities of Daily Living (ADLs) are used to measure an individual's functional independence. The activities include personal activities such as getting out of bed, grooming, bathing, going to the toilet, dressing, and eating.

Activity Theory stresses the roles and activities that older persons engage in as a means to avoid social disconnection from society. Engaging in social activities replenishes lost roles that may occur during the retirement period and contribute to the overall well-being of older persons.

Actual Autonomy is an individual's capacity to make use of their actions and the actions of others in order to contribute to the realization of that which is important to them.

Actually Autonomous represents the state of using one's actions or the actions of others to contribute to the realization of that which is important to oneself.

Acute Disease represents illnesses that develop rapidly and have short durations; examples include the common cold, headaches, or the flu.

Adult Foster Care typically offers family-style housing and support services to a small number of older adults. Available services vary considerably depending on a home's license. May be run by a license holder who lives in the home as a primary caregiver (family adult foster care) or by an agency where the license holder does not live in the home and care is provided by hired staff (corporate adult foster care).

Age in Place is the ability to live in one's own home and community safely, independently, and comfortably, regardless of age, income, or ability level.

Age Norms are widely accepted age-based standards for participation in important areas of social life (such as education, family life, and work).

Ageism is a form of discrimination and/or prejudice based on one's age, with a primary focus on older adults. It includes stereotypes and other preconceived notions based solely on one's perceived age.

Aging Network programs, services, agencies, and organizations serving older adults and often their caregivers, enabling and supporting individuals to age in their communities.

Alzheimer's Disease (AD) is characterized by neurofibrillary tangles and beta amyloid plaques. Alzheimer's is a nonreversible neurodegenerative disorder that has at least two forms: the relatively rare early onset (before age 65) and the more common later onset. The disease tends to progress gradually over a number of years and stages, with increasing confusion and severity of cognitive impairment.

Americans With Disabilities Act (ADA) is legislation that was enacted in 1990. Under the ADA, it is illegal to discriminate against persons with disabilities in employment, transportation, public accommodations, communications, and government activities.

Anti-Racist Pedagogy encompasses three interconnected components: racial content addressing institutional racism within historical and political contexts (e.g., analysis of power relations); educational method (e.g., focused on fostering critical analytical skills while empowering students); and application of anti-racist analysis within and beyond the classroom (e.g., strategic organizing for social change).

Applied Research is used to provide information in order to improve the human condition, or improve society. Is prescriptive in nature and attempts to offer solutions to practical or real-world problems.

Asset Income is money coming into one's budget/finances from property or money one already owns.

Assisted Living Facilities (ALFs) represent an extremely diverse category of housing offering services ranging from minimal to comprehensive. ALFs range in size from small home-like environments to complexes serving upwards of 600 to

800 residents. At minimum, services typically include housing, meals, assistance with one or more ADLs, and 24/7 emergency monitoring (which should not be confused with the availability of 24/7 skilled nursing care).

Autonomy is the extent to which an individual can live a life according to one's own conception of one's own good.

Basic Research is driven by curiosity and is used to increase our knowledge. Typically, it is descriptive in nature, and often is used to explain/understand a phenomenon.

Birth Rate is the number of live births per every 1,000 members of a population during a given time, often a year.

Blood Pressure is the pressure that is exerted by the blood upon the walls of the blood vessels, such as arteries, necessary to deliver blood to the brain, organs, and muscles, and that varies with the muscular efficiency of the heart, the blood volume and viscosity, and the age and health of the individual.

Certificate of Need (CON) refers to state mandates intending to contain health care costs by regulating the number of hospital and nursing home beds available. Insufficient capacity had to be demonstrated in order to get approval (i.e., a "Certificate of Need") before new facilities could be created (www.ncsl.org/research/health/con-certificate-of-need-state-laws.aspx).

Chronic Disease is an illness with slow onset and long duration, for example, diabetes, heart disease.

Civic Engagement involves individual and/or collective efforts through both political and nonpolitical processes in which citizens participate to make a difference in the life of a community.

Cohort Studies are a type of research study that focuses on a specific category or group of people that share similar sociohistorical characteristics such as baby boomers, millennials, Vietnam war veterans, and so forth.

Coinsurance represents the percentage or amount of health care services or costs one has to pay after one pays the deductible.

Community refers to a group of people living locally near each other who may provide social support and share community resources.

Compassionate Ageism is the belief that older adults are needy and deserving of governmental support based on the stereotypes that older persons are poor, frail, and/or dependent.

Continuing Care Retirement Communities (CCRCs) are a form of multilevel care typically requiring significant entrance fees in addition to monthly maintenance fees depending on level of care needed. May also be known as "Life Care Communities."

Cross-Sectional Study Designs represent a type of research design that collects data and investigates social phenomenon at a single time point.

Cultivation Theory posits that the more TV people watch, the more they come to believe that TV's portrayal of society is realistic and accurate.

Cumulative Advantage/Disadvantage Theory means that "the rich get richer and the poor get poorer across the life course." In concrete terms, this means that socioeconomic status early in life leads to increasing socioeconomic inequality and widening health disparities across the life course between same-age peers from lower and higher socioeconomic backgrounds.

Custodial Care refers to care in a long-term care facility, for example, nursing home, which includes personal care, assistance with ADLs, or other basic medical care such as medicine administration. Not included is any form of physical, occupational, or speech therapy. Medicare does not cover this form of care.

Death Rates are the number of people who die each year in each age group.

Deductible varies by health insurance plan, but makes up the out of pocket or amount of money one must pay before the health insurance begins to pay for services or supplies.

Dementia-Related Behaviors are behaviors thought to be related to a person with dementia's later life cognitive impairment (e.g., agitation, wandering). Current thought is that these actions represent communication rather than simply being an outcome of brain pathology.

Demographic Transition is a theory that describes population aging as a process during which, as countries develop/advance, the birth and death rates change from being very high to low birth and death rates, resulting in an increase in the average age of a population. The transition includes a three-stage shift—pretransition, transition, and posttransition—during which birth and death rates change from high to low.

Demography is the scientific study of human population including the causes and consequences of changes in human population.

Dependency Ratio defines how many individuals are dependent, both old and young, on individuals who economically provide for them.

Diagnostic and Statistical Manual of Mental Disorders **(5th ed., DSM-5)** is a system used in the United States for classifying mental disorders by specific diagnostic criteria (www.dsm5.org/about/pages/default.aspx).

Didactic Lectures are a method of teaching in which an expert presents on a topic of their expertise to a group of students who wish to learn. Evaluation of successful learning consists of testing factual recall of data, commonly in the form of objective tests with right and wrong answers.

Disability is a physical (i.e., mobility) or mental (i.e., mental health, cognition) condition(s) that substantially limits or presents challenges to a person's ability to participate in one or more major life activities. This can be both short and long term.

Disorienting Dilemma is an experience testing one's own beliefs.

Diversity refers to heterogeneity among people based on socially constructed characteristics such as race, ethnicity, gender, sexuality, ability, and so forth. Diversity also implies inclusiveness with regard to these differences.

Durable Medical Equipment is any equipment that provides therapeutic benefits to a patient and is required because of a medical condition or illness. Such items are reusable, ordered or prescribed by a physician, can be used in the home, and are not useful to someone without an illness, disability, or injury. Examples of such items include the following: wheelchairs (manual and electric), traction equipment, canes, crutches, walkers, and oxygen tanks.

Earnings are the money one receives after taxes are removed from the gross income of an individual.

Elderly Cottage Housing Opportunity (ECHO) Units (also known as "Granny Flats") are small, temporary, separate (i.e., not attached to or within an existing house) housing unit that can be installed in a backyard.

Evaluation Research is to examine the solution to the problem via looking at the processes and outcomes associated with the proposed solution. Evaluation research may be summative, which attempts to evaluate the proposed solution/ program. It may be formative, which attempts to improve upon the intervention/ solution.

Fertility is the addition of new members of a population due to births and the rates of these births influence population sizes and composition.

Fertility Rates are the number of live births per a single woman in a lifetime of fertility (usually from age 15 to 44).

Formal Organization is a large social group, often secondary, that focuses on efficiency and goal achievement. These types of groups are often run through a more bureaucratic structure. Communication in formal organizations often runs through a hierarchy of authority.

Formulary is a list of covered drugs for an insurance plan. Many Medicare and insurance drug plans place drugs into different "tiers" on their formularies. Drugs in each tier or level have a different cost.

Frailty is the state of being immediately dependent on others in order to meet one's daily needs.

Frontotemporal Degeneration (FTD) is a form of dementia associated with impairment to the frontal and temporal lobes of the brain. Symptoms typically include changes in behavior (e.g., reduced social screens, lack of empathy, disinhibition) and/or difficulties with speech and language. Memory and spatial skills may appear less affected early on than in other dementias.

Gender is a socially constructed set of expectations and roles that often gets attached to one's biological sex. Traditionally, gender is associated with a male/ female dichotomy, but recent social movements have broadened the definition to include multiple gender identities.

Geriatrics "is the study of health and disease in later life and the comprehensive health care of older persons and the well-being of their informal caregiver" (www.aghe.org/resources/gerontology-geriatrics-descriptions, 2016).

Gerontologists "improve the quality of life and promote the well-being of persons as they age within their families, communities and societies through research, education and application of interdisciplinary knowledge of the aging process and aging populations" (www.aghe.org/resources/gerontology-geriatrics -descriptions, 2016).

Gerontology is "the study of the aging processes and individuals as they grow from middle age through later life. It includes the study of physical, mental, and social changes in older people as they age; the investigation of the changes in society resulting from our aging population; and the application of this knowledge to policies and programs. As a result of the multidisciplinary focus of gerontology, professionals from diverse fields call themselves 'gerontologists'" (www.aghe .org/resources/gerontology-geriatrics-descriptions, 2016).

Glaucoma is a disease of the eye in which the pressure within the eye increases until a gradual loss of vision occurs.

Group involves two or more people who engage in interaction for various reasons. Individuals may share similar identity characteristics or be a part of similar social groups.

Home Health Care provides various services including nursing care, physical/ occupational/speech therapy, durable medical equipment, nursing aid assistance, and other services to clients within the client's home.

Home Sharing (also known as "share-a-home") is a living arrangement in which two or more people live together in a private apartment or a house for mutual benefit (e.g., companionship, support, and cost-sharing). Arrangements may be either formal (through a share-a-home program or agency) or informal. Often, but not always, the older person's own home is the one shared as a way to support their ability to age in place.

Hypertension is a medical condition described by abnormally high blood pressure, especially arterial blood pressure, which can cause damage to blood vessel walls and internal organs.

Ideal Autonomy is being free from interference in acting according to one's conception of one's good.

Informed Consent is given by a legally competent individual who agrees of their own free will with no pressure to participate in an activity.

Institutional Racism represents racial inequality stemming from the systematic, inequitable distribution of resources, power, and opportunity in society.

Intraindividual Changes that take place within a person.

Lewy-Body Dementia (LBD) is a common cause of dementia. LBD is a neurodegenerative disorder that, in addition to dementia-like progressive cognitive decline, also features Parkinson-like symptoms (e.g., resting tremors, bradykinesia) and fluctuations in cognitive function. Visual hallucinations and depression are also possible.

Life Course Perspective holds that in order to understand aging one must examine everything that has come before as the entire life experience has a cumulative effect and must also be taken into account within both the social, historical, and personal contexts of the individual.

Life Expectancy represents how long a member of a group is expected to live after a certain age.

Life Span represents the maximum biological number of years an organism could live if no disease, environmental factors, or medical conditions cause damage or death to it.

Longevity or a long duration of life, service, or employment; can be used in demographic studies to refer to longer-lived members of a population.

Longitudinal Study Designs is a type of research study that examines or collects data on the same group of people over a period of time.

Long-Term Care is continuing substantial medical and/or personal assistance for individuals with physical and/or cognitive challenges and is typically but not exclusively provided in an institutional setting (e.g., skilled nursing facility).

Macular Degeneration is a disease of the eye occurring when the central part of the retina deteriorates, causing impairment in the eye's ability to focus. The first stages do not affect vision; however, over time the central vision of an individual is affected first with the loss of vision slowly expanding until all central vision is gone and the person is considered legally blind.

Median Age of Population represents the midpoint or the exact age at which half the population is younger and half the population is older than that age.

Medicaid provides health insurance to individuals with low income and is jointly funded by the federal and individual state governments.

Medically Necessary Services are services or supplies that are needed to diagnose or treat your medical condition and that meet accepted standards of medical practice.

Medicare is a federal program to provide health insurance to individuals over the age of 65. It is funded by a specific tax at the federal level.

Migration is the number of people moving into and out of a geographic area and/or population.

Mission Creep represents when housing providers adjust their service offerings to accommodate changing needs of residents aging in place.

Mortality is the loss of new members of a population due to deaths; the rates of these deaths with the ages it occurs at influence population sizes and composition.

Multilevel Care refers to facility or campus environments providing more than one type of housing option (e.g., independent apartments, assisted living, and skilled nursing care) on site.

Neurocognitive Disorders (Major and Minor) is a diagnostic term in the *DSM-5* that replaces the previous "dementia" diagnostic category in earlier versions of the American Psychiatric Association's *DSM*.

Nonautonomous is on the ideal (liberal) concept of autonomy; a person is nonautonomous if the person acts or is acted upon in ways that are not a direct product of their own choices; on the concept of actual autonomy, a person is nonautonomous if the person acts or is acted upon in ways that hinder the realization of that which is important to them.

Normal Aging consists of changes associated with the passage of time.

Nursing Home see *Skilled Nursing Facility*.

Older Americans Act (OAA) was enacted in 1965; the program strove to address a lack of community social supports for older Americans. The federal program created the Administration on Aging (AoA) that today administers a network of over six state agencies on aging, 629 area agencies on aging, nearly 20,000 service providers, 244 tribal organizations, and two Native Hawaiian organizations. Services provided include a range of home and community-based services, such as Meals on Wheels and other nutrition programs, in-home services, transportation, legal services, elder abuse prevention, and caregivers support.

Older Dependency Ratio measures the number of individuals 65 and older per 100 workers (usually individuals aged 15–64).

Oral Histories are a qualitative type of research method often used to gather data from older persons. This method focuses on gathering data about socialization experiences or events that occur over the life course.

Pathological Aging refers to changes associated with disease or illness.

Pedagogy is the method of teaching, education, or instruction.

Pensions are funds to which money has been added to by an employer and/or employee during the employee's years of employment that then provide money/income upon the retirement of the employee.

Power Relations recognize that we hold different positions of power according to our race, gender, class, and other intersecting identities.

Prehypertension is a medical condition defined as a systolic blood pressure between 120 and 139 mmHg and a diastolic blood pressure between 80 and 89 mmHg; indicative as a precursor to hypertension.

Presbycusis is a gradual decline in hearing leading to difficulty perceiving higher pitched sounds and/or distinguishing between certain consonant sounds. It can be made worse by a lifetime of exposure to noise or medications that are toxic to the hearing mechanism.

Preventive Services work to identify and prevent the onset of chronic or acute illnesses or diseases.

Primary Care provides treatment for common health problems such as acute or chronic diseases or prevention services.

Primary Group is a type of group, usually small in size, that focuses on close personal relationships and involves more frequent face-to-face interactions.

Proportion of Older People in a Population is a value calculated by dividing the number of individuals over 65 by the total population. Easily converted into a percentage by multiplying by 100, the proportion allows for comparisons between countries or populations of different sizes by standardizing the groups by how much each is represented within the whole population.

Public Policy is the guiding principles/thoughts of those making decisions in a given area/concern created by government.

Qualitative Research Methods produce data that is descriptive and seeks to provide a better understanding of a phenomena or topic through individual participant's perceptions. Data is nonnumerical.

Quantitative Research Methods produce numerical data that can be descriptive or used for other methods of statistical analysis. The method seeks to translate a topic or phenomena into something that can be measured numerically.

Replacement Rate is the number of births needed to maintain a zero growth population. The rate usually is somewhere over two births on average per woman so that one child can "replace" each parent, and another to replace a peer who dies before reproducing or who never has children.

Research is a process of continuous exploration and discovery through systematic steps in order to increase knowledge or to discover new information on a particular topic or question.

Retirement Communities are age-segregated campuses or residential areas designed and equipped with amenities specifically for the interests and needs (e.g., leisure, socialization) of healthy older adults.

Secondary Care provides care to an individual who has a health issue that requires more intensive or specialized care, for example, hospitals, hematologists, or oncologists.

Senescence is a gradual reduction and degeneration of physical and cognitive function that increases the mortality risk of an organism or individual.

Senior Centers provide older adults and their families with many services, often acting as a gateway into the aging network. Centers provide services that include nutrition, information, transportation, benefit counseling, and other assistance programs. Often centers offer social, recreational, art, health, fitness, and wellness programs as well.

Senior Housing can have several meanings, including any housing where older adults live; age-segregated housing designed for older adults; and most specifically, age-segregated housing that provides limited to no additional support services. Often, the term will be applied to apartments (either market rate or subsidized) designed for independent older adults.

Sex Ratios describe the number of men divided by the number of women, usually multiplied by 100; a sex ratio tracks the proportion of women to men in a population.

Site Visit refers to an opportunity for an individual or group to observe an agency or organization first hand by touring the built environment and/or interacting with staff members and/or participants.

Skilled Nursing Care is defined by Medicare guidelines as care that can only be performed safely and by a licensed nurse.

Skilled Nursing Facility (SNF) is known by a growing number of names (e.g., "Nursing Home," "Convalescent Home," "Care Community"). SNFs are highly regulated, licensed residential facilities providing 24/7 on-site skilled medical care. While typically providing long-term care, they may also offer short-term rehabilitation services under a variety of names (e.g., *subacute care, restorative care, short-stay care*).

Social Clock is a timetable determined by societal consensus specifying the proper times for the achievement of major milestones connected to education, family, and work.

Social Location represents an individual's social position as determined by one's membership in groups based on factors such as race, gender, class, sexuality, religion, age, ability, and geographical location. Such social positions hold different degrees and intersections of privilege and oppression, which then shapes an individual's perspectives and experiences in society.

Social Security enacted in 1935 under President Franklin D. Roosevelt during the height of the Great Depression, was the first large-scale social insurance program in the United States.

Social Stratification is a hierarchically ranked categorization of individuals within society reflecting differences in income, status, and power, created by factors such as social class, ethnicity, gender, and age.

Socioeconomic Status represents one's position in society relative to one's financial status (e.g., wealth, income) and other factors deemed important by society (e.g., education, occupation).

Spirituality is a human quest for meaning, sense of purpose, and more principles in relation to one's deepest convictions and experiences about the nature of reality; a relationship with that which is sacred in life and transcends the ordinary limits of the body, ego, linear space, and time; wisdom in which the individual tries to achieve balance in life.

Stable Population is a population with no change over time. The population may be growing, declining, or remaining the same size, but the rates remain constant.

Stationary Population is a population that has fertility and mortality rates remaining constant; even with migration the population growth is zero.

Stereotypes are unfounded sets of beliefs or generalizations that are erroneously thought to apply to all members of a specific group.

Successful Aging is aging with low risk of disease/disability, along with high levels of functioning and engagement.

Transformational Learning is based on the Transformational Learning Theory developed by Jack Mezirow. Learners involved in transformational learning go beyond the acquisition of facts. In transformational learning, learners are asked to make meaning of an event or experience. Learners experience a disorienting dilemma and then they examine, assess, and reflect on this event by exploring how this experience changes the learners' future roles and actions. This process results in a fundamental change or shift in learners' perceptions, attitudes, beliefs, thoughts, and/or behaviors.

Universal Design is the design and structure of an environment so that it is accessible (i.e., ramps, signage), understood (i.e., braille, captions), and used to the greatest extent possible by all people regardless of their age, size, or ability.

Usual Aging is aging with no disease but high risk.

Vascular Dementia is a form of dementia resulting from damage caused by cardiovascular problems impairing blood supply to the brain. Symptoms may appear to progress in a step-wise fashion and/or as more localized rather than global cognitive deficits, depending on the specific areas of the brain that are affected (e.g., speech, memory, mobility).

Youth Dependency Ratio measures the number of children (usually from the ages of 0 to 14) per 100 workers in a country.

INDEX

Printed in the USA
CPSIA information can be obtained
at www.ICGtesting.com
LVHW010822140923
758110LV00006B/497

9 780826 149169